THE BARON OF WALL STREET

CLARENCE DILLON AND THE MAKING OF THE MODERN FINANCIAL WORLD

THE BARON OF WALL STREET

WILLIAM R. LOOMIS, JR.

HANOVER SQUARE PRESS

ISBN-13: 978-1-335-01643-0

The Baron of Wall Street

Hanover Square Press
22 Adelaide St. West, 41st Floor
Toronto, Ontario M5H 4E3, Canada
HanoverSqPress.com

HarperCollins Publishers
Macken House, 39/40 Mayor Street Upper,
Dublin 1, D01 C9W8, Ireland
www.HarperCollins.com

Printed in U.S.A.

Life isn't about finding yourself.
Life is about creating yourself.

George Bernard Shaw

Table of Contents

Author's Note

Researching and writing a book about someone long deceased is similar to being a detective assigned to a cold case.

I came across the name Clarence Dillon after my retirement from investment banking when I was enrolled as a graduate student in the history department at the University of California. I was intrigued, since I'd competed with Dillon Read as a banker at Lazard. Dillon's firm was so white-shoe and noncompetitive that we didn't take them seriously other than as a talent pool from which to hire promising young bankers who were frustrated there.

As I began my writing journey, I discovered that Clarence Dillon was a pioneering pirate on Wall Street in the 1920s. Much of what we consider innovations from the 1980s, such as junk bonds and private equity, were, in fact, created by Dillon decades earlier.

I had a significant breakthrough in the case when I was given the chance to read a draft autobiography that Dillon had written late in life. The manuscript was long rumored to exist but had never been published. About one hundred typed pages, with numerous corrections in Dillon's handwriting, the manuscript became an indispensable primary source.

This draft autobiography is a curious document: a highly fictionalized version of Clarence Dillon as he wanted to be remembered. While often accurate in matters of business and his married life, the most revealing passages for a biographer are those in which Dillon spins tales about his past.

His father, a successful Polish-Jewish owner of dry goods stores in Texas, is inflated to the status of "merchant banker." His Russian-Jewish mother is transformed, strangely enough, into a Swedish Lutheran. Dillon revels in being descended from a highly decorated officer named Eliezer Dylion, who fought on the side of Napoleon during his invasion of Russia. There was indeed such an officer in Dillon's bloodlines, but he fought in Czar Alexander's army *against* Napoleon, before being ignominiously cashiered for corruption.

Clarence Dillon avoided such pitfalls. By 1957, *Forbes* listed him as one of the richest Americans alive.

As you'll see in the following pages, Dillon's life is a singular, heretofore untold American story.

THE BARON OF WALL STREET

Chapter One

VERITAS

CLARENCE DILLON MAJORED in poker at Harvard. Attending classes was nothing but an afterthought. During late-night no-limit games in his Gold Coast dorm room, Clarence's skill at cards became legendary.

When anyone raised him by a hundred dollars or more, Dillon would expose his hole cards and ask: "You think I'm strong enough to call?"

Dillon studied his opponents' eyes and his lightning-quick appraisal almost always won him the pot. Decades later, the same intuitive principles of reading human behavior came into play. He often compared Wall Street to a game "more fascinating than no-limit stud poker."

Clarence Dillon's magna cum laude "degree" in poker would later serve him well on Wall Street. He knew when to open, to raise, and to fold just as he knew when a big pot was on the table and when the other players were mostly new to cards. Like J.P. Morgan before him and Mike Milken after him, Dillon's times were as much the reason for his success as were his skills. Growth, diversity, and innovation swirled around him in the 1920s, as he raised his bets over and over again. He astutely folded his cards without any major losses after the Great Crash, having anticipated it.

Dillon's closest friends at Harvard nicknamed him "The Baron." A reference to his elegant appearance, refined manners, and the fact that he was one of the few undergraduates to show up on campus driving a brand-new car: a shiny black Oldsmobile Curved Dash. The nickname was also an allusion to another champion of the period: the famed racehorse Baron Dillon, who sportswriters of the time called "cool and level-headed," a trotter with an "aristocratic air." The comparison was apt: fascinated by horseracing his whole life, an inveterate gambler, Clarence Dillon was also known for his unusual success at selecting winners.

At Harvard, Dillon seems to have barely paid attention to classwork, and by 1903 his father, Sam, was notified that his son was on the verge of flunking out of college entirely. Clarence had been charitably characterized as an indifferent student.

Make no mistake: young Clarence *was* studying. Outside the classroom. He focused all his attention, with a calculating eye, on developing relationships that would later lead to a promising job on Wall Street and marriage to an heiress with impeccable social credentials.

Like other privileged students in his Harvard class, Dillon had entered college in 1901 with a few boys he already knew. He roomed with a friend, William Phillips, from his Massachusetts prep school. Worcester Academy was a reliable waystation to Harvard, but it was not as prestigious as Groton, which in 1900 sent nineteen of its twenty-three graduates to Harvard, including Franklin D. Roosevelt.

Dillon and his roommates lived in a residential hall at 35 Bow Street, between Westmorly Court and Russell Hall, near Harvard Yard. With its grand facade, diamond-leaded windows, and oak wainscoting, Westmorly was the most ornate of the privately owned residence halls lining Harvard's exclusive "Gold Coast." Just opposite Saint Paul's Church, the building was new in the fall of 1900, when Roosevelt and Lathrop Brown moved in as freshmen. They decorated their first-floor suite with school pennants, banners, team pictures, beer steins, and social invitations.

Harvard's luxurious private dorms featured suites with chandeliers, baths, and steam heating; some even had swimming pools and squash courts. While Roosevelt chose Westmorly Court, the poet T.S. Eliot moved into nearby Russell Hall a few years later. Most students in the Gold Coast buildings went to Boston society dinners and belonged to elite clubs. There was an obvious social divide between the very wealthy boys in private rooms and those of limited means crowded into the Harvard Yard dorms, some of which lacked central heating and even modern plumbing.

Harvard's student body was more diverse than that of Yale or Princeton. Under Charles W. Eliot's long presidency, Harvard awarded more academic scholarships than any other university—rewarding merit rather than lineage. Forty-one percent of Franklin Roosevelt's class of 1904 came from public schools, many the children of immigrants. Even still, most Harvard undergrads were white Episcopalians. Less than a handful of African Americans were admitted to Clarence Dillon's class of 1905, which had about eight hundred students. In 1908, roughly 7% of the student body was Jewish and 9% was Catholic. The social hierarchy was controlled through the club system by a select group of so-called "golden boys" from private schools like Groton and St. Paul's, whose admission to Harvard was often considered a family legacy.

For Clarence Dillon and many undergraduates of the era, Harvard's opportunities for social advancement—what we would today call "networking"—were far more important than academic studies. Social sifting began in a young man's sophomore year when one hundred students, deemed an elite within the elite, were elected to the "Institute of 1770." The order of selection by the Institute of 1770 was a significant indicator of social standing—even published in the Boston newspapers and *The Harvard Crimson.*

The first group of ten was chosen by the previous class; then these new ten selected the next ten, and so on, until the limit of one hundred was reached. Only the first seven or eight groups of ten were admitted to Delta Kappa Epsilon—known as "the Dickey" (or "DKE"). Membership in DKE was essential for election to one of the seven final clubs: the Porcellian, the A.D., the Fly, the Fox, the Gas House, the Owl, or the Spee.

The Porcellian was the summit of prestige at Harvard. With more than a century's history of members from the United States' most prominent families—the Adamses, the Lowells, and the Cabots—being asked to join Porcellian offered a nearly guaranteed lifetime of privilege. Franklin Roosevelt, whose heritage included his distant relation (fifth-cousin, once removed) and Porcellian member Theodore, had anxiously awaited his election to the Institute of 1770. Instead, FDR was rejected. Years later, the nation's thirty-second president described his rejection by Porcellian as "the greatest disappointment" of his life.

The gregarious personality of Joseph P. Kennedy, class of 1912, a Roman Catholic from Boston Latin School, enabled him to be admitted to the Dickey. Yet his futile wait for the tap on his door by one of the "final clubs" convinced him that he'd forever be viewed as an outsider by the WASP establishment in America. Kennedy sometimes stood outside the Porcellian trying to imagine what it was like to be one of the select few seated in plush armchairs inside.

Clarence Dillon was neither blackballed—as Roosevelt had been from the Porcellian for some still-undisclosed but evidently irritating personality trait—nor excluded, like Kennedy, simply for being born Roman Catholic. However, he failed to gain admittance even to the Institute of 1770 during his sophomore year. By his junior year, Dillon had cleverly wrangled an "honorary" membership to the Institute. Still, he had no chance for election to the more prestigious final clubs. Despite Dillon's efforts toward social acceptance—his surname, prep school credentials, WASP roommate, and Gold Coast residence—it was a most poorly kept secret that he had Jewish ancestry.

No Harvard final club in that era would *ever* accept a Jew as a member.

On September 17, 1901, a few days before entering college, Clarence had legally changed his surname from Lapowski to the more Gentile-sounding "Dillon." His father, Sam Lapowski, a Jewish immigrant from Poland, had applied for his son's name change in the Taylor County Courthouse in Abilene, Texas. Clarence retained Lapowski as his middle name, but typically used only the middle initial both at Harvard and in his later Wall Street career. The surname change was almost surely Clarence's idea, reluctantly agreed to by his father, with the retention of the Jewish middle name as a compromise between the two. Only after Samuel Lapowski's death in 1912 did his widow and his unmarried daughter also change their surname to Dillon.

Samuel Lapowski may have had concerns about Clarence attending Harvard openly as a Jew and recognized the advantages of the new name for someone with aspirations to rise in a Protestant-dominated society. Clarence Dillon also joined Harvard's Christian Association and the Episcopalian Christ Church in Cambridge. Later on Wall Street, Freddy Warburg, the distinguished banker from a prominent German-Jewish family, and a fellow Harvard graduate, "refused to take a call from Clarence Dillon because the Dillons had changed their name from

Lapowski, supposedly to conceal their Jewish ancestry—an unpardonable sin in Freddy's eyes."

It isn't difficult, in hindsight, to understand the pragmatism behind Dillon's decision. The first report on Dillon's class of 1905 printed one alumnus's objection to the existence of the Harvard Union, which provided club-like facilities for the so-called "un-clubbed" boys and which counted Dillon among its membership, because of the "prevailing numbers of Jews that infect the place."

Jewish men were viewed by many native-born Protestants as lacking in traditional American manliness, chivalry, and courage. Even Theodore Roosevelt, a politician often sympathetic to Jewish causes, expressed that view. "The great bulk of the Jewish population, especially the immigrants from Russia and Poland, are of weak physique and have not yet gotten far enough away from their centuries of oppression and degradation," the twenty-sixth president of the United States wrote.

The extreme ostracization felt by young Jewish men in Ivy League schools was so well-known that Ernest Hemingway latched on to it for the opening sentences of his brilliant debut novel, *The Sun Also Rises*.

"Robert Cohn was once middleweight boxing champion of Princeton," Hemingway wrote. "Do not think I am very much impressed by that as a boxing title, but it meant a lot to Cohn. He cared nothing for boxing, in fact he disliked it, but he learned it painfully and thoroughly to counteract the feeling of inferiority and shyness he had felt on being treated as a Jew at Princeton."

The character Robert Cohn was a loosely fictionalized rendering of the young novelist Harold Loeb—Hemingway's onetime friend and tennis partner in Paris. Loeb was indeed a Princeton graduate and the scion of two of New York City's most prominent and wealthy German-Jewish families. Harold's mother, Rose, was a member of the Guggenheim family and his father, Albert Loeb, was a senior partner at Kuhn, Loeb & Company—a Wall Street investment bank with which Clarence Dillon would, decades later, find himself doing considerable business.

President Charles W. Eliot's policies led to a notable increase in the number of Jewish students at Harvard. By 1922, Jews made up 21.5% of the student body and won a statistically disproportionate number of academic awards. This liberal attitude among the admissions committee coincided with a nationwide nativist backlash against immigrants from Eastern and Southern Europe. Indeed, President Lowell, Eliot's successor, felt that Harvard had a "Jewish problem" and he initially proposed a Jewish quota of 12%. Public backlash forced him to settle on an unofficial cap of 15%. But to more subtly limit Jewish acceptance, Lowell's admissions committee devised various strategies, asking loaded questions such as: "What change, if any, has been made since birth to your own name or that of your father?"

Clarence Lapowski had chosen a surname suggestive of French or Irish origin, which gave rise to a mythic account of his ancestors. Years later, a rather fawning magazine article attributed Clarence's versatility to his "unusual mixture of blood . . . French, Irish, Polish, and other European strains." A less flattering magazine profile claimed that "with the few who knew him well" at Harvard, "Baron" Dillon was "immensely popular, and the delicate question of his racial strain never came up."

Supposedly—at least in his own retelling—Dillon's ancestry included Jacobites from Ireland who'd migrated to France and even an officer who'd served in Napoleon's army during the emperor's unsuccessful attempt to conquer Russia. The truth was far more prosaic. "Dylion" was the maiden name of Clarence's

Jewish paternal grandmother, Pesha Lapowski. The surname was originally Sephardic and spelled De Leon; Pesha's distant ancestors had lived in Spain prior to the expulsion of Jews by the royal decree of King Ferdinand and Queen Isabella in 1492.

Clarence was intrigued by Pesha's grandfather, Eliezer Dylion, and later in life he discreetly kept a framed photograph of him clad in Imperial Russian military uniform, a chest full of medals, wearing an extravagant-looking, oversized circular fur hat made from the tails of the finest Russian sable. Eliezer had served as a representative of the Jews of Minsk province in the Russian Empire, communicating their concerns to high government officials. He was a Russian military contractor during Czar Alexander I's war against Napoleon and received numerous medals from the czar for his services. After attaining wealth and influence, Eliezer was accused of certain still unspecified "improprieties," placed under arrest, and dispossessed of all his property. Whether his abrupt downfall and disgrace was fueled by antisemitism isn't clear, but Eliezer was eventually released from czarist prison and had his property returned to him. Eliezer Dylion never regained his relatively high social status nor his army commission and, instead, became a small-time trader in Vilna—a city which was at the time more than 40% Jewish, a hub of Yiddish culture and rabbinical scholarship. During the Holocaust, Vilna's proud and venerable Jewish community was forced into a disease- and starvation-plagued ghetto, liquidated by Hitler's SS in 1943. Today, Vilna, now known as Vilnius, is the capital of the Republic of Lithuania, and home to a minuscule number of Jews.

Proud as he was of his portrait of an austere but dignified Eliezer Dylion in Czarist military uniform, in Clarence's unpublished hand-typed draft autobiography, written decades after his student days, he omits any mention of Eliezer, Jewish ancestry, or the Lapowski surname—he barely hints at his familial origins in Poland or Russia.

Brazen self-invention is as American as the Republic itself. Long before 1776, all manner of rogues, criminals, and men of "low birth" could cut new figures for themselves out of whole cloth.

Take, for example, John Paul, a hotheaded Scots sea captain who, after killing a mutineer in the Caribbean, changed his surname, fled to Philadelphia, and as John Paul *Jones* became both a Revolutionary War hero and the revered founder of the United States Navy. Benjamin Franklin, a lowly printing apprentice in Boston, broke the terms of his apprenticeship, and fled the law, also arriving in Philadelphia to start a new and productive life.

Clarence Dillon took this uniquely American penchant for audacious self-reinvention to an extreme, at a time when our notions of a globalized, fast-paced technological marketplace were first being shaped. Like F. Scott Fitzgerald's character Jay Gatsby, Dillon attempted to fully erase his past, to slip into a fictitious one—as if deftly slipping into one of his tailor-made Savile Row suits.

Dillon's own path to reinvention was made more complex by the ugly reality of antisemitism in his era. Though he tried to pass himself off as the scion of old European money, of Irish Jacobites, of French military officers—though he claimed to be the son of a millionaire merchant banker—his true origins could not have been humbler.

Clarence's father, Samuel, was born on October 27, 1851, in Vizne, a shtetl in the Lomza district of Eastern Poland, the son of Joshua and Pesha (Dylion) Lapowski. The town had about 2,500 people in 1860, mostly devout Polish Catholics but approximately 20% Jewish. The Jews of Vizne suffered greatly during the Napoleonic wars and later during all-too-frequent pogroms unleashed by rabidly antisemitic Cossacks storming into the town's poor Jewish quarter on horseback.

As with so many Jewish communities in Eastern Poland whose populations were almost completely murdered during the Holocaust and whose synagogues and other Jewish institutions were destroyed by the Nazis, there is little documentation about Shmuel Lapowski's birth and early years in Vizne.

The most revealing information can be gleaned from an account in Yiddish which was published on June 12, 1927, in *Der Lodzer Tageblatt*—the daily paper of the city of Lodz, at the time the highest circulation Yiddish newspaper in Poland outside the capital city, Warsaw. The account was datelined Berlin, where the *Tageblatt* had a correspondent, and reprinted by the Jewish Telegraphic Agency in English. The dispatch aimed to answer a reader's question about the origins of the by-then world-famous financier Clarence L. Dillon. Dillon's name had been making headlines in 1927—for some very ugly reasons.

Nazi press organs in Weimar Germany, particularly the antisemitic *Der Weltkampf* journal and the Nazi Party's official daily publication, the *Völkischer Beobachter*, singled out Clarence Dillon as being the leading financier in an alleged vast "international Jewish conspiracy" which had a stranglehold on the world's economic institutions. The Jew-baiting press claimed that "Dillon controlled Wall Street" and was "the greatest rival today of J.P. Morgan."

In response to the reams of antisemitic attacks, the Yiddish *Tageblatt* attempted to separate the facts from fiction about Dillon's background.

"In some quarters it was said that Mr. Clarence Dillon is a converted Jew," the *Tageblatt* reported. "A well-known Jewish citizen and philanthropist who is a relative of Dillon's has given us the following interesting facts. The name of Dillon's father was Samuel Lapowski. He was born in Vizne, near Lomza and came to Lodz, where he was employed in his father's concern at the end of Constantin and Zachodni Streets. Samuel Lapowski's father, Dillon's grandfather, was Yehusha [Joshua] Lap and was the son of Berl Lap in Vilna where he is still remembered today.

"Samuel Lapowski emigrated to America in 1876." [Actually, the year of Sam's emigration was 1869, confirmed by his successful US passport application in April 1898.] "It was there that Clarence who is now a well-known financier, was born. Dillon's grandfather Yehusha Lap and his grandmother Pesha Lap are buried in the cemetery of Lodz. Pesha Lap's maiden name was Dillon. She was a daughter of Moshe Dillon."

The Yiddish spelling and punctuation in this dispatch don't convey the subtle but important fact that Moshe and Pesha's surnames were not *Dillon* but rather *Dylion*.

The article continues: "The reason why Clarence Lapowski changed his name to Dillon was as follows: Moshe Dillon's father, Eliezer Dillon of Nesficz was the chief provision agent for Czar Nicholas I during the Sevastopol war. He rode out on the battlefront with the czar and there is a photograph showing him wearing a *shtreimel* on his head, two rows of decorations bestowed on him by the czar on his chest."

Shtreimel is the Yiddish word for a then popular fur hat, almost always circular in design, custom-made from the tails of Russian sable, beech marten, European pine marten, or gray fox. Due to its expense and the requisite furriers' expert craftsmanship, a *shtreimel* like the one Eliezer Dillon sported in the photograph—framed and greatly admired by his descendant Clarence Dillon—was a great status symbol, often the most expensive article of clothing in a Jewish man's wardrobe.

The photograph of Eliezer Dillon in uniform and *shtreimel*, according to the dispatch in the *Lodzer Tageblatt*, "was in the possession of Dillon's grandmother Pesha Lapowski in Lodz on the request of Dillon's uncle, Professor Boleslaw Lapowski, who won the gratitude of Poland for his services on her behalf in America. The photograph of Eliezer Dillon in *shtreimel* and Imperial Russian uniform was sent to [Clarence] in America. When Clarence Lapowski saw the photograph, it impressed him so much that he adopted the name Dillon."

The Yiddish account, garbled in its spellings and confused about the timeline of events, nevertheless *does* contain numerous previously unreported and factual details. By 1924, Clarence Dillon and his investment banking firm, Dillon, Read & Co., were involved in high-level financial negotiations with the Polish government. Dillon agreed in mid-January 1925 to give Poland a $50 million loan—the equivalent of nearly $1 billion in today's US currency—at exceedingly high interest rates.

After a business trip to Paris in 1925, Dillon continued by rail to meetings in Germany, Czechoslovakia, and Poland, visiting the capital of Warsaw, as well as the city of Lodz. As the *Lodzer Tageblatt* reported: "Clarence Dillon's aunt who still lives in Lodz has an envelope factory on Podlunowa Street. Dillon also has a cousin in Lodz who is a well-known attorney. When Dillon was in Lodz on a visit, however, he refused to receive any of his relatives. He did not even pay a visit to the graves of his grandparents."

For most impoverished Polish Jews, emigration to America had long been a dream—an often unattainable one, at that. *Der Goldineh Medinah*—"The Golden Land," in Yiddish—was idealized as a country where Jews and other recent immigrants could live in safety, enjoy legal and civil rights, perhaps even *prosper*—a land of such supposed abundance that the streets were famously said to be "paved with gold."

While most Ashkenazi Jewish immigrants to the United States arrived between 1880 and 1924—a period which saw an influx of over 2.5 million mostly impoverished Jews from Eastern Europe and Russia—Clarence Dillon's father had arrived earlier. He was part of a movement by a group of enterprising evangelical Christians in West Texas to recruit Jews to come to the American Southwest. The reason? A sudden and urgent shortage of labor vital to the agricultural economy of both the Deep South and the Southwestern states.

After the American Civil War, with the defeat of the Confederate secessionists and the emancipation of approximately four million Black slaves, by 1865 owners of cotton plantations simply couldn't find enough unskilled workers to gather their crops. During Reconstruction, "King Cotton" may still have reigned in the South, but no planters' fortunes could be made if the mature fluffy cotton bolls went unpicked, the delicate plants left to dry out and die under the scorching sun.

Given that Jews were prohibited by law in the Russian Empire and Poland from owning land, Jewish men who worked on dairy, barley, and wheat farms were, in many ways, not much different from America's sharecroppers: such Jews could eke out a living in agriculture, but the farms themselves were almost always owned by wealthy members of the Polish and Russian nobility, to whom came most of the profits.

Why not—thought a group of inventive Christians in West Texas—entice this pool of unskilled Jewish labor to the United States? The opportunity to pick cotton in the 100-degree heat of a Texas summer may not have sounded appealing, but an escape from the constant dangers of pogroms and official Russian and Polish antisemitism certainly did.

Shmuel—the Hebrew name for the Biblical prophet Samuel—Lapowski was one such young Jewish recruit who left behind his parents and decided to emigrate with nothing more than a single rucksack on his back. In 1869, the seventeen-year-old Lapowski booked passage in steerage class on a steamship called the *Saxonia* which sailed from Hamburg in late May. Listing his occupation on the ship's manifest as "a shop assistant" and his race as "Hebrew," he sought a better future in America. As he proceeded through immigration, his Hebrew name *Shmuel* was now listed as Samuel though he left his surname untouched. That bit of assimilation would be left to his only son.

Arriving in the busy port city of Galveston, Texas, Sam was soon joined by his younger brother, Jacob. Once they'd both passed through the official formalities of immigration and were safely living on American shores, the Lapowski brothers had *no* intention of toiling, as so many generations of Black slaves had been forced to, in the cotton fields.

Instead, Sam and Jake decided to set up a small business. They saw an unfilled niche in the economy of Texas, this being the era when so many ambitious Americans were heeding the advice to "Go West, young man." Sam and Jake recognized a fruitful business opportunity in being "outfitters," supplying dry goods and other necessities to the tens of thousands of settlers thronging the cattle trails and railroad lines of the rapidly transforming Texas frontier.

The Lapowski brothers worked as peddlers of dry goods in various towns before opening a small store in Weatherford, Texas. Using the business name S. Lapowski & Bro., the brothers soon thrived financially by opening branches of their dry goods company in San Angelo, San Antonio, Abilene, Colorado City, and Gainesville. Jake Lapowski managed the San Angelo store when Sam Lapowski eventually relocated to manage the Abilene store. Their younger brother Nathan, who arrived in 1882, managed the Colorado City store, and later the Gainesville branch. The Lapowskis also opened a store in El Paso. Most of their stores were in rough cattle towns which had been added to railroad lines. Ranchers came to town with their wagons; even Jewish mercantile firms stayed open on Saturdays—the Shabbat, commencing at sundown on Friday night, twenty-four hours in which all work and financial transactions are prohibited—because these were peak shopping days. The Lapowskis' San Angelo store was soon advertised as "the biggest general merchandise store in West Texas." It grossed over $125,000 annually for about twenty years.

Sam and Jake fell in love with and married two sisters in 1881. Their names were Bertha and Henrietta Steenbock. Sam and Bertha obtained a marriage license on July 11 and were married on July 20 in Tarrant County. Jake and Henrietta married on December 11, one day after obtaining their marriage license in Parker County.

Sam and Bertha's first child, Clarence Lapowski, was born on September 27, 1882, in San Antonio, Texas, and though he later denied it, was raised in a traditional Jewish home. He had a bar mitzvah ceremony on his thirteenth birthday.

Once Clarence Dillon became well-known in the financial world, a story circulated—no doubt started by Dillon himself—that he was not *actually* Jewish through the bloodlines of his mother, Bertha Steenbock. Knowing full well that for a child to be considered fully Jewish—under Halachic law—one's mother must be fully Jewish, Dillon further muddied the waters of his ancestry by claiming that his mother, Bertha Steenbock, was actually a Scandinavian Protestant. His maternal grandfather had been a Lutheran immigrant from Sweden named Gustav Stenbock, Clarence claimed, thereby making Dillon only partially Jewish. Early in his financial career, various newsmen credulously repeated this fiction as fact. The truth was that Bertha Steenbock's father, Julius, had changed his surname from Steinbach to Steenbock when he arrived at Ellis Island.

Julius Steinbach was not Lutheran. He was not a Swede.

He was a practicing Jew who'd emigrated, much like Samuel Lapowski, from a shtetl in the Pale of Settlement, a region where Jews were legally allowed to live, of the Russian Empire—his birthplace located in today's Republic of Latvia. Bertha's mother, Jennie Levy, was an American, born in New York City, and came from an English-Jewish mercantile family. Again, much like Sam and Jake Lapowski, Julius Steenbock and his younger brother, Nicholas, worked as dry goods merchants in New York City and then Richmond, Virginia, until a lawsuit forced them to declare bankruptcy. The Steenbocks then moved to Denver, Colorado, where Julius first accumulated, then lost, a substantial amount of money investing in silver mines.

Sam Lapowski moved from San Angelo to Abilene with his wife and two-year-old Clarence in 1884. Abilene recently had been an unincorporated tent town, a place for cattlemen to ship stock on the Texas and Pacific Railway line. This was truly the edge of the "white man's civilization," in the minds of the American settlers. There'd been several so-called "Indian Fights," involving Comanche raiders on horseback, shooting it out with Texas Rangers and cowboys on August 29, 1863, in Buffalo Gap, and as recently as New Year's Day 1871, in the dusty streets of Merkel, seventeen miles west of Abilene, only a dozen years before the Lapowskis arrived in town.

Conditions on the frontier were rugged, to say the least. Catclaw Creek alternated between drought and floods. But the Texas and Pacific Railway did a fine job promoting Abilene as a boomtown, "The Future Great City of West Texas." Several hundred people had arrived and purchased lots in 1881.

Abilene became the county seat in 1883. Sam Lapowski immediately opened a dry goods store, placing advertisements in the *Taylor County News*, offering products such as silver-plated spoons for twenty-five cents and ladies' dresses—with the promise of "no two alike"—for between fifteen and thirty dollars. By

1885, Sam was building a new brick residence. Five years later, the population of Abilene reached 3,194. The town was booming as was Sam Lapowski's business. His Abilene store expanded to 12,400 square feet with $150,000—over $2 million in today's values—of inventory and more than fifteen full-time employees.

Later in life, Clarence—never shy about taking liberties with the truth—described his father as having been a successful "merchant banker" in Texas. But, of course, only the first part of that description is accurate. Sam Lapowski was a common, newly arrived immigrant merchant—albeit a successful one. In the American West, owners of dry goods stores often *did* advance purchases on credit to cattle ranchers and cotton farmers during lean periods when banks wouldn't lend to them. Clarence claimed that his father also advanced cash to his customers so that they could shop around and buy items more cheaply, and Sam Lapowski profited from the relatively high interest rates on these credit purchases and cash loans.

Though he never warranted the lofty appellation of "merchant banker," Sam Lapowski did well enough in his dry goods business to soon become a cotton broker and a land speculator. And by the time Clarence was in grade school, Sam was a millionaire and could afford to raise his son in one of the largest houses in Abilene. The Lapowski family employed an English coachman and a Chinese cook and escaped the Texas heat by spending summers taking the train to Maine, where they stayed at the elite Poland Spring resort. Bertha Lapowski helped found the Readers' Club, later called the Ladies' Shakespeare Club, in Abilene.

Since few Jews resided in nineteenth-century Abilene, the town had no synagogue. Sam Lapowski often hosted relatives visiting from other Texas towns, New York City, and even the Russian Empire, so that they could worship together privately in his home. On September 22, 1893, the *Taylor County News* reported that "the Jewish holiday Yom Kippur was duly observed by the Hebrew population of our little city . . . and S. Lapowski & Bro., E. Weil, and Mr. Kline closed their places of business."

Although Samuel Lapowski publicly observed the Jewish High Holy Days, his family barely maintained their religious traditions as they assimilated into Texas society. Clarence later recalled that his closest friends, the Keebles, were the sons of the town's Episcopalian minister.

The Lapowski home was diagonally across from the Episcopal Church of Heavenly Rest. Reverend Keeble, one of the few college-educated men in Abilene, became Sam's good friend.

After becoming a naturalized American citizen in 1891, Sam participated in local Republican politics in Democratic-dominated Texas. He was regularly elected as a delegate from Abilene to the Republican county, state, and congressional conventions. By 1897, a little more than a quarter century after arriving in America, Sam was interviewed by the editor of *The Abilene Reporter* about the nation's business outlook and his recent visit to Washington, DC, for President William McKinley's inauguration. When Clarence was nine, he began accompanying his father on twice-yearly buying trips to New York City, where Sam purchased stock for the Lapowski stores and arranged financing. They occasionally visited Sam's youngest brother, Dr. Boleslaw Lapowski, a graduate of the University of Warsaw's medical school, who published scholarly papers in *The New York Medical Journal.*

Seeing the success of his brother intensified Samuel Lapowski's desire for his son to receive the best education money could buy. Sam's New York banker advised that the quickest route for Clarence's advancement in America was a New England preparatory school, which could be a gateway to a prestigious college. Possibly even to the Ivy League.

In 1894, however, a severe drought in West Texas led to

crop failures and the loss of thousands of cattle; most of Sam Lapowski's customers defaulted on loans. Sam was hit so hard that he shuttered his Abilene store for a full year. Such was life in frontier West Texas. Boom and bust, then boom again. During the rough times, Clarence spent two years at the public Abilene High School, where his name appeared on the honor roll list in the local newspaper.

In the fall of 1899, Sam had recovered enough financially to finally send his seventeen-year-old son to Worcester Academy, one of the nation's oldest boarding schools, forty miles west of Boston, Massachusetts.

By this time, Clarence had learned from his father the importance of salesmanship, favorable publicity, and building relationships with influential figures. For the rest of his life, Dillon was also highly attuned to anticipating economic fluctuations. Seeing his father experience West Texas's many booms and busts drilled that into Clarence's psyche.

Accustomed to acceptance by non-Jewish neighbors in the less stratified society of frontier towns in West Texas, Clarence struggled to adjust to the more insular "old boys' club" atmosphere of a New England prep school. Poet Stanley Kunitz, a Worcester native who was unable to get into the academy, described in his poem "The Testing-Tree" walking by the school's ballpark where he could never hope to play because he was a Jewish boy. Ironically, however, by the mid-1890s, Worcester's population of over 100,000 included many Irish, German, French-Canadian, Italian, and Eastern European Jewish immigrants drawn by jobs in its textile mills, woodworking and metalworking factories. And years earlier, Worcester Academy had even moved its campus to a hill where a large Jewish neighborhood was also located.

Charles E. Merrill, who later founded Merrill Lynch, transferred from a public high school in Jacksonville, Florida, to Worcester Academy in 1903 for his senior year. Despite his impeccable colonial American ancestry, Merrill found himself miserable at the academy, mocked because of his thick Southern accent which, at the time, marked a boy as being of supposedly lower intellectual and social status. Not only was Merrill playing catch-up in his studies, he was also conspicuous because he was receiving financial aid. The sons of wealthy and established American families dominated the school and were highly attuned to social class in selecting friends. Practicing Jews, Catholics, Blacks, and girls were not admitted to the academy.

Young Clarence Lapowski was not an observant Jew at Worcester and immediately upon arrival, he attended the headmaster's "moral talks" in the chapel. Soon he also began attending Episcopalian Sunday services along with his classmates. Clarence, like Charles Merrill, had a distinctive Southern drawl due to his Texas upbringing, but his father was wealthy enough to pay full tuition and a higher boarding fee, paving the way for some social acceptance.

When Clarence arrived, the campus had just two dorms: Dexter and Davis. Dexter, with fireplaces in every room, housed students from affluent families like Clarence's. Scholarship students stayed in the crowded Davis, a repurposed Civil War hospital. Wealthier boys focused on classics while those with less money studied sciences. Headmaster D. Webster Abercrombie called this setup a democracy because both rich and poor mixed in dining halls, assemblies, sports, and clubs.

By January 1900, Clarence had built a close circle of friends. He enjoyed going to plays in Boston and visiting his sister at Lasell Seminary in Auburndale. During his two years at the academy, Clarence earned more C's than B's, except for A's in mathematics, science, and declamation, the then-requisite study of dramatic oration and emotive public speaking. His lowest marks were D's in French and Latin. His unspectacular grades were likely due to his spectacular record of absences: thirty in just one term.

Once he'd achieved fame and fortune on Wall Street, his former Worcester classmates recalled Clarence as "reserved and quiet, but companionable and aggressive." One classmate remembered that Clarence, despite "suffering from illness, [left] the school infirmary to win, mostly by his own wit and power, a Sigma-Lego debate." Indeed, Clarence proved to be a brilliant debater, serving as captain of the 1901 Sigma debating team. He also managed the track and field team.

In mock class elections during his junior year, Dillon was voted "Biggest Talker" and, more tellingly, "Biggest Bluffer." He was chosen to deliver the humorous "Tree Oration"—a once traditional part of the school's valedictory address—during the graduation ceremonies in June 1901.

Despite his poor academic qualifications, Clarence applied to Harvard College for admission in the fall of 1901. Headmaster Abercrombie wrote a lukewarm reference letter, supporting Clarence's application while acknowledging that he'd failed the Latin, French, and English exams for Harvard admission. "We do not know exactly how to explain his failure," Abercrombie wrote. "He is a boy of good character as far as we know . . . Self-conceit is a strong characteristic of the boy and it is quite possible that this has obscured for him a clear view of his own attainments."

A letter from Clarence's former teacher Albert Bailey was less ambiguous in its praise. "He is one of the brightest boys I ever met," Bailey wrote. "He is a fellow too who is destined to wield an influence because of that ability and because of a very attractive personality. He leads his fellows naturally. This is the cause of his recent downfall." Bailey explained that Clarence had neglected his studies by being overextended, having accepted such a wide variety of offices in school organizations.

Headmaster Abercrombie, less dazzled by Clarence's charm, observed that the boy, at last, was concerned about his uncertain academic future: "He seems now to be deeply impressed with his situation, he certainly ought to be, so I have written at his request . . . [to] the secretary of the Scientific School with recommendation that he be accepted as a special student there." Abercrombie stressed that Clarence hoped to be able to "enter the University proper by a year of faithful and successful work" at Harvard's Lawrence Scientific School.

The Lawrence Scientific School had been established in 1847 by Harvard to offer degrees in science and engineering, but it also offered boys with less than stellar high school records a kind of backdoor mode of entrance. They could do two full semesters of remedial classwork—or what we today, more politely, call "academic upgrading." Not the strongest recommendation at a time when it was relatively easy for boys from Worcester to be admitted to Harvard College.

Despite his first-year enrollment as a special student at the Lawrence Scientific School, Clarence arrived in Cambridge intent on fully participating in campus social life and extracurricular activities as if he was simply a typical new boy in the class of 1901. He tried out for the freshman rowing team and joined the freshman debating club, serving as its co-president. Nonetheless, Clarence's grades barely improved: he maintained only a C average, nearly failing both required courses in Latin and German. However, he petitioned successfully to become a "degree candidate" and gained admittance as a regular undergraduate in Harvard College by the first semester of his sophomore year.

To say that Clarence didn't apply himself to his studies at Harvard would be a massive understatement. The dean of Harvard College wrote to Clarence in July 1903 regarding the D's in his sophomore class report, warning him that unless his grades improved, he'd be dropped and put on probation. From Texas, his worried father sent a Western Union telegram to Harvard in October 1903, its syntax and spelling betraying his still less than fluent English.

Wire Condition of Clarence L. Dillon
don't secrete anything

Clarence promised to do better, but the real problem wasn't his lack of intellect or application—once again, it was simply his failure to attend classes. In January 1905 Sam Lapowski received yet another stern letter from Harvard:

"I am sorry to have to inform you that the administrative board, at its meeting last night, put Clarence on probation for absenting himself from college engagements. When I saw him on January third he had been absent no less than thirty-three college engagements."

That March, Clarence managed to persuade the college to take him off probation on the understanding that he would "attend faithfully thereafter" and do his best "to maintain satisfactory grades."

Dillon did indeed keep his word, doing the bare minimum of what was expected from him academically. Though his grades were less than stellar, he could never be accused of having wasted his time at Harvard. For well-bred men of Dillon's generation, the ideal grade at an Ivy League college was a C. As one biographer of Franklin D. Roosevelt observed, "a C was the grade a gentleman aspired to, so as not to seem too interested in studies and be considered a 'grind.'" In his first Harvard semester, the poet T.S. Eliot was so blasé about his studies that he managed only D's in every course. The few Jewish students at Harvard were usually disparaged with the epithet "grinds," and Dillon, still self-conscious about his Jewish origins, did everything he could to avoid that ignominious label.

Many years later, when he was an established investment banker on Wall Street, Clarence Dillon met a Harvard undergraduate named Francis Sedgwick.

"What are you concentrating on?" Dillon asked.

"Fine Arts and Finance," Sedgwick replied.

"Splendid. That's just what *I* did in college."

There was a *pinch* of truth in Dillon's version. He took a few economics courses in college, but his artistic education was extracurricular; he liked to spend hours in Harvard's Fogg Museum and in the many museums and galleries of Boston. Dillon enjoyed making pen-and-ink sketches; years later, he'd amassed enough money to collect those done by Rembrandt.

He also participated in the Harvard Rifle and Pistol Club, which held shooting matches. He managed the Harvard junior and senior crews. As a Phillips Brooks House Association member, he volunteered to do public service at the Cambridge Social Union, which offered adult education for the working class from nearby industrial neighborhoods.

The fact that Dillon graduated in 1905, even though he rarely attended class, is hardly surprising. Harvard was then as much a finishing school for the sons of the rich and privileged as it was an institution of higher learning. Dillon did what a gentleman was expected to do at Harvard—and did so brilliantly. He used his charm and wit to forge lifelong relationships—like those with his roommates Armin Schlesinger and William Phillips—that would propel his later career.

In less than two decades, Clarence would transform himself into the Protestant president of a leading investment bank on Wall Street, a pillar of New York society, and possibly the most innovative and influential financial mind of his time.

In their 1978 book *The Power of Their Glory, America's Rul-*

ing Class: The Episcopalians, Kit and Frederica Konolige observe: "Episcopalians are outstandingly powerful because they have bred a small, super successful, and super wealthy elite that has become, historically and today, America's aristocracy. These are the people we have called *Episcocrats*."

In a brazen metamorphosis act, Clarence Lapowski changed his name and became a member of this elite. By 1905 he had all the trappings of an Episcocrat. After his somewhat fraught time at Worcester Academy, he decided that there was no way he'd enter Harvard in 1901 bearing the stigma of low birth, labeled as the son of an unknown Polish-Jewish purveyor of dry goods in the frontier boomtowns of West Texas.

In the summer of 1905, with the zeal and confidence of someone born again—a newly minted Episcocrat and now a graduate of Harvard College—Clarence Dillon was set to take the world by storm.

Chapter Two

MIDWEST MENTORSHIP

ARMIN SCHLESINGER ROOMED with Clarence on the Gold Coast. Armin was by then an unobservant Jew. Clarence was a new Episcopalian. Their friendship would prove to be instrumental in Dillon's meteoric rise in the financial world.

Immediately after graduation, Armin arranged for Dillon to get his first job with his father in Milwaukee. Ferdinand Schlesinger was well on his way to becoming the richest man in Milwaukee by September 1905, when Clarence Dillon arrived by train in the Wisconsin metropolis. The senior Schlesinger lived in a palatial residence on Lafayette Place with a spectacular view of Lake Michigan. Fine crystal chandeliers imported from Paris illuminated the mansion's lavish furnishings and eleven live-in servants maintained the residence and its stables. In 1905, the Schlesinger estate was valued at $30 million, or over $1 billion today. Ferdinand Schlesinger served as a perfect example of what Clarence Dillon aspired to become: a self-made millionaire, an immigrant of boundless ambition, a man whose upward mobility in American society took place at a lightning pace.

While still in his teens, Schlesinger had come to the United States with nothing and, through sheer determination, charm, and hard work, became a midwestern mogul—the "Iron King of America"—by middle age. Born in 1851, seeing that as a Jew his career opportunities were limited in Prussia, he left for America alone, and arrived in Wisconsin in 1871. He took a job in tiny Kilbourn City, teaching a shopkeeper's children German, French, and Latin. Unlike many Jewish immigrants, Schlesinger could read and write English, and he learned to speak it—albeit with a thick German accent—before moving to Milwaukee.

To Dillon, Schlesinger was as impressive in the way he bounced back from financial failures as in the way he'd made his fortune. Fired from a job at Linfield's dry goods store, Schlesinger borrowed $1,600 for a stake in a hardware store that also failed. A Milwaukee businessman soon asked him to manage a grain-cleaning machine factory. Schlesinger struck an unusual deal: he'd earn a salary until generating $25,000 profit for his employer—then ownership would transfer to him entirely. In just eighteen months' time, the factory was his own. The ambitious Schlesinger then entered the milling industry by taking over a miller's business in lieu of a debt payment.

He began trading grain futures on the Milwaukee Board of Trade—winning big initially but eventually losing even bigger. Covering his debts from this loss meant giving up control of his milling company while continuing with the grain machine factory until 1887.

By 1889 things had worsened financially; he was broke again. Undeterred, Schlesinger turned toward mining—a field where he'd later become legendary for his persuasion skills.

In the mid-nineteenth century, Wisconsin was a land rich in iron ore. Schlesinger saw what others had missed: an opportunity to harness these natural resources on an industrial scale. He acquired vast tracts of land, investing heavily in mining operations. His strategy was simple yet effective—control the entire supply chain from extraction to distribution.

That same year, without using a dollar of his own money, Schlesinger managed to acquire Chapin Mine located in Iron Mountain, Michigan, valued at $2 million, by raising $1.5 million; most of the capital came from iron ore brokers in return for supply contracts.

After Schlesinger improved the operations, the mine netted over $500,000 a year. This led to investments in more mines, furnaces, and foundries. Schlesinger was eventually estimated to control a quarter of the iron produced in the Lake Superior region.

The risk-taker was, once again, quickly in debt. He had speculatively used ore brokers' vouchers for payments for his ore shipments as collateral at banks. In the economic panic of 1893, iron ore prices plummeted. Schlesinger's vouchers became worthless. Condemned as "the greatest of all plungers," he caused the failure of Mitchell Bank and damaged three other Milwaukee banks.

The blue-eyed, mustached, and bowler-hatted Schlesinger, who still spoke with a heavy Prussian accent, lost his spectacular mansion, but he once again rebounded. Schlesinger's "glib tongue and persuasive manner had as much to do with his success in securing the necessary capital as anything else," noted *The New York Times* in 1893. "Every man in Milwaukee had fallen under his spell and looked up to him as one who had accomplished much more than the average man is capable of."

By 1905, Schlesinger owned the Newport Mining Company that operated mines in Ironwood, Michigan, as well as its subsidiary, the Milwaukee Coke and Gas Company that delivered coal gas to heat residences and businesses. Schlesinger's son, Armin, became a vice president of his father's companies and Clarence came on board to prepare financial reports.

Schlesinger's business acumen extended beyond mining. He built infrastructure—railways and ports—that ensured efficient transport of iron ore to markets far and wide. This not only increased his profits but cemented his dominance in the industry.

Dillon immediately learned a great deal from Schlesinger. Dillon saw that the Prussian immigrant's success wasn't just about iron: it was about having a long-term vision and perseverance. In a time when many new Americans struggled for survival, Schlesinger turned adversity into advantage, making millions through sheer determination and strategic foresight. What most impressed Dillon about this "bold Napoleon" of the iron world was Schlesinger's emphasis on the power of persuasion to raise capital.

Now twenty-three, Dillon wasn't too proud to start doing menial work: he spent his days in the unglamorous work of drawing up payrolls and fielding company complaints, all the while learning about iron ore mining and the manufacturing of coke.

In his spare time, Dillon focused on his entrée to the city's affluent young social set. Milwaukee's location on Lake Michigan enabled it to develop into Wisconsin's major port and industrial center, drawing thousands of recent arrivals from Germany, Ireland, Italy, Scandinavia, and Poland. Though transplanted East Coasters initially dominated the Milwaukee social order, the fortunes generated by manufacturing and commerce meant that the city's elite soon included first- and second-generation European immigrants. Milwaukee emerged as a leader in wheat production, meatpacking—and as the "most German city in America"—especially in the brewing of beer. Enterprising investors in the nearby iron ore deposits filled the city with iron and steel mills, machine shops, and foundries.

Early twentieth-century Milwaukee was far more ethnically fluid than Boston society. Money mattered much more than the age of one's wealth. Or its source. Nouveau riche men, like Ferdinand Schlesinger, weren't stigmatized by "old money" families the way they would be in Boston or New York.

Beyond his financial success, Dillon saw in Ferdinand Schlesinger an example of a German Jew who had successfully assimilated in the United States. In 1876, at age twenty-six, Schlesinger married Mathilda Stern, the daughter of one of Milwaukee's wealthiest dry goods merchants. Raised Jewish though never devout, Schlesinger and his wife joined the Unitarian Church. Their son, Armin, would later become an Episcopalian and marry a well-connected Milwaukeean of Scottish ancestry. Ferdinand's grandson would later change his name from Armin McGregor Schlesinger to Armin Schlesinger McGregor.

Armin Schlesinger was a member of the University Club and Clarence Dillon took a room there. With his suave good looks, smart sense of fashion, and a voice that retained its Texas drawl, Clarence was one of the few Harvard-educated men in the largely blue-collar city. At the University Club, Dillon made friends with other college men from Princeton and Yale over billiards, poker, and meals. Clarence's post-college circle of friends was starting careers in related industries, and some were fellow members of Harvard's Institute of 1770.

As one of the city's most eligible bachelors, for months, Clarence was primed by his friends to meet a very special young lady: Anne McEldin Douglass. Kathleen McCulloch, the soon-to-be-wife of Armin Schlesinger, was eager to introduce the two immediately. "Wait until you see Anne," she said, whenever the tall, impeccably dressed bachelor spoke about his romantic interest in other women.

Kathleen was the granddaughter of a prominent banker-lawyer. Her friend Anne was the youngest child of another leading Milwaukee business family. Benjamin Douglass, Anne's grandfather, and Robert Graham Dun, her great-uncle, had created the precursor company to Dun & Bradstreet, the first credit reporting service in the United States. Anne's patrician pedigree included generations of canny Scottish Presbyterian merchants and Sir George Yeardley, an English-born slaveowner who served as the governor of the Colony of Virginia in 1616.

From July to October 1905, Clarence waited to be introduced to this intriguing-sounding young lady. Anne, twenty-four years old, was then traveling in Europe with her brother and sister. Anne had already come out as a debutante after attending the German-English Academy in Milwaukee, then Madame Le Fevre's exclusive finishing school in Baltimore, where the future Duchess of Windsor, Wallis Simpson, was later a student. Anne had been pursued by many suitors; the months-long European trip may have been a way of fending them off.

Finally, when Anne returned to Milwaukee, one October night she and Clarence were both invited to a dinner party given by their mutual friend, Alice Prime, another leading lawyer's daughter, who belonged to the Milwaukee equestrian set.

Dillon—always cocksure—already had a clear picture of Anne in his mind's eye. He wrote that she was going to be "rather tall, strong, ruddy complexion, graceful, athletic figure, friendly eyes, soft brown hair . . ."

But now, across the room, Dillon spotted a young woman of a completely different type—someone with whom he was immediately smitten. She was a small girl, perhaps five foot three, with hair which, in the lamplight, seemed like shimmering gold, hanging almost to her waist.

"Her complexion wasn't ruddy but a transparent pink," Dillon later wrote. "And her lips were a deeper pink." In that instant, he recalled, "'Anne' was forgotten." He weaved his way through the crowded room and stood next to the petite and stunning blonde.

She smiled up at Dillon, and her friends all moved away.

"I feel I've known you for a very long time," she said. "But how does it go? But when or where or how we met—"

Just then Kathleen McCulloch interrupted.

"Aren't you going to let me introduce you?" she asked.

But when Dillon turned his head, Kathleen had abruptly disappeared somewhere into the crowd.

"I'm afraid I've offended her," Dillon said. "She wanted to introduce me to someone."

As they were called to dinner Dillon's new acquaintance with the translucent pink skin looked up at him, her light blue eyes squinting playfully.

"Shall I help you find your place? What's the name?"

"Dillon."

"I know *that*," she said, looking through the neat white pyramids of place cards. "These have only first names."

"Then look for Clarence," Dillon said. "Or maybe Baron."

"Here's *Baron*."

"Who's sitting next to me?"

"Anne."

Dillon's eyes widened. "Wait, that's the girl I was supposed to meet."

"Anne?"

"*Shhh*—"

Dillon pulled out the chair for the long-awaited Anne now realizing, sheepishly, that while he'd been oblivious, she'd known who he was all along. Anne was flirtatious but told Dillon to spend his dinner talking to their hostess while she politely chatted to the man seated on her left.

After dinner, they played roulette. Clarence banked the game. Anne lost one dollar. As everyone was saying good night, Anne offered Clarence a lift in her chauffeur-driven car and dropped him off at the University Club.

The next day, Clarence received a hand-delivered envelope, containing a note from Anne and a one-dollar bill.

"Gambling debts, I understand, must be paid before sunset the following day."

Clarence bought flowers and sent them with his own flirtatious message.

"And I understand such payment must be promptly acknowledged."

It was not long before Clarence Dillon became a fixture at the Douglass dinner table. Years later, Dillon wrote of the tradeoff.

"What I saved on food, I spent on flowers."

The couple made a striking impression as the tall Clarence and the petite blonde Anne drove around Milwaukee and walked through Anne's bucolic neighborhood. In 1906, however, they came to a mutual decision: they wouldn't be able to marry for some time. Dillon bought a bronze box and placed Anne's love letters in it and returned them to her. He told Anne that the letters were still his property but that he was leaving them in safekeeping with her. It wasn't a matter of a lack of passion or love; Dillon knew that he didn't yet have the financial means to provide the life to which Anne was accustomed.

Clarence and Anne's romance was accelerated by an accident almost too freakish and bizarre to be believed. In July 1907 after a weekend visit with Anne and her family at their North Lake vacation retreat, Clarence and Anne's mother were standing on the platform waiting for the arrival of their train to Milwaukee. Another train, the Pioneer Limited, was running two hours late and thundered through the station at far too great a speed.

The locomotive's cow catcher hit a large Saint Bernard crossing the tracks, killing the dog and throwing it high into the air.

The full-grown Saint Bernard—weighing well over a hundred pounds—struck Dillon in the chest, and he in turn fell against Mrs. Douglass, knocking her to the ground.

The back of Dillon's head hit an iron post, and he collapsed unconscious on the brick pavement. Mrs. Douglass's arm was broken. Dillon fared much worse. He'd fractured his skull on the bricks, and lay unconscious, bleeding heavily on the railway platform.

He was gingerly transported back to the Douglass home where, in the weeks ahead, Anne was to become his devoted nurse. In a near-comatose state, Dillon hovered close to death. Initially, a local doctor named Nixon attended to him. Anne's father, George Douglass, called in the best specialists from Milwaukee, but Dillon later credited that "old country doctor," Dr. Nixon, with saving his life.

When the specialists decided that Dillon needed to be rushed by ambulance to a Milwaukee hospital, Dr. Nixon blocked them, insisting that no one touch his patient.

"What do you want to see?" Nixon asked. "Suppose you find that his skull's cracked. What are you going to do about it?"

The specialists acknowledged there was nothing even the best hospitals in the city could do for Dillon. With a linear fracture of the skull, the only treatment was weeks of rest and close observation with the patient's head slightly elevated.

"Then why risk moving him about and having the blood spread all over his brain?" Nixon said. "Leave him where he is. Do *not* touch him."

The specialists left the Douglass residence and Dillon lay on a simple cot on the floor.

"Dr. Nixon cut my clothes off and I was not moved for a couple of days," Dillon later wrote. "Then he allowed me to be put on a stretcher and carried upstairs to a bedroom. Dr. Nixon got down on his hands and knees under the stretcher. With it resting on his back he crawled up the stairs. I was unconscious for eight or ten days, Anne watching over me. When I regained consciousness, I was frightfully dizzy and no one could hold my head tight enough."

It was weeks before Dillon was able to sit up in bed. By then, Samuel Lapowski had received news by telegram that his son was near death and traveled the nearly 1,200 miles from Texas. By the time Lapowski's train arrived in Milwaukee, Clarence was conscious—even smiling at his father's surprise appearance in his bedroom; the most dangerous days of a cerebral hemorrhage or stroke had passed. Clarence would simply have to lie prone, as Anne nursed him, until the bones of his skull knit back together. Relieved, Sam kept his visit to Milwaukee short; before he returned to Texas he spoke curtly to his son.

"You're a very lucky man," he said. "And we're a very lucky family."

Clarence nodded, taking in the unstated meaning of his father's words. Sam Lapowski was telling his son to heal up, get back on his feet and waste no time in asking Anne McEldin Douglass to marry him.

Dillon followed his father's advice. When he'd recovered enough to return to normal activity, adhering to formal etiquette, he first asked George Douglass for permission to propose to Anne. Douglass had no doubt that Clarence would provide financially for his daughter. In fact, as Dillon later recalled, Douglass seemed more interested in the day's baseball scores than in Dillon's proposal. "Listen, how'd the game come out today?" Douglass asked. Dillon could only shrug—he told his future father-in-law that he didn't follow professional baseball.

George Douglass's only remark about Dillon marrying his youngest daughter was a humorous warning.

"You know what you're getting yourself into," he said. "She's a regular little spitfire."

Although the Douglass-Dun family was part of the American upper class and typically would have frowned upon a marriage to an *arriviste* like Clarence Dillon, Anne's maternal relatives had established a precedent for unconventionality. Anne's mother's brother, Edwin Dun, had served as a US diplomatic envoy to Japan and, rather scandalously for the time, married a Japanese woman. Anne's aunt, Minnie Dun, had married the English explorer-naturalist Thomas Blakiston who had traveled up the Yangtze River in China in 1861, "going further than any Westerner before him." Anne's eldest sister, Elizabeth, resided in Cairo for ten years after marrying an English lawyer.

Once Anne accepted Dillon's proposal, the society section of *The Milwaukee Journal* dutifully reported the engagement on October 17, 1907, and the wedding announcement on January 20, 1908.

> Mr. and Mrs. George Douglass have issued invitations for the wedding of their daughter, Anne McEldin Douglass, and Clarence Dillon at 4 Tuesday afternoon Feb. 4 at the residence of the bride's parents on Waverly Place. The ceremony will be performed by the Reverend Paul B Jenkins of Immanuel Presbyterian Church in the presence of relatives and a few intimate friends and will be followed by a small reception at 4:30. The bride's only attendant will be her sister, Miss Elizabeth Douglass.

The wedding was small but tastefully elegant. The Douglass home at 14 Waverly Place had a picturesque view of Lake Michigan's blue horizon. Arrangements of lilies of the valley, Easter lilies, and roses filled silver bowls in the rooms. A chamber group played from behind a bank of palms. Anne wore an empire gown made of white satin. Her maid of honor wore an imported Irish point lace dress.

The Milwaukee Journal listed no Lapowskis in their account of the wedding. This was by design: Clarence clearly wanted no members of his immediate family in attendance. The matrons and misses in the assisting party were all the wives and daughters of Milwaukee's elite. Conscious of appearances, Dillon didn't ask Armin Schlesinger to be his best man. Instead, he picked Walter McKown Jones, an Institute of 1770 member whose parents were listed in the Boston Blue Book. Jones gifted Anne a gold mesh bag studded with diamonds and sapphires.

If Dillon had begun a calculated metamorphosis from the Texas-born son of a Polish-Jewish immigrant before entering Harvard—legally changing his surname, joining the Episcopalian Church, styling himself at Harvard as "The Baron"—his marriage to Anne made the transformation complete.

Dillon surely marveled at the fact that his new bride was a member of the Colonial Dames of America, descended, through Sir George Yeardley, from one of the First Families of Virginia. While his own forebears were living as unemancipated Jews in the Russian Empire, without the rights to own property or to travel outside the Pale of Settlement, Anne descended from an Englishman who'd governed Colonial Virginia one hundred and sixteen years before George Washington was born.

Their marriage, though, was not merely a matter of cold calculation; Clarence and Anne were very much in love—and proved to be quite a spirited and compatible couple.

After arriving in New Orleans and having lunch in their honeymoon suite, they visited the Fair Grounds racetrack where Dillon thought he could impress Anne with his skills as a professional gambler. He made wagers on each race, but only after thorough studies of the records of the horses and carefully going over the "dope sheets."

He proceeded to lose every single bet.

When it came to the final race of the day, Anne handed Clarence a five-dollar bill and gave him the name of an obscure horse.

As Dillon later recounted:

"Proud of my knowledge of racetrack lingo, I asked, 'To show?' 'No,' she said, without looking up. 'On the nose.' I was relieved that she did not see my astonishment. Apparently, she was just as familiar with racing lingo—maybe more so—and I made up my mind then and there never again to try to show off in front of her."

Still, Dillon considered his wife a betting novice: Anne's horse had odds of 40 to 1; it was a ridiculous bet, Dillon thought, but he placed her money on the longshot, nonetheless. Then he went with his own mathematical and "professional doping" to choose his own horse.

"I returned to the stands after placing our bets. Anne said, 'Did you get my money up?' I told her I had. A few minutes later, they were off, and there was great excitement; it was the big race of the day. As they came into the stretch, there was one horse well out front, I felt it was mine and was quite proud of myself. But as they drew near and you could see the numbers; it was Anne's horse, running three lengths in front of the field.

"She collected two hundred dollars. The booth where I'd placed our bets was for small wagers, so Anne's winnings were handed over mostly in one-dollar bills—the dirtiest money I've ever handled. She took her victory in a calm and matter-of-fact fashion."

When they got back to their hotel room, Dillon laid the two hundred dollars in small bills on the table, feeling that the cash "was so dirty that I hated to touch it. Anne simply said, 'You take it.' . . . Then I asked her, as I could no longer contain myself, how in the world she had picked that horse? 'I didn't,' she said. 'I picked the *jockey.* His name was the same as the man you are working for.'"

Clarence and Anne found they had a more serious mutual passion: old furniture. In the French Quarter of New Orleans, they discovered numerous antique shops in which to look for bargains and rare collectibles. "Antiquing was great fun," Dillon later wrote, "and we worked hard at it. . . . It was not long before we knew all the antiquaires in New Orleans, both the better-known ones and the smaller dealers who had shops in the side streets."

Their honeymoon pastime was born out of practicality; they needed sofas, ottomans, tables, and chairs for the empty house they'd rented in Milwaukee. Holding hands, wandering side streets, whispering the confidences of young lovers, they spent days learning the nuances of the antique business and before long were posing as experts. "Whether we fooled any of the [antiquaries] I do not know, but we got fun out of it and learned something," Dillon wrote. "The main thing was that we were now fired with the desire to collect."

Severe headaches and bouts of vertigo continued to plague Clarence Dillon long after the accident. The injuries prevented him from returning to his position at the Schlesinger companies. Dillon filed a $25,000 damage suit against the Milwaukee railroad, but the jury failed to agree on a decision in June 1908. Eventually, Clarence Dillon was awarded a settlement of $8,000—more than $200,000 in today's currency.

He used the money to finance a long trip to Europe with Anne as he attempted to regain his health. In October 1908, they crossed the Atlantic on "the Cunard *Carpathia*," Dillon wrote, "later to achieve fame as the first ship to go to the rescue of the *Titanic*," and joined Anne's parents who were exploring Europe in their chauffeur-driven Peerless touring car.

The newlyweds lived less grandly than did the Douglasses by staying in "pensions" except when Anne's parents took them along to what Dillon called "swell hotels." A few family members took a side trip to Cairo to visit Anne's sister before returning to Europe. Leisurely touring with this party of well-to-do Americans, Clarence served as a good son-in-law by organizing all the practical details. He also pursued his fascination with art, architecture, and gourmet cooking; and took Anne on a grand tour of France, Monaco, Italy, Germany, and Switzerland.

An article appeared in the *Abilene Reporter* on January 22, 1909, announcing that Samuel Lapowski of El Paso intended to travel to Europe later that month to meet "his son and daughter, Mr. and Mrs. C. L. Dillon, in Paris, France, and they will see the Eastern country together." But Sam Lapowski never made the trip due to a crisis in Texas.

In February 1909, Lapowski's mercantile company filed for bankruptcy. It owed over $100,000 to 351 creditors. An involuntary petition in bankruptcy had already been filed several weeks earlier by some of Lapowski's creditors who accused Sam of trying to transfer property to other creditors while insolvent. Lapowski himself said that he'd hoped to pay back his creditors but had not been able to weather the Panic of 1907 and the subsequent Depression.

Clarence and Anne, meanwhile, were preoccupied in Geneva with the arrival of their first child, Douglas, who was born on August 21, 1909. Despite his business hardships, Clarence's father sent a small American flag to the Dillons. Sam Lapowski's note asked that Clarence and Anne place the flag in the baby's room "where the future President of the United States will first see the light."

Dillon thought of himself as a typical doting father, but "not being used to the appearance of small babies I initially thought Douglas's back was crooked." In a panic, he called in a team of French medical experts. "When I asked the doctors about it, they measured him centimeter by centimeter and then announced that they would order a plaster cast for the child, so that his back would grow straight. Next day I inquired if the cast was ready. 'Oh, no, monsieur,' they said. 'It will take three weeks.' Of course, by the time the cast arrived, Douglas was twice its size—and there was nothing the matter with his back, anyway."

The damage Clarence Dillon himself suffered during the Wisconsin train accident was graver. Due to an irreparable rupture of the inner ear, he would continue to suffer unexpected attacks of vertigo for the rest of his life. During their tour of Europe, however, Dillon's headaches and dizziness became less frequent and eventually ceased altogether. The months spent traveling together throughout Europe, touring the finest palaces and museums, were idyllic. When Clarence and Anne were comfortably ensconced at the Hotel Trianon in Versailles, the $8,000 railroad settlement was nearly depleted.

Dillon needed to shelve his artistic preoccupations and sail back to America with his young family. The shock of his father's financial difficulties sparked Clarence's eagerness to get back to work by March 1910.

Clarence Dillon was no longer an employee of the Schlesingers. Instead, he went to work for one of the Douglass family companies, becoming vice president of a subsidiary of the Milwaukee Machine Tool Company founded three years earlier by his brother-in-law George Angus Douglass. Anne's parents provided the $10,000 Clarence needed to purchase a half interest in the small firm. In 1910, Clarence lived with his wife and son in his father-in-law's Milwaukee home. In stark contrast, Armin

Schlesinger built the "largest and most imposing" residence in a prestigious district of Milwaukee by spending $150,000 on a grand Tudor Revival house.

Dillon began selling Milwaukee Machine Tool Company bonds to a local bank and building a new factory for it. His superb salesmanship skills combined with his industrial inexperience, however, nearly closed down the firm. In 1913, when a fire destroyed the plant of an Indiana automobile company, Dillon journeyed to the site and acquired an order to replace all that company's lathe equipment. The huge order was more than the Milwaukee Machine Tool Company could manufacture. To cope with the crisis, Clarence deftly negotiated the sale of their own business to a nearby competitor, Kearney & Trecker, for partial ownership. Dillon learned that it's often smarter to receive payment in stocks rather than cash.

Meanwhile, a Texas sheriff had sold Sam Lapowski's El Paso property to satisfy a judgment against his firm by the State National Bank. Clarence's father traveled to Salt Lake City and then to San Francisco to set up new dry goods businesses.

Without warning, Sam Lapowski developed a brain tumor and died in San Francisco on June 30, 1912.

"At the time of his death," the *El Paso Herald* reported on August 5, 1912, "Mr. Lapowski was engaged in business in Salt Lake City, Utah, but had been in San Francisco for four weeks before his death . . . The funeral services were held in San Francisco."

Clarence and Anne, who was then pregnant with their second child—a daughter they would name Dorothy—took the train to San Francisco to pay their respects.

According to a report on August 13, 1912, in the *Abilene Semi-Weekly Reporter*: "The remains were buried in Santa Barbara . . . where his wife and one of their daughters, Miss Jeannie Lapowski, were living."

Dillon's own description of his father's final years, typed in his unpublished memoir, is just one sentence:

"He retired from business in 1910, and went to California, where he died."

Clarence added a second handwritten sentence immediately following, but then crossed it out:

"He never saw Douglas and died before Dorothy was born."

After learning much about the iron mining business from Ferdinand Schlesinger, Dillon found a second Milwaukee mentor in George Peckham Miller, Milwaukee's leading lawyer, who was George Douglass's counsel. Since Miller had no son of his own, Dillon wrote, "he was always interested and helpful in whatever I was doing."

By then, Clarence and Anne were living in one half of a double house in a desirable Prospect Avenue neighborhood. After the sale of the Milwaukee Machine Tool Company, Dillon had decided that he wouldn't take a job working for anyone else; from then on he would go out on his own—a plan encouraged by the then fifty-five-year-old Miller who saw immense potential in the young man. For his part, Dillon received an invaluable tutorial in the art of negotiation from Miller.

In 1908, Anne's father received by inheritance ownership of a one-tenth interest in R. G. Dun & Company. Founded as the Mercantile Agency in 1841, R. G. Dun & Company, the predecessor firm to Dun & Bradstreet, was the first successful commercial reporting agency in the United States and a pioneer in the industry of credit reporting.

George P. Miller advised Anne's father to place his one-tenth interest in a trust in December 1910, with Miller, his son, George Angus Douglass, and son-in-law, Clarence Dillon, as trustees. A dispute soon arose between the Dun heirs. George P. Miller suggested that regular financial audits of R. G. Dun & Company should be made with full information disclosed to George Douglass as owner of one-tenth of the business.

The owners of the other nine-tenths in New York staunchly opposed an audit and felt that George Douglass should be satisfied with receiving his share of the earnings when there were distributions.

"They felt the nature of the mercantile agency business was such that any form of publicity would be injurious," Dillon later wrote. "Mr. Miller did not feel publicity need result from the fact that the owners received statements such as he was requesting."

Miller, Dillon and George Douglass went to New York to negotiate the dispute with the Dun heirs and their legal team. At the New York conference, Dillon took in the gamesmanship with fascination. The Dun heirs' chief counsel was Francis L. Stetson, one of America's most prominent corporate lawyers, a past president of the New York State Bar Association in 1909, and the personal counsel to J. Pierpont Morgan.

Stetson didn't even bother engaging at first; he let his younger colleagues do all the talking.

"The lawyers for the owners of the nine-tenths threatened that if we did not settle on their terms the business would go up at auction," Dillon recalled. "And they could very easily bid it in and pay Mr. Douglass out at their own price while we, representing only one-tenth, could not buy nine-tenths."

Clarence watched as Francis Stetson coolly sat at his desk, thumbing through a copy of *English Country Life*, and let the younger lawyers continue to play hardball. Only when the discussion arrived at an impasse did Stetson nonchalantly look up at Miller.

"Well, if you can't come to terms," he said, "your client will be ruined at the auction block."

George Miller didn't reply. He sat silent for a long moment. "A very thin man of cadaverous appearance"—as Dillon described him—Miller finally stood up, went over to Francis Stetson's desk and extended his long thin arm.

"Till we meet at the auction block," he said, leaving the room.

Clarence and his brother-in-law accompanied Miller back to the Plaza Hotel where the thin, pale lawyer quickly arranged for three tickets on the Twentieth Century Limited train west, before approaching the hotel desk clerk.

"A friend of mine will be calling me," Miller told him. "Please say that we've checked out and are leaving on the 2:30 train for Chicago."

Dillon took a short walk with Miller and Douglass in nearby Central Park, and when they returned to the Plaza, the clerk said: "You have had a call from Mr. Doyle and we gave him your message."

During the short taxi ride to Grand Central Station, Miller smiled. "He'll be at the train," he told Dillon.

Doyle, one of Stetson's junior lawyers representing the nine-tenths owners, was indeed waiting at their gate when the Miller team arrived for the Twentieth Century Limited. Doyle said he was sorry that they'd taken offense, and that Mr. Stetson had not meant his comment to sound so crass and so threatening.

"Won't you please stay in New York?" Doyle asked.

"I'm sorry," Miller said, "but we can't. I've made other arrangements, and I must be in Milwaukee tomorrow."

On their sixteen-hour ride to Chicago, Miller turned again to Dillon, smiling with confidence.

"They'll be in Milwaukee next week."

Doyle indeed arrived in Milwaukee the following week and Miller agreed to resume talks. Quietly, Miller proposed a tentative price to George Douglass for his one-tenth interest. He prepared the signed settlement papers for delivery.

Already confident in young Dillon's abilities, Miller told him, "No use my going—you go on to New York."

Upon arriving in New York with his brother-in-law, Dillon read the expressions on the faces of the Dun heirs like the expert poker player he was. "When we got there it was apparent the others were anxious to get the thing settled," Dillon wrote. With no price mentioned yet, he stayed silent, waiting for the opposing counsel to speak first. The Dun heirs' lawyers named a price much higher than what Miller had suggested.

Dillon said he needed to first phone Miller—buying time to decide whether to hold out for even more or accept their offer. He and George Douglass—a blood relation to the Duns, after all—chose to accept the offer "to keep family relations as pleasant as possible."

The adrenaline rush and satisfaction of the experience sparked Clarence Dillon's lifelong appetite for tough negotiations.

Clarence shared the amusing story of his success with his former Harvard roommate, Bill Phillips, who by then worked as a bond salesman for William A. Read & Co., a New York investment banking firm, and had traveled to Milwaukee to see if he could sell securities to Clarence's father-in-law. Bill Phillips laughed at Dillon's account of the negotiation with Francis Stetson's team, then looked his old classmate up and down.

"Listen, Baron, this is no place for you," he said. "You need to be in New York—not out here in the sticks."

Back in New York, Phillips promptly told his boss, William A. Read, a savvy Wall Street trader himself, how Clarence Dillon had outfoxed the legendary Francis Stetson. Read was visibly amused.

Always on the lookout to recruit new talent, impressed by Dillon's cool shrewdness, he asked to meet this tall young Texan who styled himself "The Baron."

The next time Dillon was in New York City, Bill Phillips introduced him to William Read.

It was Dillon's first encounter with a Wall Street trader of the old school. Read was born in Brooklyn in 1858, forty years before the borough was incorporated into New York City. He was educated at Brooklyn High School and the Brooklyn Polytechnic & Collegiate Institute and began his finance career at Vermilye & Co., eventually becoming the senior partner in 1904 when the firm was renamed William A. Read & Co. Renowned for his expertise in securities, Read held directorships at the Bank of New York, Central Trust Company of New York, Alliance Assurance Company of London, Twin City Rapid Transit Company, and Interborough Rapid Transit Company.

As Dillon would soon learn, Read was a well-read man—a lover of history—and an avid book collector with a library celebrated for its artistically bound volumes. In 1894, he married Caroline Seaman, daughter of Samuel Seaman of the Cromwell Steamship Company. They had seven children who reached adulthood; their four eldest sons all served as US Navy aviators.

The Reads divided their time between their brownstone at 4 East 62nd Street in Manhattan and the lavish Hillcrest estate in Purchase. They often summered in Lenox, Massachusetts.

"William Read's reputation as a financier is beyond question," *The Wall Street Journal* wrote in a 1915 profile while *The New York Times* described him as "a man of great financial ability and conservative views."

His conservatism was clearly reflected in his appearance. With his well-trimmed gray handlebar mustache, Read seemed like a man stuck in the previous century. During business hours, he wore a traditional black cutaway coat, revealing the waistcoat beneath, with two knee-length tails. In the buttonhole of his narrow-peak left lapel he always had a fresh violet.

Over lunch, Read wasted little time: he offered Clarence a job. The aspiring Wall Streeter didn't accept; he said he would have to discuss it with his wife.

"Anne did not like the idea of leaving Milwaukee, but she said, 'Of course, I will do whatever you want,'" Dillon later wrote. "We decided not to go to New York, but we accepted Mr. Read's second proposal to go to the Chicago office. Meantime, I would commute and spend weekends in Milwaukee."

In 1913, Clarence began serving a bond salesman apprenticeship under the supervision of William Meade Lindsley Fiske II, a worldly, articulate man whose Puritan ancestors had emigrated from England to Massachusetts in the seventeenth century. Dillon immediately admired Fiske who, like himself, had become a Francophile after a European tour. Dillon focused on making an impressive debut in his new position by acquiring substantial bond-buying clients that no one in the Read organization had been able to land.

He struck paydirt almost immediately. George P. Miller was the personal attorney to a most unlikely multimillionaire named William Horlick and recommended that he buy bonds from Dillon.

Horlick had become wealthy through a humble baby-food supplement, malted milk, a powder made from malted barley, wheat flour, and evaporated whole milk—first developed by his brother, the London-born pharmacist James Horlick, as a nutritional supplement. When James joined William in Racine, Wisconsin, in 1873, the brothers incorporated as J & W Horlick and began manufacturing their brand in nearby Chicago. Ten years later, they received a patent, and by 1886 had trademarked the name "malted milk."

Lightweight, nonperishable, and packed with nutrients, tins of malted milk powder became a favorite among explorers who carried them on expeditions around the globe. Admiral Richard E. Byrd was so grateful for the supply of malted milk that he named the Horlick Mountains in Antarctica in their honor. In 1890, James returned to England and was later made a baronet. In the United States, the Horlicks brand became a staple at soda fountains and gained even more popularity when combined with ice cream in "malts" (or "malteds") which inspired thousands of malt shops across the country.

The decades-long vogue for malteds made both Horlick brothers extremely wealthy. After George Miller introduced William Horlick to Clarence Dillon, the food magnate was so impressed, he not only bought bonds from Dillon but decided to turn over his entire investment portfolio to him. In short order, Horlick became one of William Read & Co.'s best clients.

On the strength of Clarence Dillon's ambition and remarkably rapid success in the Midwest, William Read now insisted that Dillon move immediately to the Manhattan office.

The bond business may have little cachet today but in the first two decades of the twentieth century, being a bond salesman was akin to what being a young hedge funder is today. By the 1920s, bond selling was a career followed by so many ambitious young Ivy League--educated men that F. Scott Fitzgerald in *The Great Gatsby* has his book's narrator Nick Carraway saying:

"The Middle West now seemed like the ragged edge of the universe so I decided to go East and learn the bond business. Everybody I knew was in the bond business, so I supposed it could support one more single man."

Clarence Dillon's ambitions were considerably higher than Nick Carraway's—and much more akin to Jay Gatsby's.

Dillon left Milwaukee and Chicago behind—never looking back.

He was a man in a hurry. He set out for New York with one priority: to accumulate his own fortune.

That did not take long.

Chapter Three

RISK AND REWARD

CLARENCE DILLON'S NEW employer was an independent thinker with a knack for calculating precise bids in uncertain markets. William Augustus Read didn't shy away from competing against Wall Street's giants. Despite this fearless streak, for decades William A. Read & Co. remained a small firm focused on municipal debt financing.

In January 1914, however, Read achieved a significant and unexpected victory by winning the bid for a $51 million New York state bond issue alongside Kuhn, Loeb & Co. Read himself had made the winning bid and then, summoning his new protégé into his office, as Dillon later wrote, "he left the details of the arrangement pretty much in my hands."

It was a huge responsibility for a Wall Streeter of such little experience. Dillon walked the short distance to the Bankers Trust Building at 14 Wall Street. Entering Kuhn, Loeb's offices on the second floor, Dillon was introduced to Jacob Schiff, a man who, since 1885, had been one of Wall Street's most powerful and influential figures—second only to J.P. Morgan.

Diminutive and silver-bearded, always impeccably dressed, Schiff had made his reputation reorganizing the Union Pacific railway and by financing the Empire of Japan in its war against the Empire of Russia in 1905.

When Dillon walked in, Schiff was already glancing at his pocket watch; the old man was known for being scrupulously punctual, focusing on using every *instant* of his day profitably. Dillon knew Schiff's reputation; the sixty-six-year-old German Jew could get frighteningly impatient and didn't suffer fools gladly; if he felt someone was wasting his time, his steely blue eyes would bore through them with withering scorn.

A staunch member of the Reform Judaism movement, Schiff helped establish both the Hebrew Union College and the Jewish Theological Seminary. As one of American Jewry's top philanthropists and leaders, Schiff donated generously to nearly every major Jewish cause. In New York alone, he supported institutions like the Montefiore Home for Chronic Invalids and the Young Men's Hebrew Association.

Schiff's Orthodox upbringing in Frankfurt had instilled in him the rabbinic teachings on philanthropy. He often explained to non-Jews that the Torah spoke in terms of *tzedakah*, or justice, and that he objected to the word *charity*:

"The ancient Hebrew lawgiver knows no such word as charity; to him even giving to the poor is only an act of justice, and justice is the expression he solely applies, when he urges his people to their duty to the needy and dependent."

Following the ancient teachings of Jewish sages, Schiff believed that true philanthropy meant providing a job for the unemployed. It was "something terrible," he said, for a person to want honest work and not find it. In 1901, Schiff was one of the founders of the Industrial Removal Office, which relocated tens of thousands of unemployed Eastern European Jewish immigrants—crowded in unspeakably bleak, unsanitary conditions on the Lower East Side—throughout the United States to smaller cities where Jewish communities and jobs existed.

Schiff supported relief efforts for victims of pogroms in Russia—especially the horrific Kishinev massacre of April 1903—by establishing an additional port of entry for immigrants in Texas. Eventually known as "The Galveston Movement"—or "Galveston Plan"—between 1907 and 1914, tens of thousands of impoverished Jewish immigrants arrived through Galveston, Texas. "The Galveston Movement" is not to be confused with the much smaller Christian missionary–sponsored, post–American Civil War emigration to Galveston, made by Samuel Lapowski. Behind the scenes, Schiff spearheaded the movement with $500,000 of his own money—equivalent to about $17 million today—while British-born Rabbi Henry Cohen of Galveston's B'nai Israel synagogue became the figurehead, personally welcoming ships at Galveston's docks and guiding newcomers through the complex arrival process and assimilation into rural America.

Schiff lived by Maimonides's famous "ladder of tzedakah" in which one of the highest *mitzvot*—good deeds—is to give donations anonymously. He wouldn't permit his name to be attached to the buildings he sponsored, with the notable exception of the Schiff Pavilion at Montefiore Hospital in the Bronx. Because of his secrecy, the exact amount of his philanthropic donations is impossible to calculate (though some estimates place his total philanthropic donations at between $50 million and $100 million dollars).

The handshake between Clarence Dillon and Jacob Schiff was, in a sense, a meeting of two different philosophies: Old World thinking versus American modernity; proud religious insularity versus unabashed assimilation. It also reflected the difference in social status between New York's German Jews—earlier immigrants to America who saw themselves as more cultured, sophisticated, and educated, a higher stratum within Jewish society compared to the "gauche" working-class Polish-Jewish community to which Samuel Lapowski belonged.

Ferdinand Schlesinger, though Prussian-born and German speaking, wasn't cut from the same cloth as the established New York German-Jewish financial families, many of whom, like Jacob Schiff, had a lineage of European banking going back to the late 1700s in Frankfurt with Mayer Amschel Rothschild, founder of the Rothschild dynasty.

Clarence Lapowski had made the calculated decision before entering Harvard to obscure his Jewish origins, becoming an Episcopalian and taking on all the outward trappings of being from old WASP money to succeed in New York, whereas America's pioneering German-Jewish bankers had taken another tack entirely.

Back in the late 1860s, Abraham Kuhn and his brother-in-law Solomon Loeb had faced employment barriers at Gentile firms on Wall Street; rather than be shut out of the old boys' club, they simply created an insular world of their own. They formed a powerful all-Jewish investment bank which would compete aggressively with any firm on Wall Street. Jacob Schiff, married to Solomon Loeb's daughter, Therese, was by the turn of the century securely at the head of the firm. Indeed, all Kuhn, Loeb & Co. partners were related by blood or marriage.

At the conference table on the second floor of 14 Wall Street, Clarence Dillon was charged with negotiating the terms of the "spread"—how the two underwriting firms would divide the risk. In layman's terms, working out the details of the spread is akin to the way a bookie will lay off bets to other bookies, to minimize his own exposure in the case of a loss.

During the meeting, one of Kuhn, Loeb's junior partners, flanking Jacob Schiff, pointedly asked Dillon whom he proposed would get "top billing" in the forthcoming advertisement in *The New York Times.*

"Mr. Dillon, will it be Kuhn, Loeb or William Read listed first in the advertisement?"

Dillon recalled his late father often saying, "Where McGuire sits, that's the head of the table." (Sam Lapowski had been fond of that famous nineteenth-century proverb, a slight misquoting of Sir Walter Scott's novel "Rob Roy": *Where MacGregor sits is the head of the table.*) In other words, the great man makes the place rather than the place the man.

"If you have a preference," Dillon said, without blinking, "make your choice."

Normally inscrutable, Jacob Schiff couldn't stifle his smile. The experienced old German trader was clearly impressed by this lean young Texan's swagger and acumen at the negotiating table. As Dillon later wrote, upon seeing the taciturn Schiff smile, "I felt I'd made a new friend."

When one of the junior partners suggested that Dillon return later that afternoon to finalize the details of the deal, Schiff cut him short: "There'll be no need for that." Schiff decided that William Read & Co. would "be on the left"—he magnanimously decided that the smaller firm would be the one running the deal.

In a quiet but authoritative voice, the old man said: "Mr. Dillon will keep the books."

"William A. Read & Co., in association with Kuhn, Loeb & Co., yesterday secured the award of the $51,000,000 New York State bond issue," *The New York Times* reported. "The syndicate headed by J.P. Morgan & Co. was expected to get the issue, but Read & Co.'s bid, which was lower by ⅛ of 1 per cent, won the day."

The Kuhn-Loeb-Read offering was a tremendous success; within two hours, all bonds sold out. William Read was as impressed as Jacob Schiff by the skillful work of Clarence Dillon. The young man had the sort of self-assuredness and negotiating savvy that belied his years—an almost innate quality that Read knew could not be easily taught.

Read encouraged Dillon to rent a house in Westchester County in Harrison near his own estate named Hillcrest in Purchase.

Once Dillon had found his own classy but modest home in Harrison, the two men often commuted together in Read's chauffeur-driven Rolls-Royce, discussing business, history, and world affairs during the forty-five minutes it took them to get to Wall Street. When Anne was out of town, Clarence sometimes accompanied Read to the Metropolitan Opera, where in the 1914–1915 season they had the chance to see the great Italian tenor, Enrico Caruso, appearing in *Pagliacci*.

Dillon found his new boss to be an extraordinary man, cautious and never impulsive or rash, though Dillon noticed that Read was sometimes overly confrontational in his approach. During his time at Vermilye & Co., Read was known to be quite litigious, several times suing rivals over petty matters. Dillon believed that Read didn't spend enough time courting others—taking a softer touch, using the power of persuasion he'd observed so closely in Ferdinand Schlesinger.

Read gave Dillon no specific instructions during his first year in the New York office. Wanting to test his protégé's mettle, he let Dillon take the initiative. Dillon quickly saw that the firm had no aggressive sales force to distribute securities. He devised a simple plan to incentivize the team. He told the firm's bond salesmen, who had felt inferior to the corporate finance staff, that they could quickly become the most important division of the business. Dillon said that from now on they would be rewarded by compensation based on performance.

Clarence worked with his old friend Bill Phillips to sharpen the sales force's effectiveness and found customers among trust companies and brokerages.

During a slow business period in March 1914, Dillon showed his salesmanship again. He went back to Milwaukee and created a financing plan for Newport Mining Company. Then he sold an issue of notes in Cleveland. By the time Clarence returned to New York, he had made a handsome profit of $100,000 for the firm.

William Read was pleased with his resourceful young colleague, and doubtless, also pleased with his own sharp judgment of talent.

The unexpected assassination of Austro-Hungarian Archduke Franz Ferdinand and his wife in Sarajevo on the morning of June 28, 1914, threw the world into chaos and thus Clarence Dillon's future. Following the murder of the archduke by Gavrilo Princip, a nineteen-year-old Bosnian Serb nationalist, Austria-Hungary saw an opportunity to assert its dominance in the Balkans. With Germany's backing, they issued an ultimatum to Serbia laden with demands that were nearly impossible to meet. Serbia's partial compliance was not enough for Austria-Hungary, which declared war on July 28.

The declaration set off a cascade of alliances and treaties coming into play. Russia mobilized in defense of Serbia; Germany responded by declaring war on Russia. France was drawn in due to its binding alliance with Russia. When German forces violated Belgium's neutrality as part of their strategy against France, England entered the fray to defend Belgian sovereignty.

The modern age had introduced new technologies and methods of warfare that defied traditional military strategies. Yet despite these advancements and the clear risks involved—both in terms of human life and national stability—the nations involved felt compelled by honor, alliances, and perceived threats to engage fully in what would become one of history's most devastating conflicts.

With war clouds looming, Clarence Dillon had foreseen an immense risk to William Read & Co. He remembered his father's losses during financial panics and Texas droughts. Dillon felt that the firm should liquidate its large inventory of bonds to carry fewer liabilities during wartime.

William Read brushed off what he saw as Dillon's alarmism about global affairs. This was not the Napoleonic era with hordes of cavalrymen slashing at each other with sabers or slow-advancing infantrymen armed with muzzle-loaded muskets. By 1914, there were new technologies and methods of warfare and military strategies—tanks, airplanes, long-range artillery, even deadly chemical gases—and the conservative-minded Read couldn't see the European leaders being so illogical and foolish. All the frightening news out of Europe was surely gamesmanship, Read thought.

"They can't fight, Dillon," he said. "Not today—not in an industrial world. They can't go to war."

Dillon didn't disagree. A world war in 1914 made no sense. Yet Dillon was more of a realist—certainly, he was more in tune with the changing zeitgeist than his mentor in his impeccably tailored Victorian-style cutaway suit. Showdowns between powerful egos, involving family connections and promised alliances, did not follow the rules of logic.

In no-limit Texas Hold'em, Dillon knew a man would go "all in" with stacks of chips, strictly based on an emotional decision, not rationality or common sense. Read was right about the changing nature of warfare in the industrial age, however Dillon could see that all the nations involved were driven by motives other than logic.

For Dillon, it boiled down to one simple question.

"Who's going to back down?" he asked his boss.

Read didn't answer; he sat pensively, then let the matter drop. He didn't give his young protégé an answer until the next morning when he called Dillon into his office.

"I've been thinking about it," he said. "Who *is* going to back down?"

"That's what worries me."

Read nodded.

"Let's get an early start. Go ahead and liquidate the inventory."

When the first shots were fired between the French and Germans at 5:00 a.m. on August 7, in the Battle of Mulhouse, William A. Read & Co. was safe because of Dillon's foresight.

Though Read was quietly impressed by Dillon's intuition, he strongly disagreed with Dillon's next ambitious move. In midsummer 1914, the New York Stock Exchange did something unprecedented in its one-hundred-twenty-two-year history: it shut down trading indefinitely. On July 31, panic selling surged as fears of war gripped investors. Liquidity worries and potential bank runs added to the chaos.

The US government intervened, closing the Exchange to prevent further destabilization. Markets in London and Berlin had already ceased trading due to panic among investors. The proximate cause was Austria-Hungary's war declaration on Serbia on July 28.

The NYSE had previously shut down during financial panics or political crises—after the assassination of President Garfield;

during the opening salvos of the Spanish-American War—but only for a matter of days. The closure in the summer of 1914 was different—the Exchange didn't reopen until four months later, on November 28, with new restrictions and strict regulations aimed at curbing speculation.

While the Exchange was shuttered, bond brokers had no choice but to halt all sales. Many Wall Street firms reduced their sales teams or gave employees vacations at half pay. Bond dealers, frustrated by the ban, suggested resuming securities sales but only with their own clients and for cash transactions. By any measure, the bond market was at a nadir during the early months of the First World War. William A. Read & Co. participated in only one underwriting from June 1914 until year's end.

Six months into the war, on a brisk evening early in 1915, Dillon was having dinner at the Metropolitan Club with two friends working for J.P. Morgan's purchasing group formed to buy critical war supplies in America on behalf of England and France.

Waddill Catchings was a friend whom Clarence knew in Cambridge, through Harvard's debating club. Catchings had coached the senior debate team as a first-year law student in 1902. Dillon's other dinner companion, Grayson Mallet-Prevost Murphy, had graduated from West Point and once made an intelligence trip to Colombia in 1903 for President Theodore Roosevelt regarding plans to construct the Panama Canal. As they settled into their seats at the dinner table, Catchings casually asked about the latest news out of Europe.

"Dillon, have you been reading the papers? Both the French and British are running desperately low on phenol. They're searching everywhere to buy some."

Dillon was immediately curious. Why was phenol so desperately needed?

"Baron, phenol is positively *essential*—you can't make picric acid, TNT, or any other explosives without it."

Catchings further explained that phenol was primarily obtained as a byproduct of coal tar distillation and coke manufacture. These natural processes yielded very limited quantities of phenol, making it scarce and expensive.

Dillon began to strategize aloud at the dinner table. If natural sources were finite, could phenol possibly be made synthetically? And if it could be made synthetically, could it be produced on an industrial scale? Perhaps, with the right machinery, and the right expertise . . .

Dillon immediately thought of his roommate from Harvard's Gold Coast.

"You remember Armin Schlesinger?"

"Of course," Catchings said.

Dillon mentioned his experiences in Milwaukee with the Schlesinger coke ovens. Catchings and Murphy could see the wheels turning in their friend's mind. There was surely money to be made here—perhaps a fortune—as in any wartime shortage.

First, Dillon had to run the idea to invest in synthetic phenol production by his boss. William Read immediately told him it was foolishly risky. Read knew nothing about the chemical industry and, for that matter, *neither* did Dillon.

"Mark my words," he said. "You'll lose both your money and your friends."

Dillon forged ahead nonetheless, meticulously researching the chemical industry to assess opportunities and risks. He contacted Armin Schlesinger who discussed the proposal with his father. The Schlesingers agreed that synthetic phenol could *potentially* be a lucrative proposition. In May 1915, the Schlesingers' chemists and engineers began experimenting with phenol synthesis using benzol recovered from coke-oven gas at their Milwaukee facilities.

Their innovative approach enabled large-scale synthesis from benzol through distillation processes, separating valuable benzene and toluene components. This breakthrough would immediately address the wartime phenol shortage.

Dillon negotiated a tough but fair deal with the Schlesingers: they would own 51% of the new "synthetic phenol production" company while he would hold 49%. Dillon assumed the responsibility of finding customers and selling the product; the Schlesingers financed its manufacture. Dillon continued his full-time work at William A. Read & Co. and knowing the old man's disapproval, and pessimistic prediction, Dillon treated synthetic phenol production as a private and personal sideline.

Dillon's first customer was already an American legend: Thomas Edison. Edison invented the phonograph in 1877 while experimenting with an automatic method of recording telegraph messages. He used phenol to produce his so-called "Diamond Discs." Edison began stockpiling phenol strictly for phonograph production, wholly unaware that the chemical would soon become vital in global affairs.

With the onset of World War I, the US imported much of its phenol from Germany, which sourced coal tar from Britain to synthesize the chemicals. When Britain imposed a wartime embargo on Germany, it led to a phenol shortage in the United States. This left Edison scrambling for ways in which to obtain phenol.

Edison built a plant in Silver Lake, New Jersey, in 1915 to produce phenol domestically. Clarence Dillon saw an opportunity here—not only to make a profit but also to contribute significantly to the Allied war cause.

Thomas Edison soon sent Dillon a list of companies that were also interested in purchasing benzol. Edison wrote in a letter dated April 21, 1915, that he intended to use all the benzol he could get for his own production of phenol. Edison therefore suggested that the other customers contact Dillon's startup venture which was expected to begin production in Milwaukee that May.

There were other reasons for Edison's haste to begin operations. On April 21, 1915, he wrote to the investment banking firm, Lazard Frères:

"I shall have in operation a plant for [manufacturing] Carbolic Acid [phenol] in about twenty-five to thirty days. I infer that the French government is desirous of obtaining a considerable quantity for making Picric Acid Explosive." Edison continued: "More than a dozen groups of speculators are after me to purchase my output of 4,000 pounds daily up to January first, but they all appear to be irresponsible."

Edison hoped to negotiate a deal through Lazard Frères with the French government as a large buyer. By early June, Edison was also corresponding with Edward Stettinius at J.P. Morgan about his contract with the British government to provide toluene for the manufacture of TNT.

While Americans were busily making profits from exporting war materials to the British and French, Germans within the United States were seeking to thwart such shipments. The linchpin of this internal espionage plot was Dr. Hugo Schweitzer, one of Germany's most important intelligence assets in the US during the first year of the war.

The fifty-five-year-old Dr. Schweitzer, who wore a mustache brushed up at the ends to resemble Kaiser Wilhelm II, had earned a doctorate in chemistry prior to immigrating to the US in 1889, where he joined the German-owned Bayer Chemical Company in New Jersey. Before the outbreak of the war, Schweitzer was receiving an annual retainer from the German War Office as a spy to supplement his Bayer salary. With the outbreak of war in 1914, Schweitzer's loyalties became evident with his publication of pro-German propaganda designed to evoke American sympathy.

Heinrich Albert was a German American businessman and agent who played another crucial role in what would later become known as "The Great Phenol Plot." He was a close associate of Hugo Schweitzer and worked as a liaison between Schweitzer's front companies and the German government.

To any casual observer, Albert appeared to be an ordinary European businessman. Born in Hamburg in 1874, Albert studied chemistry before moving to the United States, where he was the manager of Bayer's New York office, overseeing its export department. In truth, Heinrich Albert was no businessman; he was a spymaster managing cells in America for the German military intelligence agency Nachrichten-Abteilung.

Albert financed Dr. Hugo Schweitzer's phenol purchases from Thomas Edison through a front company called Chemische Fabrik Griesheim-Elektron, further obscured by a shell company, J. A. Schulz and Co., or "JASCO." JASCO was a wholly fictitious outfit solely set up by Albert to conceal the identity of the buyer—Schweitzer and the German government—and to facilitate their secret purchases of phenol from Edison's facility.

Their scheme dramatically impacted US markets: prices for picric acid and phenol soared, unintentionally benefiting ventures like the Newport Chemical Corporation owned by Clarence Dillon and the Schlesingers.

From the Germans' perspective "The Great Phenol Plot" proved to be one of World War I's most successful espionage missions.

"One and a half million pounds of carbolic acid have been kept from the Allies," Albert wrote to Schweitzer. "This tremendous quantity of explosive material has been withheld by your contract." Albert estimated that Schweitzer's purchases were the equivalent to destroying at least three railroad trains loaded with explosives.

Despite their layers of front companies and use of encoded messages, Albert's espionage activities attracted the attention of the United States Secret Service and its senior man in New York City, Special Agent Frank Burke. On the afternoon of July 24, 1915, Burke canceled his plans to go to the New York Giants–Pittsburgh Pirates baseball game at the Polo Grounds and joined another Secret Service agent surveilling the Hamburg America Line offices on Lower Broadway.

Heinrich Albert emerged, instantly recognizable by his Prussian mustache and elegant tailored three-piece suit. Rather than drawing attention to himself by using a chauffeured car, Albert took the elevated L-train uptown. The agents hopped on board, sat behind and across from Albert until his stop at 52nd Street whereupon Frank Burke snatched Albert's bulging leather briefcase and ran to catch a trolley, telling the operator not to stop because "a madman" was chasing him. Albert was running and flailing, giving credence to Burke's description.

At the German American Club on Central Park South, Albert and his staff, having no clue that they'd been under Secret Service surveillance, assumed that a common thief had stolen the briefcase. They placed an ad in Monday's newspapers, offering a paltry reward of $20. By then, however, the contents of the briefcase with details of the espionage plot were beginning their journey to Washington, DC, and directly to President Woodrow Wilson's desk.

Special Agent Frank Burke contacted Herbert Bayard Swope, editor of the anti-German *New York World* and offered an exclusive scoop—on the strict condition that Swope would never reveal his source or the true story of how the briefcase was stolen.

On Sunday, August 15, the *World*'s front page ran the exclusive under explosive headlines:

HOW GERMANY HAS WORKED IN THE U.S. TO SHAPE OPINION,

BLOCK THE ALLIES AND GET MUNITIONS FOR HERSELF: TOLD IN SECRET AGENTS' LETTERS

The *World* reproduced letters in both German and English and the public ate up the story of the "The Great Phenol Plot."

Swope kept his word: the *World* never revealed its sources; while competing daily newspapers reported the disinformation planted by Special Agent Burke, that Heinrich Albert's briefcase was stolen in July on the Lower East Side of Manhattan, in the vicinity of Fulton Street and Broadway. They reported that a thief either broke into Albert's office or snatched the briefcase at a nearby restaurant while Albert was distracted and made his getaway on the crowded sidewalks.

The thief—supposedly—unaware of the briefcase's contents, sold it to a secondhand dealer on the Lower East Side and eventually, the briefcase made its way to the US authorities.

While the stories about the theft were pure fiction, the contents of the stolen briefcase were indisputable evidence. Inside was a trove of documents: incriminating letters and telegrams from Hugo Schweitzer, contracts and invoices for the phenol purchases from Thomas Edison, coded messages and German military encryption keys.

Heinrich Albert was exposed as a fraud: fronting as Bayer's export department manager in New York while spying for the German military intelligence agency Nachrichten-Abteilung, helping Dr. Hugo Schweitzer to monopolize the world's supply of phenol for Germany.

After the plot was exposed, Albert was arrested and charged with espionage, but he managed to escape prosecution by fleeing back to Germany.

Although the plot was not illegal at the time, it garnered significant attention in neutral America's newspapers during the summer of 1915.

Thomas Edison was tarred by association because of his phenol production. The weeks of salacious headlines and public pressure forced Edison to halt his phenol business, leaving Clarence Dillon's venture with the Schlesingers as his sole option for the vital chemical.

Despite William Read's dire warnings about losing all his money *and* his friends, phenol made Clarence Dillon a multimillionaire. By June 1915, Dillon's success allowed him to buy a large property with a two-story house on Milton Road in Rye, New York, even closer to his boss's own Hillcrest estate. Dillon hired an Irish chauffeur, a Swedish maid, and, for his two young children, a French governess.

On June 11, Edison sent Dillon a gift—a Diamond Disc phonograph and records as thanks for being a reliable benzol supplier who also appreciated good music.

Dillon wrote Edison back with a story about how his son, Douglas, now six years old, became quite argumentative with his father, insisting that while Thomas Edison had certainly invented the light bulb, he was *not* the inventor of the phonograph.

Yet in August 1915, Edison turned down Dillon's offer for an additional quantity of benzol and stated that he currently had an oversupply. He advised Dillon to "sell for spot delivery & at same time look out for a long contract."

Dillon quickly realized that his company needed to advance from benzol production to the synthesis of phenol to remain profitable. He proposed a joint project with the experienced Edison. On October 12, 1915, Edison responded:

> *Let me say that I have given a good deal of thought to the co-operation which you proposed, and . . . I have about decided to go it alone. As you are aware, I am interested in the phenol question, as I am a very large and constantly increasing user of it myself, and during the development of my second phenol plant, many promising possibilities have presented themselves, and it looks to me now that I shall spend about a year on working out a simplified and better process. I could not do this unless the plant were absolutely my own, leaving me free and unhampered to pursue my experimental ways in the manner to which I have been accustomed for so many years.*

As Dillon had done with the earlier sale of his brother-in-law's company, he wasted no time turning his position of disadvantage into one of advantage. On January 3, 1916, Edison wrote:

> *My dear Mr. Dillon:*
>
> *I have been awaiting with more or less patience the receipt of some word from you in regard to continuing my contract for benzol up to the end of the present year. . . . I trust that you have not forgotten about me, and allowed somebody else to step in.*

Dillon and the Schlesingers had decided to build their own phenol production plant called the Newport Chemical Works at

Carrollville, Wisconsin, and arranged their own contract directly with the French government. Dillon soon revealed to Edison that they were now reserving most of their benzol for their own refining.

Dillon reassured Edison that he was "their favored customer" and that any excess benzol would be offered to him first. Edison was grateful when he was finally able to renew his contract for benzol with them. On July 15, 1916, Edison wrote that "the purest benzol comes from the Milwaukee Coke & Gas Company [where] Mr. Clarence Dillon has charge of benzol matters."

As wartime scarcities drove prices up, Edison noted that Dillon was claiming that he could get "reliable parties to take the benzol for ninety cents for pure." Edison advised Dillon to "close with them as there will be overproduction in the fall in case war ends then. Ninety cents is a little too high for me, as I am helping out the little people at moderate prices for phenol."

The Schlesingers' Newport Chemical Works had become a highly profitable competitor with Edison's phenol plants. Newport's 1916 advertisement offered phenol, benzol, and toluol, with the slogan: "American Made and Actually Available."

Newport Chemical was soon a major operation and Dillon noted that "by the end of 1915 we were going great guns, and my monthly dividend was very substantial." With just a small investment of his own money, Dillon found himself now an extremely wealthy man.

Foremost in his mind was his father's instruction:

"Whenever you make money, save it—be sure you never have less."

Clarence divided his new fortune into seven parts: one-seventh for himself and six trust funds with the remainder: one for his wife, one for his son, Douglas, one for his daughter, Dorothy, one for his mother, and one for each of his sisters.

William Read was impressed by his young protégé's accomplishments in the phenol business—though his ego may have been a bit wounded that Dillon had so brazenly ignored his cautionary advice.

On April 1, 1916, William Read offered Dillon a partnership in the firm. At thirty-three years old he was by far the youngest partner. When Dillon's name was added at the end of the list of William A. Read & Co. partners, Read told his brother-in-law, Joseph H. Seaman:

"You see this new name at the bottom? When we rewrite those papers next year, it will be at the top."

Read never returned to the office. A mere six days after making that prophetic remark, the seemingly healthy fifty-seven-year-old Read became suddenly ill and died of pneumonia inside his East Side Manhattan home.

Read left an estate valued between $5 and $6 million—roughly $140 to $170 million in today's currency. In addition to bequests to his family and charitable organizations, Read gave $25,000 to each of his eight partners and stipulated that his executors could loan up to $2 million to the firm.

Even though Clarence Dillon was a junior partner with less than three years' experience at William A. Read & Co., he believed that he should be Read's replacement as head of the firm. He'd been a more dynamic producer than any of the other partners, most of whom had started at the company decades before him, and he'd certainly brought more innovative ideas to the table.

The week after Read's death, Henry Davison, the senior partner of the J.P. Morgan firm, visited Dillon at William Read & Co.'s offices and asked whether there was anything his firm could do for him. Within a few months, Dillon was offered a directorship in the Morgan organization which was loaning capital to the government of France to fund its war efforts. In January 1917, the chairman of the board of the Central Trust Company invited Dillon to take William Read's place on the board.

"This was rather a signal recognition by the Street in general of my position as leader in our firm," Dillon later wrote. "And it established that position securely for the future as all of my partners were very flattered and pleased that after Mr. Read's death, we should have been given a place not only on the Board, but on the Executive Committee as well."

The committee included many of the leading men of Wall Street, including Jacob Schiff and James Cox Brady.

Dillon's position of leadership was growing in strength, but by consensus, all the other William A. Read & Co. partners—R.L. Taylor, James W. Horner Jr., James Dean, R.W. Martin, William A. Phillips, W.M.L. Fiske, E.J. Bermingham and the founder's son, William A. Read Jr.—agreed to carry on the business without naming a head.

Fully aware that the other partners had more seniority and experience than himself, Clarence Dillon calmly stood up, walked into Read's office and simply took the old man's seat behind his oak desk.

But Dillon would have to delay his formal leadership of the firm for reasons beyond his control.

Chapter Four

CAPITOL AND CAPITAL

ON APRIL 2, 1917, President Woodrow Wilson asked a joint session of the United States Congress to declare war on the German Empire and its Allies. Congress did so two days later, and Wilson signed the formal declaration of war on April 6, 1917. A mood of patriotism swept the heretofore neutral and isolationist nation. Clarence Dillon and his family were as eager as any other Americans to volunteer in any way possible.

Clarence's nephew, Seymour Weller, an associate at Dillon Read, sailed to France on July 4, 1917, serving as an ambulance driver with the American Field Service. Two of Weller's younger brothers followed soon after. Clarence's wife, Anne, joined the Red Cross as a volunteer, rolling bandages for the wounded American boys.

Even Dillon's eight-year-old son, Douglas, donated to the cause. Using Douglas's savings, Clarence and Anne purchased an ambulance for the US Army, inside of which was affixed a brass plate engraved with these words:

"Given by C. Douglas Dillon because I'm too little to fight."

His six-foot father was obviously not too little. However, at age thirty-four, he *was* too old to be drafted by the Selective Service Act. Clarence Dillon had pledged to help the war effort nevertheless, and volunteered to serve overseas, or domestically, in any capacity needed.

Dillon's personal physician was Dr. Lewis Atterbury Conner, a pioneering cardiologist who later cofounded the American Heart Association. Conner served as a private in the US Army during the Spanish-American War, and by the time the country entered World War I, he was in uniform again, now a senior medical officer and chief of the Army Medical Corps Division of Internal Medicine. Conner wore the dark maroon uniform of a major in the US Army Medical Corps when Clarence Dillon entered his office to discuss the sudden pain he'd been experiencing on the left side of his abdomen.

The discomfort had initially been mild and intermittent, but now the stabbing sensation was growing unbearable, so intensely painful that Dillon feared that, without prompt treatment, the condition could prove to be life-threatening. It didn't take Dr. Conner long to discover that Dillon had a stone in his left kidney. During his childhood in West Texas, Dillon suffered from a severe kidney infection. In the throes of a particularly high fever, the doctors in Abilene were worried that Clarence wouldn't make it.

Afterward, Sam and Bertha were so hypervigilant that they refused to allow their only son to take so much as a sip of Texas tap water. His parents, Dillon later wrote, "remained fearful of a recurrence [of infection] or that I might develop a stone in my kidney [and] when they found that the water from Poland Spring contained no calcium or other minerals, I would always drink large quantities of it at the spring." Sam Lapowski even paid for crates of bottled water from Poland Spring, Maine, to follow Clarence throughout his childhood in West Texas to his young adulthood in Massachusetts. "We would have it shipped to us, directly from the spring, wherever we might be," he recalled.

Given Dillon's complex history of infection, Dr. Conner was decisive: instead of waiting for the stone to pass or removing it with minor surgery, he advised taking out Dillon's left kidney entirely. Immediately. Without such aggressive action, Conner warned his patient that he could develop a recurrence of his infection. And given that thirty-four did, at the time, make Dillon "a man of middle age," Conner felt his patient might not recover from yet another severe internal emergency.

In 1917, the operation was extremely risky, but within twenty-four hours of his diagnosis, surgeons removed Dillon's left kidney at Roosevelt Hospital on Tenth Avenue on Manhattan's West Side. Extremely anxious, Anne drove daily from their house in Rye to visit her husband at Roosevelt Hospital, where he lay bedridden for two weeks.

Once discharged, Dillon took the train to Greenbrier Resort at White Sulphur Springs, West Virginia, in September 1917 to recuperate. The imposing white-columned hotel and its spectacular cottages were built near mineral springs in a sheltered green valley below the Allegheny Mountains. White Sulphur Springs had been a preferred retreat for numerous dignitaries since the nineteenth century.

By coincidence—or providence—US Secretary of the Treasury William Gibbs McAdoo was also at Greenbrier Resort and Dillon quickly introduced himself. Dillon had talks with the cadaverous-looking, long-legged McAdoo about how the United States government should fund war expenses. Dillon felt that the forty-four-year-old McAdoo didn't appreciate the difficulty of financing a war of this magnitude. This was hardly surprising: nothing on the scale of the "Great War" had ever occurred in human history.

McAdoo decided that only one-third of the war expenses

should be covered through tax increases, with the rest borrowed by selling government bonds. McAdoo began his two-week Liberty Loan bond drive in June 1917 with a goal of reaching $2 billion in sales.

This seemed overly ambitious to most bankers. Such an amount of money had never before been raised in this or any other way. McAdoo set an interest rate of 3½%, which was a lower return on the bonds than the market price at that time. He believed that patriotic Americans would subscribe in large numbers, even though most of the public had no experience with buying bonds.

After a whirlwind promotional campaign, McAdoo exceeded his goal, announcing he'd exceeded $3 billion in sales. *The New York Tribune*, however, derided the Liberty Bond drive as a failure. McAdoo's figure of more than $3 billion had been inflated, the *Tribune* wrote, because many banks had subscribed to the bonds for reasons that were hardly patriotic: just to resell them later at higher interest rates. Large purchases had also been made by the Federal Reserve. But sales to the American public? They were not great at all. Selling Liberty Bonds to Main Street had been "hard sledding," the *Tribune* claimed.

Determined to prove his naysayers wrong, Secretary McAdoo kicked off a second Liberty Loan drive in September while still recuperating at White Sulphur Springs and having long financial discussions with Clarence Dillon. Though there's no definitive proof, Dillon's advice to McAdoo was likely instrumental in the strategic change in the next bond drive.

For the Second Liberty Loan campaign, McAdoo raised the interest rate to 4%. In a speech to the West Virginia Bankers' Association, McAdoo also made the stakes clear, using stark and frightening language. It was left to the United States of America to "rescue civilization from the dark abyss into which this military despot of Germany has thrust it," McAdoo declaimed, adding that "it was the privilege of every American to subscribe to the bonds."

Privilege was an inspired and highly persuasive choice of nouns on McAdoo's part. Even more inspired was McAdoo's idea to enlist the country's three biggest silent movie stars, Mary Pickford, Charlie Chaplin and Douglas Fairbanks to headline Liberty Bonds rallies across the country. Thousands of fans of Pickford, Chaplin, and Fairbanks swarmed to rallies in Chicago, Washington, New York, and numerous other cities, just to hear their screen idols speak. In this silent film era, of course, many people had never heard the stars' voices. After leaving the rallies, thousands of people were inspired, persuaded, and determined to exercise their patriotic "privilege." Almost overnight, Main Street rushed to buy the second issuance of Liberty Bonds.

In hindsight, this marked a watershed moment in twentieth-century financial history. After the Second Liberty Loan drive, the bond business, and the American public's relationship with personal investing, would never again be the same.

Just before his thirty-fifth birthday, while recovering from his surgery at White Sulphur Springs, Clarence Dillon received a surprising Western Union telegram. The cable was from the United States War Department, informing him that General John J. Pershing, commander of the American Expeditionary Force, was requesting that Dillon report to France for wartime service.

Dillon was a bit perplexed and figured that Charles G. Dawes, the president of the Central Trust Bank in Chicago, was the man behind this War Department appeal. General Pershing had placed Dawes, his old friend and a future US vice president, in charge of the general purchasing board in the summer of 1917.

Though not a close friend, Dillon knew Dawes well. Dawes

had previously asked Dillon to negotiate financing for the lieutenant colonel's family business, Dawes Brothers, Inc., a holding company for a nationwide network of utilities and oil companies. A shrewd businessman, Dawes now had absolute authority to buy anything from the French and the British that US soldiers overseas needed in combat.

Instead of cabling back an immediate "yes" to Pershing's request, Dillon, typically circumspect, decided to do some detective work. He called an old Harvard friend, Gordon Auchincloss, the son-in-law of Colonel Edward M. House, a powerful advisor to President Wilson. House was now posted to the State Department, where he was tasked with gathering financial intelligence. Dillon asked Auchincloss to find some background intel on this unexpected War Department request.

"My Dear Dillon," Auchincloss wrote on September 17, 1917. "Finally, after digging through the files of the War Department, I have the following information for you. A similar telegram to that sent to you apparently was sent to the Guaranty Trust Company asking that Mr. Dean Jay come over to assist Lieutenant Colonel Dawes." The Guaranty Trust Company's reply to the War Department was that the bank appreciated an opportunity to do whatever they could to help the nation in wartime, and that "Mr. Jay awaits your command." Auchincloss also reported that a nearly identical telegram had been sent by Pershing to Mr. Abbott of the Central Trust Company.

Dillon sent a quick reply to Auchincloss: "There's probably no further information obtainable over here so I shall cable Dawes that if I am needed, I am ready to go."

Looking fit, rested, tanned, and fully recovered, Dillon left White Sulphur Springs and took the train to the nation's capital. When he showed up for the standard physical exam by the Medical Board in Washington, a normally perfunctory step before receiving a US Army officer's commission, Dillon was taken aback. In the examination room, he came face-to-face with his personal doctor, Major Lewis Atterbury Conner, now a member of the army's Medical Board.

"Afraid you're out of luck, Dillon," Conner said. "If there'd been anybody else sitting here, the examination would have been perfunctory—and they would have passed you." Conner narrowed his gaze, and lowered his voice: "Unfortunately, I *know* you've got only one kidney."

Dillon protested, asking what difference it made whether a man had one or two kidneys, insisting that he was fully recovered and as fit as he'd ever felt in his life. The major quickly showed him the book of US Army Standards for Medical Fitness. Dillon saw it in black-and-white: a man with one kidney was disqualified for an army commission. Dillon could still serve his nation in wartime, but he'd need to do such service on the domestic front.

Bernard Baruch was an elegant, white-haired financier with sharp, patrician features. Clarence Dillon and he had first met in William Read's office, in 1915, when Baruch was already one of Wall Street's most famous and admired men. Born in 1870, in Camden, South Carolina, the son of a Jewish physician who'd served as a Confederate officer in the Civil War, Baruch got his start as a broker for A.A. Housman & Co., fast becoming one of the best traders on the floor of the New York Stock Exchange. By 1904, Baruch had saved enough to buy himself a seat on the Exchange.

By age thirty, he was already worth many millions, having made smart investments in Hawaii's sugar market and in the rubber industry. Baruch contributed generously to President Wilson's 1916 reelection campaign and assisted his good friend, Treasury Secretary McAdoo, "by subscribing $5 million to help put the first Liberty Loan over the top." McAdoo in turn gave Baruch a position on the Advisory Committee of the Council of National Defense in 1917, and less than a year later, he became the chairman of the War Industries Board. Despite being a financial titan with a sterling reputation, not every military officer was pleased by Bernard Baruch's arrival in Washington. For example, Colonel Edward House at the State Department strongly, if privately, opposed Baruch's appointment.

"I do not believe the country will take kindly to having a Hebrew Wall Street speculator given so much power," House wrote in his diary.

Baruch immediately invited Clarence Dillon to come to Washington to be one of his three executive assistants on the War Industries Board. Since, as chairman of the board, Baruch reported solely to President Wilson, he wielded immense power—the authority to take bold and decisive action for the government's war industry needs. Baruch made decisions on how best to increase production, on where and when to build new factories or convert existing ones to emergency wartime use, and could also dictate the prices paid to industrialists by the government.

In early 1918, the War Industries Board had de facto control over almost the entire US economy. Ethics guidelines were strict: no one connected to the board could have financial interests in firms profiting from government contracts. Clarence Dillon agreed that he'd cease to be active as an investment banker with William A. Read & Co. during his War Industries Board tenure because he "might have something to say about contracts that were given to various companies."

Before accepting his position in 1918, Dillon was, in fact, a munitions maker in his role as partner at Newport Chemical Works. In 1916, the Schlesingers' Milwaukee Coke and Gas Company and Newport Chemical Works were so profitable that they raised wages for their 1,200 employees three times that year alone. By the time America entered the war in 1917, the partners had built a second phenol plant in Carrollville, Wisconsin—this one strictly for government orders. During the latter part of World War I, Newport Chemical Works produced 130 tons of phenol daily for picric acid, accounting for 40% of the US output.

President Wilson staunchly opposed war profiteering, and in March 1917, the first excess profits tax was enacted, taxing a percentage of profits above prewar levels. Dillon complained about this tax in a letter to his wife, saying it prevented future earnings while protecting those who already had money. The ordinary income tax—the federal tax on wages, salaries, and interest paid by individuals at marginal rates—was still new for Americans, only becoming law when the Sixteenth Amendment was ratified by Congress in February 1913.

Dillon said that he and the Schlesingers had transferred management of the phenol plant to the government to avoid war profits while he was on the War Industries Board. But in the 1930s, a former associate accused him of being both a banker and munitions maker, as well as a government official and taxpayer. This associate also alleged there'd been manipulation of Newport Company's records from 1918–1922. He accused Dillon of committing fraud against the government. Dillon insisted that after 1918, he handed his stake in the plant over to his partners. They then built a thriving chemical company without any involvement from him.

When Clarence Dillon arrived in Washington in spring 1918, it was an exciting place for anyone who had ambitions for national power. Although the War Industries Board was portrayed as a business self-regulation clearinghouse, the board intervened if Baruch believed commodities or labor could be used more efficiently for the war effort. Dillon interacted with many of America's top businessmen seeking government contracts or redress.

A later *New Yorker* article described the scene:

"Capitalistic whales swam daily into the offices of the War Industries Board, spouting complaints and threats," *The New Yorker* later reported. "They were received by [Dillon,] the assistant to the chairman." Dillon was a relaxed-looking banker who "seemed to know a lot without saying much," handling situations with diplomatic but tough efficacy. Bernard Baruch was a "casual administrator" but in terms of staffing, "a scrupulous picker of detail men."

Baruch called his three most crucial financial aides his "flying executives," due to their ability to quickly assess and sort out sudden problems. The other members of the trio, besides Dillon, were Harrison Williams, who later headed the largest public utility holding company, and Herbert Bayard Swope, the Pulitzer Prize–winning reporter who would go on to edit the *New York World*.

In 1918, Dillon found the nation's capital to be full of paper pushers, lobbyists, foreign diplomats, suffragettes demonstrating for the right to vote, khaki-uniformed American and blue-gray uniformed French soldiers. This caused a severe housing shortage. Dillon initially lived at an elite gentlemen's club, the Metropolitan, and kept a horse at the Riding Club. The government provided him with a car and driver. The War Industries Board offices were in an uncomfortable ramshackle building and in summertime the heat in its halls sometimes topped 100 degrees.

The government later requisitioned a large house for Dillon. He staffed it and began hosting dinners for many of the brilliant men Dillon had met in the capital—including Joseph P. Cotton Jr., a Wall Street lawyer serving at the Food Administration, who would become one of Dillon's most trusted attorneys.

Clarence's wife, in ill health, temporarily stayed with her parents in Pasadena, California. Clarence's son, Douglas, attended a boarding school in New Jersey, while his daughter, Dorothy, lived with Dillon in Washington and attended the private Holton-Arms School.

During his eight months at the War Industries Board, Clarence Dillon developed a lifelong hatred of government bureaucracy. Still, Dillon learned to tackle military supply chain bottlenecks with sharp psychological insight and improvisation.

One of his first tasks was mediating a conflict between the army and navy over priorities of using the port of Norfolk, Virginia. The War Industries Board considered hiring a research team to help sort out the dispute, but Dillon told Baruch that would be a waste of time, money, and manpower. Baruch smiled; he didn't mind if his men did something different or unconventional, as long as they got the job done.

But the ever-affable Baruch was curious. "Dillon," he said, "how are you going to sort this out?" Dillon said he'd talk personally first with the admiral and then the general and see how flexible, or how dug in, they both were.

Dillon's next move was ingenious. He told both the admiral and the general that he believed that as experienced military leaders, they knew far more about this Norfolk Harbor situation than any civilian like himself. If it was left up to him, Dillon said, he'd have no choice but to use his personal 50/50 policy.

In the current dispute, he'd rule in favor of the navy, but the next time, he'd go with the army. Navy, army, navy, army, and so on, until this war in Europe ended. He told both officers he felt he couldn't go wrong. No, it wasn't a random coin flip before a football kickoff; more like a traffic light timed to consistently turn red then green, red then green. In the final analysis, Dillon said, things would even out—all traffic would flow smoothly.

Miffed by Dillon's flippancy—which was, of course, mere

gamesmanship—the admiral and general decided they'd work out their argument without him. And for the rest of the war, no high-ranking officers ever came to Dillon to resolve their disputes, instead settling everything between themselves.

Dillon later convinced Navy Secretary Josephus Daniels, a former newspaper editor, to redirect an unused $40 million earmarked for destroyers to instead build badly needed dock facilities in Newark, New Jersey. Time was of the essence; troops and supplies needed swift transport from Newark to France. Waiting for Congress's approval wasn't an option. Secretary Daniels balked, worried both about the bureaucratic paper trail, and about how he would justify his decision later.

"If I use that money for dock facilities," Daniels said, "what am I going to say to Congress after the war when they start investigating all these things?"

Dillon gave it a moment's thought. "Well, if I were you, I'd be more worried about our men overseas who are in dire need of the reinforcements and supplies that are being held up."

"Okay, then," Daniels said, "will you approve of the appropriation being used in the Newark docks?"

"I will."

Dillon knew, of course, his words were meaningless. He had no official standing with the US Navy or its appropriations, his "approval worth nothing more than the approval of some office boy." But he also knew, or at least intuited, that after the Allied victory there would never be a congressional investigation into such a minor matter.

The Great War finally ended when an armistice was declared on November 11, 1918. The War Industries Board, however, was not officially shut down until the president's executive order of January 1, 1919. On a bright sunny day in January, standing in a tailored cashmere overcoat on the deck of the SS *Lapland,* Clarence Dillon watched as the New York Harbor faded slowly into the misty distance. He was on his way to Europe for the first time in ten years. A private citizen again. An international banker. Clarence had in tow the foxhunting son of a Boston sugar refining tycoon, Joseph B. Thomas Jr., a self-described "engineer by profession and artist by choice."

Dillon wrote in his passport application that he was traveling to visit William A. Read & Co.'s London office and meet with his partners there. He would continue on to Paris for a business engagement and to consult with clients in Norway and Sweden. Thomas was Dillon's technical advisor in connection with some of his firm's unspecified prospective business interests in Europe.

The cabins of the SS *Lapland*—a luxurious 606-foot passenger steamer of the Belgian Red Star Line—were full of financial experts assigned to the commission to assist in the treaty-making process between the former World War I adversaries and to structure a plan for German reparation payments. On board Dillon saw several men he knew from Wall Street, the bankers Thomas W. Lamont, Harvard class of 1892, and George Whitney, Harvard class of 1907, both of whom were partners of J.P. Morgan. Also sailing with Dillon were Frank A. Vanderlip, president of National City Bank, and Albert Strauss, vice-governor of the Federal Reserve Board, en route to the Paris Peace Conference at the request of Secretary of the Treasury Carter Glass.

Lamont had been appointed as one of the US Treasury's representatives on the American Commission to Negotiate Peace.

The Paris Peace Conference officially opened on January 18, 1919. Bernard Baruch was already waiting in Paris, having sailed from New York Harbor on the SS *George Washington* on New Year's Day 1919. After Baruch resigned from the War Industries Board, President Wilson appointed him as an advisor to the American delegation. He also served on the Reparations

Commission. Baruch decided he needed a larger staff and asked Dillon to sail to France as part of the economic section of the American Commission to Negotiate Peace. Herbert Swope was now in Paris as a journalist, seeking exclusive stories about the Peace Conference. He later printed the first copy of the League of Nations Covenant for the *New York World*.

Dillon's European trip contrasted sharply with the luxurious Grand Tour he and Anne had taken a decade earlier. The first thing he noticed was the danger and constant anxiety; when he took a channel boat to France from England all passengers were ordered to put on life belts, in case the boat struck a German mine.

More shocking were the war-torn landscapes of France and Belgium. Gordon Auchincloss captured the devastation: "For miles and miles, the ground is just a mass of deep shell craters, filled with water, and there are dozens of tanks, all shot to pieces, lying about the fields," he wrote. "I have never seen such horrible waste and such intense destruction."

In postwar Paris, by contrast, life was vibrant with lavish meals for conference delegates, opera performances, races at St. Cloud, and dances at the Hotel Majestic.

The American Commission to Negotiate Peace was enormous—nearly 1,300 members strong. Clerks and bankers from New York joined Washington bureaucrats in Paris as fifty-eight committees debated future global policies. Bernard Baruch acted as a "roving ambassador," enjoying President Wilson's complete trust. He grumbled that J.P. Morgan & Co. representatives were so ubiquitous at the conference that it seemed as if the company "was running the show."

Hotel Crillon, near the Place de la Concorde, served as headquarters for the American delegation, where Lamont, Baruch, Norman Davis, Vance McCormick, and his counsel, John Foster Dulles, debated with the Allies in daily sessions of the Reparations Commission. Assisting Baruch, Clarence Dillon listened to the arguments as the Anglo-French demands diverged from President Wilson's vision of "Peace without Victory."

Gordon Auchincloss worked closely with Colonel Edward House during the Peace Conference and welcomed President Wilson to France in December 1918 before his grand entrance into Paris.

Clarence Dillon shared his thoughts later, with uncharacteristic candor, in a lengthy *New York Times* interview: "Conferences of bankers and economists can formulate theories, but if these are not put into practice, they count for nothing," he said. "It is not with formulas that one can re-establish equilibrium in the economic conditions of the world."

In a clear echo of economist Adam Smith's invisible hand theory, Dillon said: "Everyone must think first of all of his own particular business. In so doing, he will render a service to himself and others."

What was Dillon's view, the *Times* asked, on the enormous financial reparations that Britain and France were demanding of the defeated Germans?

"The question of reparations," Dillon said, "although it has the greatest economic consequences, is fundamentally a political question and cannot be solved by bankers and economists."

Immediately upon his return to New York, Dillon faced official scrutiny about his overseas business activities, particularly an "investigative" trip that Joseph Thomas had taken to Scandinavia. The foreign exchange division of the Federal Reserve Board was concerned that now that the war was over, funds would be "transferred at usurious rates to Germany for reconstruction work by purchasing securities in Switzerland, Denmark, and Sweden."

It took only a few conversations and letters for Dillon to convince Frank Polk at the State Department that neither he,

Thomas, nor anyone else at his firm had done anything even remotely improper. "The explanation is entirely satisfactory," Polk wrote back. "I will see that your name and the name of your firm is entirely cleared in the matter."

Dillon had returned from Europe in comfort on SS *Rotterdam*, a fast 650-foot luxury steamer that was the flagship of the Holland America Line. On board he met Henning Plaun, an official with the Landmandsbanken in Copenhagen, who told him about his firm's organization of the Trans-Atlantic Company expanding into Russia and Siberia.

Dillon wrote in his business diary that he should get as much information as possible about international projects that could be lucrative to the firm, like the Landmandsbanken's Siberian railroad project.

Although the Bolshevik victory in the Russian civil war ended his possible investment in the Trans-Atlantic Company's venture, during his time in Washington with the War Industries Board and in postwar Europe, Dillon had developed an appetite for international finance.

Dillon returned to New York in April 1919 with a fierce determination to both challenge the established heavyweights of Wall Street, like J.P. Morgan, and to make a name for himself abroad.

According to Paul Nitze, a later partner at the firm, "Dillon thought of himself as the David from Texas who was to slay the Goliaths of Wall Street."

Chapter Five

CONTROL

THE FIRM HAD drifted through the First World War like a ship without a captain. William A. Read & Co. was staffed by a skeleton crew; most of the bond salesmen and partners were either in uniform or doing volunteer service for the nation. Only the sale of Liberty Bonds and a few minor transactions kept the firm afloat. Read's estate needed to loan the firm $1 million for a year to keep the operation up and running.

Dillon seized the opportunity to become head of the firm when the estate of William A. Read announced the withdrawal of its majority interest after the war and "the question was where and how the firm would get the capital to carry on." Having made a fortune from the phenol venture, Clarence Dillon was ready to take command.

Years later, *Forbes* reported that Clarence Dillon's fellow partners had suggested changing the firm's name to Dillon, Read & Co. Dillon (with scarcely believable modesty) declined at first. Interviewed in *The New York Times*, Dillon gave this version: "After a year or two—I can't say exactly how long—the group of partners came to me one day and delivered something that sounded like a speech. They said that too many captains often spoiled a cruise and they wanted me to take the helm . . . They were determined, and I was ready enough to try, if they wished it."

Neither of these accounts smacks remotely of the truth.

Dillon bided his time until January 1921 when he announced at a partners' meeting:

"Gentlemen, I've brought in eighty-five per cent of the business here," he said. "From now on the name of the firm will be Dillon, Read & Company." He shot his piercing brown eyes around the conference table to see if there were any changes of expression, any faces taking offence or even objecting. Then he said: "Those who don't like the arrangement can withdraw."

None of the partners did.

The plaque on 28 Nassau Street and the bond letterhead were soon changed to read "Dillon, Read & Co." Dillon took over William Read's office—officially now—and had it redecorated.

When Dillon wrested captaincy of the ship in 1921, it was the dawn of the most dynamic business decade in US history. Coming out of the war, two firms towered above the competition on Wall Street. J.P. Morgan & Co. was led by John Pierpont Morgan Jr. Everyone called him Jack Morgan, and he was known to be unabashedly racist and antisemitic. Morgan once told a meeting that "he did not trust Jews: that they had killed his father" and that in the future he was going to "get even with them."

Kuhn, Loeb & Co. was no longer headed by Jacob Schiff, who'd died at his Fifth Avenue home in Manhattan on September 25, 1920, at age seventy-three. Schiff was succeeded by Otto Herman Kahn. Born in Mannheim, Grand Duchy of Baden, Kahn was a musical prodigy in his youth; cosmopolitan, good-humored, soon famed in New York as a philanthropist, art collector, and the city's leading patron of the opera and theater.

The international balance of power had shifted during the

war; New York City emerged as the world's new financial capital. The United States had been a net debtor of more than $3.7 billion in 1914. By 1917, the nation had become a net creditor with a surplus of $5 billion. While the war had severely drained European financial reserves, New York financial institutions possessed the capital for deals. William A. Read & Co. had once been described as a firm that "had done a highly lucrative, if limited business. . . . [but] had never aspired to leadership." It would quickly become known as: "a collection of new men, ambitious arrivistes led by a buccaneer of exceptional ability who was determined to push his firm into the very front ranks of Wall Street."

In July 1919, Dillon rewarded his roommate from Worcester Academy and Harvard, Bill Phillips, by making him a partner. Phillips, once described as a "bland, bespectacled personality," was a good manager of the retail sales force and understood the bond market. Most importantly to Dillon, Bill Phillips was both loyal and discreet. Phillips had been at William A. Read & Co. longer than Dillon—since 1905—but he was quite happy stepping to the side and playing the role of Dillon's right-hand man for years to come.

The two had the kind of tight friendship of boys bonded together from prep school through college. They were almost like brothers. During their student days, Phillips often invited Clarence to his family's house in Connecticut when the young Texan couldn't make the long train trip to see his parents on Thanksgiving or Christmas break.

Now that he was head of the firm and his name had pride of place on the office plaque, Clarence Dillon felt an upgrade in his living situation was also in order. He leased a grand apartment at 635 Park Avenue on the southeast corner of 66th Street. The thirteen-room flat occupied the entire seventh floor. The elevator opened right into the expansive sun-drenched home with its thirty-foot-long living room, twenty-seven-foot-long dining room and eighteen-foot-long salon. The building was listed by *The New York Times* in its "Top Ten: Great City Apartment Buildings," and the paper noted that designer "J.E.R. Carpenter produced one of the two best floor plans in Manhattan."

With Anne's health improved after a long California stay, she and seven-year-old Dorothy lived with Clarence in this spectacular Park Avenue apartment where the family's staff included four women: the cook, Johanna; chambermaid, May; waitress, Alice; and laundress, Tillen. Dorothy was enrolled in one of the most prestigious private schools in Manhattan, Miss Chapin's School for Girls.

Many weekday mornings Clarence walked hand in hand with Dorothy the ten blocks from their building to Miss Chapin's School on East 57th Street, with his Scottish-born chauffeur, Matthew Hay, following slowly in a new Rolls-Royce.

"Pa and I would burst out of the apartment and head downtown on the west side of Park Avenue," Dorothy later wrote. "I had to be in line at school, coat and whatever else hung up, ready to march to prayers at eight forty. Our chauffeur would follow us down, block by block, and if time ran too close, would whisk me in and rush to 57th Street and Madison."

Only after Dillon had hugged and waved goodbye to his daughter and seen that she'd safely entered the townhouse of Miss Chapin's School did he relax in the back seat of his Rolls, then head down to 28 Nassau Street, usually in silence, reading the morning's edition of *The Wall Street Journal*.

As much as he'd admired and appreciated William Read, Clarence Dillon saw his late mentor as a relic, with his cutaways, black tails, and fresh-cut violets tucked into his lapel, a formal disciplinarian with the waxed handlebar moustache of a Victorian gentleman. Read's company now seemed, indeed, to have been *stuck* in the Victorian era. Dillon needed to remold this staid conservative firm completely. In fact, he was intent on not just modernizing the company but reinventing it in his own image. For that he would need fresh blood, a team of younger, hungrier, more ambitious banking minds.

Dillon inherited six partners who'd been handpicked by Read. He considered only two first-rate: William Fiske, his former supervisor in the Chicago office, and James Dean, who'd been Bill Phillips's former manager in the Boston office.

Starting a lucrative Wall Street career had changed from what it had been a quarter of a century earlier when a messenger boy with brains and ambition could rise as rapidly as his work ethic allowed. By 1919, leading investment banking firms expected applicants to have been educated in the Ivy League. It was the very definition of an old boys' club; recent college graduates could obtain lucrative jobs solely through connections, recruited by friends and classmates from Harvard, Yale, and Princeton.

Dillon had no particular chauvinism about his Crimson pedigree. In fact, he recruited his first steady stream of new partners not from Harvard but from Princeton.

F. Scott Fitzgerald, class of 1917, set his semi-autobiographical debut novel, *This Side of Paradise*, at Princeton: "Two tall spires and then suddenly all around you spreads out the loveliest riot of Gothic architecture in America, battlement linked on to battlement, hall to hall, arch-broken, vine-covered, luxuriant and lovely over two square miles of green grass." The Princeton campus is still regularly ranked "most beautiful" in the nation.

"Gilded youth," as Fitzgerald put it, sons of the Rockefellers, Harrimans, and Morgans, blue bloods from New York and Philadelphia who'd gone to "Midas academies" like Groton made up most of Princeton's student body. Yet 20% of the college came from public high schools and middle-class homes—like the Minneapolis-born, first-generation American Francis Scott Fitzgerald. These less privileged Princeton men strove mightily to climb the social ladder and achieve success in finance, politics, and the arts.

By the spring of sophomore year, as every other Princeton man did, Fitzgerald focused his attention on the epicenter of the school's social life: the eating clubs on Prospect Street.

Much as Harvard has its distinct culture of clubs—the Institute of 1770, Delta Kappa Epsilon, the Porcellian—the row of majestic mansions on Prospect Street (often simply called "the Street") adjacent to the Princeton campus are unique among the Ivies. Although Princeton had been home to some of the country's earliest fraternity chapters, all Greek membership had been prohibited under threat of immediate expulsion since the mid-nineteenth century. In place of Greek life, the school's eating clubs defined an upperclassman's status on campus—as well as his future career.

The process of club selection at Princeton was, and still is, called "bicker." During "Street Week" in late spring, sophomores become "bickerees"—the rough equivalent of fraternity pledges—having a series of formal conversations with current members in the hopes that they'll be well-liked enough to receive a "bid."

A lot was riding on one's choice of club and getting a bid. When he successfully bickered in the spring of 1915 at University Cottage Club, F. Scott Fitzgerald felt that his future social success was all but guaranteed. He began eating three meals a day with Cottage's "impressive mélange of brilliant adventurers and well-dressed philanderers." Fitzgerald began writing his first novel in the elegant library of Cottage.

Cottage is one of the so-called "Big Four" eating clubs, the unique character of which Fitzgerald describes in the novel. The

Ivy Club (or "Ivy") the oldest and most patrician: "detached and breathlessly aristocratic"; Tiger Inn (or "T.I."): "broad-shouldered and athletic, vitalized by an honest elaboration of prep-school standards"; and Cap and Gown Club ("Cap"): "anti-alcoholic, faintly religious and politically powerful."

A proud member of Cottage, Dean Mathey had started his career at William A. Read & Co. immediately upon graduation from Princeton in 1912. He began as a bond salesman, making just fifteen dollars a week. A Brooklyn-born stockbroker's son, Mathey had been a star tennis player, winning the national interscholastic championship once, and the national clay court doubles championship twice.

His lifelong devotion to Princeton began with an interscholastic tournament on its courts when he was a sixteen-year-old visitor. It was a "lovely starlit early May evening" when, as an overnight guest of an upperclassman in Blair Hall, he heard the seniors singing on the steps of Nassau Hall, by the campus's Gothic buildings, including "Blair Arch with its spectacular steps, the clock in the tower." (Blair Hall, and its magnificent arch, are today part of Princeton's residential college named for Dean Mathey.)

When William Read had asked Mathey to recruit bond salesmen for the company in 1915, Mathey took the passenger train from Penn Station to New Jersey, transferring at Princeton Junction to the one-car steam-powered train making the five-minute shuttle to the Princeton campus—known, then as now, by all undergraduates as "The Dinky." When the Camden and Amboy Railroad and Transportation Company was building the first rail connection between Philadelphia and New York in 1839, the trustees and alumni of Princeton lobbied successfully for the tracks not to come directly through the quaint, quiet college town—thus keeping the hoi polloi from spoiling Old Nassau's bucolic charm.

Stepping off the Dinky platform and onto the flagstone path toward Nassau Hall, the first thing Mathey wanted to find out was which upperclassman was the editor of *The Daily Princetonian.*

Mathey had, himself, worked on the editorial staff of "*The Prince*," and knew that many of the sharpest minds in the Ivies were the editors of the college dailies.

He stopped one passing student and asked: "Do you know who's running the show at *The Prince*?"

"James Forrestal."

"If you don't mind, can you tell me a bit about him?"

"Well, I think he transferred here in his sophomore year from Dartmouth. He's a good all-around fellow."

"How can I get in touch with him?"

"He eats at Cottage."

"This was exactly what I wanted, for I also was a member of Cottage and repaired there for lunch," Mathey wrote in his 1966 memoir, *Fifty Years of Wall Street and Anecdotiana.* "I met Forrestal and asked him what he was going to do when he graduated. He said he didn't exactly know, but he thought he was committed to work his first summer for the American Tobacco Company because his friend and classmate, Bob Christie's father, had suggested it" and "the Christie family had been very kind to him.

"I then told him something about the bond business and the firm of William A. Read & Co. I explained to him that selling bonds basically meant the channeling of money seeking investment to business and corporate bodies who needed capital for expansion. 'If you are interested at all I think you should come to New York sometime and meet Mr. Phillips, who is my boss and whom I think would be worth your while talking to.'"

Five foot eight, pug-nosed, his mouth fixed in an almost permanent dour expression, Jim Forrestal didn't look like Princeton's typical child of privilege. He had the whiff of the streets and the battered face of a pugilist—unsurprising, Mathey learned, since Forrestal had been an amateur boxer before college.

Jim Forrestal had always been a fighter, growing up the son of an Irish immigrant in Beacon, New York. At sixteen, he began a journalism career working for three newspapers in Dutchess and Westchester Counties: the *Matteawan Evening Journal*, the *Mount Vernon Argus* and the *Poughkeepsie News Press*. Upon arriving at Princeton, he found himself forced to keep battling, albeit not with his fists: he was an outsider trying to scrap his way into the elite inner circle, a middle-class boy in a rich man's school, an Irish Catholic in perhaps the most WASP-dominated of all the Ivy League schools.

He'd been paying his own way through college by still working full-time as a journalist and editor during summer break.

Forrestal often complained that eating clubs were too elitist. He wasn't wrong. The eating club system had always been controversial, since "bicker" rewarded a sophomore's familial heritage, social status at birth, especially prizing "old money." Merit was irrelevant, Catholics and Jews for example, could never get a "bid" to Ivy, the oldest club on the Street.

Woodrow Wilson, Princeton class of 1879, tried to ban the eating club system—without success—not because it was elitist or racist, but because its raucous social life detracted, in his opinion, from a boy's focus on academia. Wilson served as president of Princeton from 1902–1910 before going on to win the presidency of the United States in 1912. For decades, the longstanding joke among Princeton men was that Wilson had taken a step *down* in prestige, going from the position of president of Princeton occupying Nassau Hall, to commander in chief occupying the White House.

As Dean Mathey and Jim Forrestal had lunch in the Cottage Club dining room they sat near the crackling fireplace, underneath the club's motto: *Ubi Amici Ibidem Sunt Opes*. "Where there are friends there are riches." Forrestal took one possible interpretation of the motto to heart, with a singular determination to become one of the wealthy.

Forrestal's mother had urged him to consider the priesthood, but on the contrary, Forrestal became a lapsed Catholic at Princeton. Forrestal's classmates had voted him "Most Likely to Succeed." They also had voted him "The Man Nobody Knows" and "Biggest Bluffer" (the same jocular title Clarence Dillon had earned in prep school).

His classmates should perhaps have voted Jim Forrestal "Hardest Worker." No one on campus was more determined and dogged. "Forrestal would often stand at the gate of Nassau Hall," recalled William Long, another Cottage Club member, referring to the university's heavily trafficked main street entrance. "If he didn't know your first name when you passed by the first time, he'd look it up."

In fact, Forrestal made a point of memorizing faces, names, and especially nicknames, so that on his way to class he could nod and say things like: "Morning, Chip," or "Hello, Hampton—see you Sunday at Palmer Stadium?"

Long claimed, with surely some exaggeration, that by the time Forrestal left Princeton, he'd memorized not only the names of every other undergraduate but also how much money each of their families was worth. Henry Merritt, class of 1915, who later worked at William A. Read as a bond salesman, acknowledged Forrestal's brilliance but viewed him as a "young man on the make," an opportunist cultivating only "the people who counted."

To the surprise of almost everyone on campus and his family, about six weeks before graduation, Forrestal withdrew from

Princeton and never received his bachelor's degree. Although the reasons for his decision are unclear, financial problems and course difficulties likely played a significant role. According to some accounts, he faced a serious financial crisis when the paying editorship of *The Daily Princetonian* rotated to another student midyear.

More significant, perhaps, was his failing a mandatory English course which he refused to retake. Forrestal later said that a certain professor in the English department disliked him, leading to an argument after which Forrestal stopped attending the lectures. Just before midterm exams, Forrestal recalled, this professor told him that missing the lectures meant he'd get an F regardless of his exam scores. Forrestal kept skipping lectures and flunked English.

When Princeton notified him that he'd need to repeat the course in the fall semester and not graduate with his class, Forrestal was furious. He packed his bags and left campus as a matter of pride and principle, without getting his bachelor's degree.

In the summer of 1916, Forrestal hustled around Manhattan's East Side, selling cigars for Bob Christie's father. He hated the job. By late August he decided to take Dean Mathey's advice to come down to 28 Nassau Street and interview with Bill Phillips.

Phillips was so impressed he hired Forrestal on the spot, made him a bond salesman with the major responsibility of covering upstate New York, running the Albany office.

The hiring policy at Dillon Read began to epitomize a phrase that would later become a commonplace business aphorism: *It's not what you know, it's who you know.* Dean Mathey had recruited the slightly younger Jim Forrestal in 1916. In 1919, Forrestal recruited his friend Bob Christie, Princeton class of 1915 and yet another member of the Cottage Club. Christie, in turn, brought on board his friend, Ferdinand Eberstadt, class of 1913, another former editor of *The Prince*. The half-Jewish son of a German immigrant, Eberstadt would prove to be a pivotal figure at Dillon Read in the years ahead.

Clarence Dillon had by no means forgotten his days in Cambridge: he hired Ralph Bollard, a former *Harvard Crimson* editor, and William A. Read and Duncan H. Read, both Harvard men and sons of the late founder of the firm, as well as Westmore Willcox Jr., Harvard class of 1917. Clifton M. Miller, Stanford class of 1914, opened the Pacific Coast office of the firm in 1920.

Almost all the new recruits had just returned from wartime service and were hustling to make up for lost time. "Here was a new generation," Fitzgerald wrote, "dedicated more than the last to the fear of poverty and the worship of success."

The Read brothers had been naval aviators in the First World War. So had James Forrestal. Westmore Willcox was a lieutenant in the naval aviation reserves. Clifton Miller was an officer in the US Army Air Service. Bob Christie had gone overseas as an aide to John D. Ryan, assistant secretary of war, accompanying him on an American Expeditionary Force inspection tour. Robert Hayward had served with the War Trade Board. Edward Bermingham had been a navy officer aboard the USS *Arkansas* and witnessed the surrender of the German fleet at sea. Dean Mathey had enlisted in the army and fought with the 79th Division of the 314th Infantry Regiment, participating in the Meuse-Argonne Offensive that ended World War I.

"When we all returned to work by the middle of 1919," Mathey later wrote, "things were humming at 28 Nassau Street."

By January 1920, Forrestal had left Albany and returned to Dillon Read's New York offices. As a bond salesman, Forrestal had a ferocious work pace that others could not or would not match. He was often the first man through the front door and rarely left the office before 9:00 p.m. Forrestal was (though the word had yet to be coined) a textbook workaholic. In his first year, he became one of the highest-salaried people at the firm and would soon succeed Bill Phillips as manager of the entire retail sales force.

Critic Malcolm Cowley wrote that this Great War generation "had been taught to measure success, failure, and even virtue in monetary terms." Wealth was the key to the glamorous Jazz Age life blooming in New York; wealth rather than birthright could now buy social status, luxurious Manhattan apartments—like the Dillon family's floor-through at 635 Park Avenue, and the elegant Long Island estates Fitzgerald describes so vividly in his 1925 novel *The Great Gatsby*.

Jim Forrestal studied everything Clarence Dillon did, fascinated by "the absolute self-assurance" of his boss's "superbly agile mind."

And Dillon saw in Forrestal a younger version of himself. The son of an immigrant, an outsider, viewed as a "nobody" when he arrived in the Ivy League. No one at Dillon, Read & Co. worked harder than Jim Forrestal, and no one shared his almost monomaniacal drive to achieve greatness. Clarence Dillon saw all this instantly and singled out Forrestal to become his protégé.

Mathey described Dillon, in a fawning but accurate passage in his Wall Street memoir, as being a master at "getting the best out of his associates and using their initiative and knowledge to supplement his own abilities. He had a knack, almost a genius, for inspiring his trusted associates. Although at times he was a hard taskmaster, he had a keen sense of humor and he was, most of the time, great fun to work with in spite of his occasional tantalizing and provoking moods."

By 1921, Dillon, Read & Co. had many partners.

But Clarence Dillon truly had no partners. The firm was now his operation, his personal fiefdom. He was shrewd enough to take into consideration the advice of his partners, but in the end, all important decisions were his alone.

The office at 28 Nassau Street was deliberately drab and

unimpressive. Dillon insisted it be kept that way. Housed in an "old fortress-like, block-square stone building," even the firm's entrance looked dull and outdated. An oil painting of one of the founders of Vermilye & Co., the predecessor firm of William A. Read & Co., was the first thing anyone saw when getting out of the elevator. Never a man beholden to the truth, Dillon ordered that painting's title be altered, to make it appear that his firm's history extended back to 1832.

The furniture and the carpet in the small reception room were old and worn. In the firm's large main room, the partners' desks were on one side and those of the salesmen on the other. Not even the most senior partners had privacy. The carpets and upholstery gave off such a musty smell that a visitor might be forgiven for thinking he'd somehow stepped back in time and entered a real-life version of the counting house of Scrooge & Marley.

In Clarence Dillon's private office, located one floor above, everything gleamed and sparkled, the large windows bathing the room in sunlight. Expensive etchings and tasteful bookshelves lined the room. A wood-burning fireplace was often roaring in the winter. Dillon's mahogany desk was covered with old Italian-tooled leather in dark brown, purple, green and black. He always kept the desk uncluttered by anything other than a simple lined notebook, a well-sharpened pencil, and his shiny black telephone.

Clients and guests were invited to sit on the fine antique sofa covered in brown tapestry or one of the four Queen Anne armchairs—all gifts from Anne, and a daily reminder to Clarence of their mutual love of antiquing, dating back to their honeymoon in New Orleans.

All this pretense and posturing caused the establishment of Wall Street, men whose money truly *was* old, to sneer. They derided

Dillon as an arriviste: "aggressive, opportunistic, and flamboyant." His attempts to reinvent the office by staffing it with talented, ambitious first-generation Americans like James Forrestal and Robert Christie, while also pretending that the firm had a lineage back to 1832 (even J.P. Morgan & Co. was only established in 1895), seemed so shady as to be almost sinister. One contemporary likened Dillon Read to "a pirate ship roaming the market for booty."

That the metamorphosis happened in five years was, indeed, remarkable. William Read's bank of 1916 was unrecognizable as the Dillon-led firm of 1921. He'd hired a team of Young Turks with Ivy League backgrounds, men much like himself, the sons of recent immigrants eager to make their own fortunes, while making sure that these men in their early twenties were steered by a handful of middle-aged partners with decades of experience and unimpeachable reputations on the Street.

Under old Mr. Read, the company had been willing to settle for second- and third-bracket positions in underwritings. Dillon demanded that his firm become a *first-level* underwriter. This wasn't only a matter of prestige; if Dillon Read was sole manager of a syndicate, it wouldn't have to share fees with any other bank. Dillon Read's profits would grow, as would its stature in the investment banking community, leading to even more major deals.

Dillon was primed to go "all in"—to use his no-limit poker terminology—ready to challenge anyone, unintimidated by established power, the titans of the financial world. He'd either lose his shirt or take home the whole pot in the high-stakes game that was Wall Street in the roaring twenties.

Chapter Six

BARON AND LITTLE NAPOLEON

ON THE SNOWY morning of January 11, 1921, Clarence Dillon was summoned to an emergency conference: America's largest tire manufacturer, Goodyear Tire & Rubber Company, faced imminent bankruptcy. Goodyear's failure could have a domino effect, triggering a national financial panic. Paul D. Cravath, the counsel for Goodyear, called the meeting at his firm's offices at 54 William Street, inviting leading bankers from New York, Boston, Cleveland, Pittsburgh, and Chicago, as well as key cotton and rubber suppliers.

"If Goodyear goes down," Cravath warned, "it'll take some other big companies with it."

Despite recognizing the economic danger, executives at J.P. Morgan, Goldman Sachs, and other leading Wall Street banks declined to take part in any rescue plan for Goodyear.

"It's an unpromising situation," said Joseph Cotton, the canny New York lawyer who'd become friends with Dillon in wartime Washington, DC, and was representing some of Goodyear's creditors at the meeting.

Cotton proposed Dillon, his client, as someone who might be

shrewd and inventive enough to solve Goodyear's crisis. Yet the young banker—despite his overweening ambition—had never tackled such a complex project.

Like Napoleon, Frank Seiberling, founder and president of Goodyear, excelled in advancing but struggled with defense. He often addressed financial challenges through public offerings led by Goldman Sachs or undisclosed personal loans from Goodyear to himself. Despite the successful sale of common stock in 1916 and preferred stock over the next three years, Goodyear's balance sheet was cash poor, reflecting its low credit rating.

Anticipating a postwar boom, Goodyear had increased its inventories of raw materials significantly. By early 1920, it held $36 million in rubber and cotton fabric and had committed $55 million for future deliveries. This proved disastrous. Rubber prices plummeted by about 50% below what Goodyear had paid. Tire sales dropped sharply from 837,000 to 118,000 within eight months. Retailers needed to unload tires by selling below cost.

In February 1920, accountants estimated the company needed $24 million to cover excess inventory costs while only having $19 million in cash. Conditions worsened weekly. Goldman Sachs provided bridge loans during this crisis, but the problem became larger as the nation dipped into a brief but sharp recession in 1920 and 1921.

Seiberling understood growth. He was brilliant at creating new products. He was one of the first American businessmen to understand what we now call branding.

In 1901, Goodyear had introduced the first straight-sided tire that didn't have to curve inward to stay attached to the rim. Goodyear was a pioneer in the use of brand logos and advertising with its now-iconic Wingfoot trademark symbol. Seiberling personally designed the Wingfoot, inspired by a statue in his home of Mercury, Roman messenger of the gods and the patron of travel and commerce (and of thieves).

In 1906, Goodyear developed the quick-detachable tire, a revolutionary design that made it easier for tires to be removed from the wheel rapidly. This new tire became wildly popular. Seiberling ran a bold publicity campaign, with ads reading "Quick, Detachable, 10% Oversize, No Rim Cut, Straight Side Tire" in magazines like *The Saturday Evening Post.*

Yet for all his gifts as a creative thinker and business innovator Seiberling was hopelessly out of his depth as a businessman. He lacked financial acumen. He didn't even understand his own balance sheet. He was lost when looking at the implications of managing a manufacturing company with long lead times for delivery of commodities like rubber, whose prices were so volatile.

Bankers and creditors were surprised when Goodyear operated at a loss and without the cash to meet obligations due in December 1920 and for the following year. Goodyear's preferred stock was down 75%. The common stock price was at less than 5% of its previous high.

At this point, Seiberling retained Paul Cravath who was well into his tenure at the helm of the white-shoe law firm now known as Cravath, Swaine & Moore. At that time, no bankruptcy laws like today's existed; companies could be taken over by creditors without a judge's order. To protect against this, Seiberling stationed guards at his Akron headquarters. Things were so unstable that Goodyear's employees no longer accepted paychecks; they insisted on getting their wages in cash at the end of each workday.

The proposal Dillon and Cravath came up with was nothing short of revolutionary. They aimed to avoid receivership through voluntary financial restructuring—a precursor to today's Chapter 11 bankruptcy code.

Simply stated, both Dillon and Cravath saw one thing clearly: Goodyear was a good business with a bad balance sheet.

The company had pressing liquidity issues. The production side of the tire company was strong. The financial management was weak. The board of directors had been unable to rein in the imperious Seiberling.

The first stage of the reorganization plan addressed trade creditor claims and other balance sheet issues. The second stage of the proposal was directed at management issues. This included the sacking of Seiberling and an overhaul of the board. When Cravath received Clarence Dillon's memorandum outlining his plan on January 14, 1921, he became firmly convinced that Goodyear should and could be saved. The voluntary reorganization of the financial affairs of Goodyear would be the largest and most complex restructuring up to that time.

To provide needed capital and to address creditors' demands, Dillon's financial plan proposed new issues of bonds and a preferred stock that would have precedence over the preferred stock issued in 1919.

Dillon Read and Goldman Sachs agreed to underwrite $30 million in secured bonds, contingent on creditors underwriting $27.5 million in unsecured bonds and accepting $33 million in new preferred stock for claim settlement. This arrangement ensured minimal risk for Dillon Read by leading the mortgage bond underwriting while Goldman Sachs took on most of it, maintaining its previous unsecured loan to Goodyear.

Though the term "junk bonds" didn't yet exist, these securities were early high-yield bonds with interest rates—far exceeding the usual 5% for high-grade securities. Issued at discounts, they offered effective yields of 14–15%. Trade creditors received 125% of their claims in new preferred stock. The high yields aimed to persuade buyers to put money into a floundering company. Some trade creditors resisted and filed lawsuits to block it.

Cravath now proved his skill as an attorney; he managed to get the Ohio legislature—Goodyear's headquarters were in Akron, Ohio—to pass a law asserting Goodyear's right to proceed despite this litigation. Since common shareholders also had to approve the plan, Cravath's firm trained the Goodyear tire salesmen to function as proxy solicitors. Dillon remained resolute: either his plan or receivership were the only options for Goodyear.

Clarence Dillon effectively gained control of Goodyear by a new issuance of ten thousand shares of management stock to Dillon Read and two creditor committees. Dillon selected brand-new Goodyear board members from his firm or trusted friends, like Armin Schlesinger and Schlesinger's Steel & Tube vice president, Edward G. Wilmer.

Seiberling was shoved aside. Wilmer, who had no experience in the tire business, and knew nothing about the rubber industry, replaced him as Goodyear's president. Strangely, Wilmer didn't work *directly* for Goodyear but instead received a salary of $50,000 a year from a firm called Leonard Kennedy & Co. Dillon had made the retention of Leonard Kennedy & Co. nonnegotiable.

The Kennedy firm was paid $250,000 a year plus a bonus equal to 5% of Goodyear's future earnings, within a range of $10 million to $20 million. Dillon called this industrial consulting firm "highly trained and unusually capable executives."

But who was Leonard Kennedy—really?

Though Leonard Kennedy didn't work long at Dillon Read's predecessor before leading his own company, Clarence Dillon often called him a "great friend from my office." Despite Kennedy being little more than a Yale-educated clerk, Dillon always enjoyed rubbing shoulders with the country's Protestant elite.

In 1931, in the sober atmosphere following the Wall Street Crash, financial journalist John T. Flynn published a book called *Graft in Business*. In a chapter he called "Rubber Stocks and Rubber Fees," Flynn gives us the most cogent and comprehensible account of the Goodyear bankruptcy. "The great secret of corporation management is secrecy," he writes. "Behind closed doors—doors closed so tight that not even stockholders can peer into the directors' rooms—indeed behind other doors and series of doors that shut out from view even some of the less important and favored directors—the business of the corporation is transacted."

Far from being a team of "highly trained" executives, Kennedy & Company had never undertaken such a job. According to Flynn, "It had a single small office in which the personnel was Mr. Kennedy and a secretary."

Sketchier still than Leonard Kennedy's involvement in the reorganization was the newly formed Nassau Company.

"Forty-five per cent of the stock of the Kennedy Company belonged to the Nassau Company," Flynn writes. "And who was the Nassau Company? It was a private corporation, the stock of which belonged to the family of Mr. Dillon. So the contract for the management of the Goodyear company at a price which yielded nearly a million dollars for two years' work was made with a company which belonged to the extent of one-half to the bankers employed by the Goodyear company to put it back on its feet."

Nassau was in fact a dummy corporation which Clarence Dillon later registered under the name Anne Douglass Dillon.

Since underwriting the most senior securities was contingent on a successful underwriting of the more junior securities, Dillon's plan meant that his own firm faced no risk.

The profits came from buying Goodyear bonds at a steep discount and then selling them at much higher prices to institutions and retail investors. Goodyear sold its securities to the two investment banks at discounts dictated by the bankers when Dillon Read controlled the company's financial affairs.

Dillon Read also received an option to buy 170,000 Goodyear common stock shares at $1 per share, an option soon worth several million dollars. Although the Leonard Kennedy & Co. contract was very lucrative for Clarence Dillon personally, the terms of the new securities burdened Goodyear with high-interest payments for the next six years.

How was all this possible? There's a well-known adage, still used on Wall Street today:

"Hope and fear provide the greatest opportunities for investment bankers."

When Clarence Dillon was approached by lawyers, bankers, and creditors for ideas on saving Goodyear, like a great white shark he sensed both fear and opportunity. The recapitalization plan he crafted with Dean Mathey was straightforward yet lucrative. They completed it in just three days. This plan primarily served Dillon Read's interests over those of Goodyear or its debtors and shareholders. It removed risk from his firm while giving him control over a major client dominating the market for a crucial auto industry product. As the recession quickly ended, Goodyear's revenues and profits surged with America's growing car purchases.

Like the deposed Emperor Napoleon returning to France from exile in Elba, in 1922 Seiberling stormed back into the picture, ready for battle, trying mightily to regain control of the company he had personally created. He backed several lawsuits filed by Laura Weiss for Goodyear's common stockholders. These suits challenged the legality of Goodyear's reorganization plan, aiming to return control to previous shareholders.

They sought to annul the Leonard Kennedy & Co. contract, arguing that the $560,000 paid from May 1921 to May 1922 was excessive and against stockholders' interests. The outcome removed Kennedy's bonus of 5% on profits over $10 million and secured five board seats for "Little Napoleon" and his allies. Clarence Dillon blamed his lawyers for this setback, citing poor legal drafting rather than admitting excessiveness.

Yet Dillon's legal troubles with Goodyear were just beginning.

The Goodyear lawsuits led to the first public attack on his character. In 1926, a lawsuit sought to recover over $15 million allegedly taken from Goodyear's assets by Dillon Read.

Clarence Dillon and John Sherwin were accused of fraudulent actions in their dealings with the murky-seeming Leonard Kennedy & Co. contract. The lawsuit called for their removal from positions of trust and demanded that Dillon Read be barred from any benefits gained through managing the company, insisting they account for all profits linked to breaches of duty.

An even bigger lawsuit filed on November 19, 1926, by nine stockholders became known by one of the plaintiff's names as the F.C. Tomlinson suit. The nine stockholders wanted to reclaim control of Goodyear from Wall Street bankers for its shareholders. Despite being profitable again after five years without dividends due to high-interest burdens from the reorganization plan, Goodyear struggled financially—earning $49 million but paying nearly $60 million in interest and debts during this period. While the company was saved, it came at a steep cost.

Frank Seiberling initially appeared as just an interested observer of this legal battle, but later testimony revealed that he secretly put up $10,000 of his own money to support litigation against Goodyear's current management.

The case posed a serious risk to Clarence Dillon, threatening both his past profits and his reputation.

To defend himself, he took no chances. He assembled what might be described as the first-ever legal "Dream Team." At an enormous cost, Dillon retained four former US Cabinet members. Charles Evans Hughes, once secretary of state and soon-to-be chief justice of the Supreme Court, led the defense. George W. Wickersham, a former US attorney general, represented Dillon Read. Emory Buckner, law partner of Elihu Root—secretary of state under President Theodore Roosevelt—played an active role in the defense strategy. Newton D. Baker, secretary of war under President Woodrow Wilson, defended John Sherwin alongside Dillon as codefendant.

For such a huge legal squad, Dillon Read needed a war room; they rented office space on one floor of the Equitable Building at 120 Broadway.

On November 8, 1926, James Forrestal summoned Dillon Read's Cleveland office manager to New York immediately. Despite a fresh year-long lease, the Cleveland office was shut down the next day. Dillon Read pulled out of Ohio entirely.

This swift retreat only delayed legal action in a stockholders' suit. They sought to dismiss service on him personally and as president of Dillon Read. Dillon's high-priced lawyers argued that Clarence Dillon wasn't an Ohio resident and had no business there; Akron's Summit County Common Pleas Court lacked jurisdiction over him. However, since Goodyear was an Ohio corporation with management stock issued under state law, the court ruled that Dillon's role as stock trustee did fall under its jurisdiction.

The nine stockholders' attorneys arrived in New York City to gather depositions from Dillon and his firm members for the Ohio courts in February 1927.

Dillon's and Forrestal's depositions appeared at best evasive, at worst dishonest.

Dillon insisted he knew nothing about the Ohio office or its closure, attributing it to the Cleveland branch being part of Dillon Read, a Delaware corporation, not the New York-based joint stock association, Dillon, Read & Co. Opponents argued that this dual structure masked a single entity and that legal papers from Ohio could reach the joint stock association's offices.

During questioning, Forrestal seemed uneasy, drinking water repeatedly as he denied ordering the Cleveland office closure—contradicting their manager's deposition there.

Dillon's answers under oath sounded so implausible that he and the firm were pummeled in the press. Dillon had never received such bad coverage. It must have unnerved him to see the scathing headlines in *The New York Times* on February 3, 1927.

DILLON DIDN'T KNOW HE HAD OHIO OFFICES.

FORRESTAL UNAWARE HE WAS VICE PRESIDENT OF COMPANY

BOTH TESTIFY IN GOODYEAR ACTION—DENY TRYING TO DODGE SUIT

CLEVELAND BRANCH NOT CLOSED BY THEIR ORDERS

THEY INSIST—EXPLAIN DUAL CONTROL

Ferdinand Eberstadt, having returned from Weimar Germany, masterminded a strategic counterattack against Seiberling. He used Mrs. Katherine Benedict, wife of Remington Typewriter tycoon Henry Harper Benedict and a Goodyear stockholder aligned with Dillon Read, as a figurehead to file a lawsuit in Toledo shortly after the Tomlinson suit emerged in Akron.

This countersuit accused Seiberling and other trustees of misconduct. It led to Frank Seiberling's revealing testimony about borrowing company funds for personal use without informing stockholders during his tenure as Goodyear's CEO, though he claimed all loans were repaid by fiscal year-end.

Eberstadt's countersuit was part of his strategy to force an out-of-court settlement of the Tomlinson case. Meanwhile, Clarence Dillon prepared for a potential trial by organizing witness depositions in his defense including one from Robert Swaine from Cravath's law firm.

On March 7, 1927, Dillon's team filed responses emphasizing Goodyear's improved financial state post-reorganization and clarifying that Dillon Read had not borrowed from Goodyear while earning modest profits for its services.

The defense argued that management stock issued was meant to protect reorganization securities and highlighted increased stock value as evidence against further complaints from plaintiffs who benefited from these changes. Despite some misleading claims—such as asserting that Leonard Kennedy & Co. saved Goodyear—damaging details emerged during Leonard Kennedy's testimony on March 14, 1927.

Kennedy admitted using Clarence Dillon's backing as leverage but could only recall telling one person: Harrison Williams—a friend and business associate of Dillon. He revealed that his firm mainly relied on the significant Goodyear contract while operating with minimal staff in the Wall Street offices.

After nearly six weeks of legal proceedings, on April 15, 1927, Clarence Dillon took the stand in Ohio. The opposing lawyers approached him with caution, focusing their questions on only a few contentious issues.

Dillon tried to appear cool and composed in the witness box, stroking his chin with one hand, while the other tapped constantly on a glass of water, only showing indignation when the stockholders' charges against him were read. Trying to justify the dubious Leonard Kennedy & Co. contract, Dillon brazenly exaggerated the management problems Goodyear had faced when he came to the company's rescue in 1921.

"There was not only a question of financing this company," he explained, "but it was a question of reorganizing probably the most thoroughly disorganized and discredited company that I have ever known anything about, and we had to have a man of outstanding ability."

And why choose this man, Edward Wilmer, formerly an executive in one of Armin Schlesinger's ironworking businesses in Milwaukee, to be Goodyear's president in 1921?

By this time, feeling the heat, Wilmer had stepped down from being president and became chairman of the board at Goodyear—a part-time role with a salary increase to $125,000 annually—about $2.34 million in 2025.

Dillon testified, falsely, that he had originally asked various industry leaders to assume the Goodyear presidency but that each had declined to do so.

Only then, Dillon claimed, had he turned to Edward Wilmer and Leonard Kennedy & Co., at the suggestion of his friend, Armin Schlesinger.

Dillon testified that he had discussed the Kennedy company with both the merchandise and bank creditors' representatives, but he couldn't remember having told any of them of his own individual interest in the concern.

"I assumed that everybody knew it," Dillon said.

The oddest part of the cross-examination, published in *The*

New York Times, was the stockholders' lawyer confronting Clarence Dillon with a question about his family heritage in West Texas.

"Are you the son of Samuel Dillon?"

Dillon was taken aback; the momentary surprise in his brown eyes flashed to anger—but he quickly regained his composure.

"Samuel Lapowski was my father," he said.

"Objection," Ferdinand Eberstadt shouted, rising to his feet. "Your honor, how is this line of questioning relevant?"

"Sustained," the judge said, ordering the exchange immediately expunged from the court record. In cross-examining Clarence Dillon about his ethnic origins, was the stockholders' lawyer trying—not so subtly—to remind the court that Dillon was born Jewish? Was he trying to invoke, for the jury and the American public, negative stereotypes about Jews as being greedy, money-hungry and untrustworthy?

The next day, perhaps by coincidence, Dillon had an acute attack of the vertigo he'd been afflicted with ever since the near fatal train-and-dog incident in 1907.

While eating lunch with Ferdinand Eberstadt and two colleagues in the dining room at 120 Broadway, Dillon complained of "dizziness, ringing in the ears, and nausea, and before medical aid could be summoned, he lapsed into unconsciousness." A private ambulance rushed him to his Park Avenue apartment.

The timing of this incident suggests that Dillon was rattled by his turn on the witness stand, by having to publicly acknowledge the Lapowski birth name after so many years trying to conceal it and to reinvent himself.

Ferdinand Eberstadt worked quietly to negotiate an out-of-court settlement. He skillfully balanced pressure with compromise to move closer to resolution. Paul Litchfield, who became

Goodyear's president in 1926, asked Dillon to meet with him and Owen Young—the mediator—to help quickly resolve differences and protect the company from harm.

The trial date was delayed until May 16. At this point there were nine different lawsuits still pending; fifteen of the leading law firms in New York and Ohio were involved representing the different sides.

Throughout that afternoon and evening, long-distance calls were made frequently to Seiberling and others in Ohio. Just after 10:00 p.m., news came from Dillon Read's legal offices at 120 Broadway: a settlement had been reached.

The official statement was crafted carefully so neither side admitted guilt.

"The charges and countercharges which have been made and have been denied, will all be dropped and disposed of so that they will not obstruct the great benefits now possible to the company, and can never in the future again embarrass the prosperity of the company," the statement read. "All of the parties recognize the constructive nature of the reorganization of 1921, which was sponsored by Messrs. Dillon, Read & Co. and as a result of which the company, then facing disaster, has been rehabilitated. Messrs. Dillon, Read & Co. will [continue to] act as bankers of the Goodyear Company."

Such careful wording shielded Dillon from blame. But the terms marked an unmistakable defeat. Dillon Read had to pay all legal fees, which came to $2,225,000—a staggering amount of money in the 1920s.

Under the agreement, the management contract with Leonard Kennedy & Co. was terminated. Dillon Read also agreed to forgo its commission and underwrite a $60 million bond issue with a 5% interest rate, "the proceeds of which were used to retire some of the higher yielding bonds and preferred stocks issued in 1921."

The litigation deeply impacted Dillon. From that moment on, he honed his due diligence skills. Throughout the rest of his financial career, he focused on meticulous legal details.

John T. Flynn, in his chapter on Goodyear in *Graft in Business*, singled out the Dillon Read and Leonard Kennedy contract with Goodyear as the "perfect example" of graft: "a profit drawn off from some perfectly legitimate business enterprise for some unnecessary service, perhaps for some service forced upon it. It is a device by which men tap the ordinary processes of production and distribution to drain away for themselves some portion of the product without giving anything in return."

Largely due to the secrecy in which corporate business was then conducted, Flynn added, such graft "is a parasitic growth which devours the substance of business."

Clarence Dillon and Paul Cravath pioneered what would become our contemporary bankruptcy code by proposing voluntary procedures to avoid receivership for Goodyear. Dillon showed how an investment banker could work alongside a lawyer to save a struggling company, marking his rise as a Wall Street leader with his adept handling of Goodyear's crisis.

Dillon emerged from the Goodyear litigation with his reputation as a financial genius, somewhat bruised, but intact. The sanitized wording of the settlement *almost* exonerated him in the forum of public opinion.

Goodyear was Dillon's first opportunity to become a serious player on Wall Street. Cravath had given Dillon a week to figure out a solution; Dillon came up with a plan in three days. By preserving a good corporation caught in a bad financial situation, Dillon announced his arrival as a Wall Street leader. One press account even referenced Dillon's "wizard-like salvaging" of Goodyear.

Leaving a positive legacy for American society was certainly never Clarence Dillon's objective when he took on the daunting task of reorganizing Goodyear in 1921.

Dillon wanted just one thing: to make money. He saw an opportunity to rake in millions of dollars for himself, his friends and close business associates.

All his actions in rescuing Goodyear were done in his own self-interest.

And in this, Dillon seemed to embody, almost perfectly, the fundamental theories of Adam Smith, the father of modern economics.

"It is not from the benevolence of the butcher, the brewer, or the baker, that we expect our dinner, but from their regard to their own interest," Smith famously wrote in his magnum opus *The Wealth of Nations.*

Using the famous metaphor of an "invisible hand," Smith's theory holds that self-interested people—like Clarence Dillon—operating in a free market economy often benefit society as a whole *unintentionally*.

"Every individual necessarily labors to render the annual revenue of society as great as he can," Smith wrote. "He generally neither intends to promote the public interest, nor knows how much he is promoting it. He intends only his own gain, and he is, in this, as in many other cases, led by an invisible hand to promote an end which was no part of his intention."

Rescued from bankruptcy, Goodyear Tire is today one of the US's most enduring corporate brands. Highly profitable once again, Goodyear is now one of the "big four" tire manufacturers worldwide, behind only the Japanese firm Bridgestone and France's Michelin.

The Goodyear Blimp, which first took flight on June 3, 1925, is an iconic American symbol of corporate advertising, known for its distinctive shape and the instantly recognizable Wingfoot logo on its sides. The Goodyear Blimp has floated over virtually every major sporting event from the 1955 Rose Bowl through the 2025 Super Bowl.

Dillon and Cravath created a template that did not become codified in law for half a century until it was approved by an act of Congress. The Bankruptcy Reform Act of 1978 established a uniform bankruptcy law—Chapter 11—which permits reorganization available to every financially troubled business—corporations, partnerships, and sole proprietorships.

The Chapter 11 code has been used to rescue many of today's most successful companies. General Motors, Texaco, Marvel Entertainment, Six Flags, Delta Air Lines. Even Apple—yes, *Apple*, as of this writing, ranked the largest company in the world with a market cap of $3.59 trillion—was on the verge of filing for bankruptcy in 1997.

Goodyear marked a watershed, for Dillon and the nation's economy.

Seeking to enrich himself and his friends through chicanery, subterfuge, and graft, in rescuing Goodyear, Clarence Dillon had inadvertently done good.

Chapter Seven

SOUTH AMERICAN BONANZA

BY THE BEGINNING of the 1920s, Clarence Dillon had made his mark with domestic successes like the Goodyear Tire bankruptcy restructuring. He now shifted his focus to opportunities for foreign financing. In the decade before government regulation, Dillon was one of the first financiers on Wall Street to seize on the opportunity to sell high-yield—and high-risk—bonds issued by foreign governments.

Though many other Wall Street firms followed suit, Dillon, Read & Co. was the most aggressive Wall Street underwriter of bonds for what was then considered the Third World, but what we now more politely call "emerging global economies."

The success of the Liberty Bond campaigns during World War I had created a large new pool of Main Street Americans who were comfortable investing in bonds but were not well-informed about geopolitics or creditworthiness.

With South American governments eager for American capital after the war's strain on European money markets, Dillon could elbow aside conservative American banks and the once-supreme British bankers in these Latin nations.

Dillon singled out Robert Hayward, the Yale graduate and lawyer, who'd been hired by William A. Read in 1916, served as a War Trade Board representative and was now head of Dillon Read's foreign department. In 1919, Dillon had dispatched Hayward on an exploratory four-month tour of Brazil.

As Dillon had witnessed himself in Paris, all investment in Europe was overshadowed by the immensely complex issue of Germany's war reparations. Brazil was a promising nation for American capitalists because of its vast natural resources and its exports of coffee, sugar, rubber, and cocoa.

Several Canadian entrepreneurs had already planted their flag in Brazil, creating Canada's largest foreign holding, the Brazilian Traction, Light and Power Co. In 1899, Sir William Mackenzie, son of Scots immigrants to Ontario, known as Canada's "Railway King," had taken over an old mule-drawn tramway in São Paulo and reorganized it as the São Paulo Tramway, Light and Power Company. In 1904, Mackenzie and his partners had similar success with the Rio de Janeiro Tramway, Light and Power Company. Ownership of these two corporations was assumed in 1912 by the newly created Brazilian Traction, Light and Power Company, known to millions of Brazilians simply as "The Light."

The company provided Brazil's industrial southeast with electric power, tramway, telephone, and gas services until late 1978, when these assets were sold to the Brazilian government.

Examining the lucrative properties of Brazilian Traction was the ostensible reason for Robert Hayward's journey. He traveled by powerboat on the broad turbulent waters of the Amazon River to the Brazilian state of Pará and then he continued to Uruguay.

Brazilian Traction had arranged a loan through William A. Read & Co. when the overburdened British banks had withdrawn their financing participation during World War I. In the immediate postwar period, Brazilian Traction asked Dillon

Read to renew their loans for three years. Not content with only floating securities for Brazilian Traction, Clarence Dillon and Robert Hayward also wanted to expand the firm's business in South America by using Sir Alexander Mackenzie, Brazilian Traction's president, as their primary contact with the Brazilian government. Mackenzie was, by 1920, the single most influential foreigner in the country.

The London firm of N.M. Rothschild & Sons had been the Brazilian government's exclusive bankers for almost a hundred years. No investment bank before or since has ever wielded so much clout with foreign governments.

"For most of the nineteenth century, N.M. Rothschild was part of the biggest bank in the world which dominated the international bond market," writes historian Niall Ferguson in *The House of Rothschild*. "For a contemporary equivalent, one has to imagine a merger between Merrill Lynch, Morgan Stanley, JP Morgan Chase & Co., and probably Goldman Sachs too—as well, perhaps, as the International Monetary Fund, given the nineteenth-century Rothschild's role in stabilizing the finances of numerous governments."

The timing was right to make inroads into Brazilian financing. Hayward learned that the Brazilian government was looking for a new loan and, on the basis of Mackenzie's strong recommendation, Dillon Read became Brazil's exclusive American banker.

Dillon had insisted that the exclusivity of the relationship was nonnegotiable.

"It was our idea that if Brazil should come into the American market for funds," Hayward later said, "which it had not done up to that time, we should establish ourselves in the same position of responsibility and advisership that Rothschild had held before."

In 1921, as N.M. Rothschild and the Brazilian government debated terms, Clarence Dillon emerged, like a python from the

Amazon rainforest. His firm secured a $50 million underwriting deal—the first external dollar loan ever for Brazil. They bought Brazilian bonds at $90 and sold them to Americans at prices between $97 and $98.50, reaping significant profits.

For the next decade, Brazil consulted both Rothschild and Dillon Read before financing decisions to determine whether London or New York offered better terms. Despite Rothschild's legendary name and reputation, Dillon Read often had the upper hand.

That summer, Hayward met with Rio de Janeiro's mayor, Carlos César de Oliveira Sampaio. The mayor was looking for a loan from Wall Street to demolish Morro do Castelo—Castle Hill—a prime location in the heart of Rio, then Brazil's capital city. The hill's slopes were covered with a sprawling and unsightly slum, home to some five thousand impoverished people.

As the year 1922 was the centenary of Brazilian independence, Mayor Oliveira Sampo ordered a complete destruction of the hill in order to modernize and make Rio "more European." Once Morro do Castelo was demolished and flattened, its thousands of poor Black residents evicted, the city could profit enormously by selling valuable real estate lots. Dillon Read envisioned excellent profits in the demolition of the hill and agreed to underwrite $12 million of this loan by acquiring bonds at $89 and selling them at $97.75, earning about $1.5 million in gross spread plus fees.

On a date still infamous in Brazil, one of the city's earliest landmarks, Morro do Castelo, was leveled, leaving five thousand evictees, mostly poor Afro-Brazilians, homeless and forced into sordid favelas. Once the flattened real estate was developed, the evictees would be replaced by wealthy or middle-class *luso-brasileiros*—meaning Brazilians of pure Portuguese descent—as well as by the many new immigrants from countries like Italy, Spain, and Germany, all in an official and openly stated campaign to "whiten" Rio de Janeiro and turn it into the "Paris of the Tropics."

In financing the Rio project, Clarence Dillon employed an all-too-familiar strategy from his Goodyear bankruptcy reorganization in 1921: he used the front company of Leonard Kennedy & Co., despite their lack of expertise in mountain removal work—no public bidding was allowed for engineers on this project either.

Once again, Dillon secretly controlled Leonard Kennedy & Co., holding a 45% stake through the dummy corporation Nassau Company, with trustees Clarence Dillon, Robert Hayward, and Bill Phillips overseeing it all—thereby all three were getting paid twice for the same transaction.

To secure Rio's loan deal further required settling the prior claim of Imbrie & Co.—a bankrupt US-based firm—with a $120,000 payment. Dillon used Leonard Kennedy's contract to help recoup that cost while making an additional profit of around $350,000 on the Morro do Castelo demolition alone—around $6.6 million in today's currency paid out overall between both firms involved in the deal, both headed by Dillon himself.

Hayward claimed that Leonard Kennedy & Co. secured the Morro do Castelo contract because they wanted someone trustworthy for the job. But it was clear that Leonard Kennedy's firm got the contract solely to benefit Clarence Dillon and reward Kennedy for his role as a front man in their consulting company.

Hayward had a long-standing connection with Kennedy, dating back to their days as Yale classmates and members of the secret society Scroll and Key. Both also had shared ties through the Society of Mayflower Descendants, and Kennedy was an usher at Hayward's wedding.

Hayward frequently traveled to Brazil in the early 1920s to manage projects like Rio's railway electrification and secure more underwritings for Dillon Read. In 1922, they issued $25 million in bonds for Brazil's Central Railway Electrification. Dillon Read underwrote a $60 million Brazilian loan using coffee instead of cash as security—a novel approach at the time—and continued securing significant investments from Brazil through 1927.

Brazil became such a vital business partner that Hayward studied and became proficient in Portuguese and joined the American-Brazilian Association's board of directors. From 1921 to 1927, Dillon Read raised over $180 million in Brazilian bonds, establishing itself as a key player in the nation's capital market.

Despite Hayward's glowing reports of Brazilian prosperity in US newspapers and the resulting South American bond-selling frenzy of the 1920s, it wasn't until 1929 that Rio de Janeiro was able to sell any of the flattened land left by the Morro do Castelo removal. Only about $250,000 worth of this supposedly prime real estate was sold by the onset of the Depression. Except for a few years immediately after the Brazilian securities were purchased, most US investors received no returns on their bonds.

Dillon Read's loan profits were generated by the originating, underwriting, and sales fees, shielding the firm from losses, while the naivete, or dishonesty, of South American financial agents led to numerous contract approvals.

In the 1920s, the US State Department promoted stabilization loans to South American governments through Wall Street firms. While, starting in 1922, bankers had to submit loan proposals to the State Department for review, if the loans met US political criteria, they were swiftly approved. The State Department never denied a single application in the 1920s and did not assess the business merit of these loans. Despite warnings that a "no objection" ruling from the State Department hardly guaranteed economic soundness, investors often saw it as an endorsement of quality.

The boom in the stock market throughout spring and summer of 1929 was marked by a high demand for credit and an increase in global interest rates which elevated the costs of maintaining inventories and diminished the demand for primary goods exported by Latin America. The hike in interest rates further strained Latin America through its impact on capital markets.

In the 1920s, the United States emerged as a significant provider of foreign capital, presenting both opportunities and challenges for Latin America. While these vibrant new markets in the Western Hemisphere were crucial due to diminishing capital surpluses from traditional European banks, this new borrowing from American firms like Dillon Read came at a high price.

"In the smaller republics the new lending was intertwined with US foreign policy objectives and many countries found themselves obliged to submit to US control of the customs house or even national railways to ensure prompt debt payment," writes Victor Bulmer-Thomas in *The Economic History of Latin America Since Independence*. "In some of the larger republics the new lending reached such epidemic proportions that it became known as 'the dance of the millions.'"

According to Bulmer-Thomas, an esteemed British academic and historian specializing in Latin America, "little effort was made to ensure that the funds were invested productively in projects that could guarantee payment in foreign exchange, and the scale of corruption in a few cases reached enormous proportions. US officials might occupy customs houses in pursuit of fiscal rectitude, but they had little or no control over US bankers issuing bonds to cover widening public-sector deficits."

Competition among US banks for profitable South American deals grew fierce. Traditional investment banks treated Latin America like the Wild West, engaging in audaciously unethical practices. J. & W. Seligman & Co., a respected New York bank, paid an outright bribe to the son of Peru's president to land new business opportunities.

Dillon Read avoided such crass tactics as open bribery to heads of state; the firm navigated South America's ethically gray areas with slightly more finesse. Clarence Dillon offered "finders' fees," a phrase which sounds far more respectable than "bribes," which were paid to intermediaries (businessmen acting as buffers), who then distributed funds discreetly to corrupt government officials and advisors needed for securing deals.

Dillon turned again to the idyllic campus of Old Nassau in New Jersey to find the man who would become—we can now say in hindsight—a "partner in crime." His name was Professor Edwin Walter Kemmerer, a distinguished professor of economics at Princeton University. Kemmerer rose from humble origins in Scranton, Pennsylvania, to become a full professor at Princeton in 1921. By then, the globe-trotting Kemmerer was famed as "The Money Doctor."

In the aftermath of the First World War, with South American governments badly wanting access to American financial markets, the US State Department often advised these republics to hire Professor Kemmerer to advise them on fiscal restructuring. Although Kemmerer was seen as an independent advisor, his missions allowed the US government to covertly guide international financial reforms without stirring nationalist opposition. Kemmerer's years of official travel as the State Department's favored "Money Doctor" are a paradigm of what Victor

Bulmer-Thomas describes as Wall Street banks' "lending [being] intertwined with US foreign-policy objectives."

Dean Mathey, proud Princeton man, first introduced Edwin Kemmerer to Clarence Dillon. Dillon could see how Kemmerer's work would benefit his firm in Latin America. In October 1922, Dillon, Read & Co. paid the professor $1,000 for his summer services in South America. By 1923, after a successful mission to Colombia, Dillon, Read & Co. decided to retain Kemmerer, under strict confidentiality, paying him $3,000 annually for advice and lobbying efforts with various South American governments.

Kemmerer, a brilliant economist, no doubt, was also quite cunning. Unlike so many other academics, he had some street smarts. Kemmerer made sure to leave a paper trail as "evidence" that everything he was doing was aboveboard. Kemmerer memorialized in a letter dated November 7, 1923, that his ties with Dillon, Read & Co. would end whenever he worked for a foreign government—and he'd continue to have no contact with Dillon Read for sixty days thereafter. In other words, there could never be any possible conflict of interest, Kemmerer claimed, in his work for the US government and for Wall Street investment banks.

But in practice, the professor consulted Dillon Read before and after his South American missions. He consulted the firm *during* his missions. Like any other good employee, or independent contractor, Kemmerer wanted to make sure his boss was happy and kept in the loop.

We can clearly see the role that Kemmerer played in Dillon Read's South American bonanza through a series of letters he exchanged with Dean Mathey and Robert Hayward. Before engaging Kemmerer, the firm had already invested heavily by sending a representative to Colombia. After months of waiting, nothing had happened.

In July 1922, Mathey wrote that if Kemmerer thought Colombia might trust them with their financial plans, they'd gladly send yet another envoy to Bogotá to build a lucrative and long-standing banking relationship like J.P. Morgan had with France. Mathey also wrote that he'd received Kemmerer's fiscal reform plan for Colombia and planned to review it over the weekend while relaxing at Clarence Dillon's country estate up in Maine.

Hayward and Kemmerer exchanged letters about Dillon Read's unsuccessful attempts to become the exclusive bank for the Republic of Colombia. Initially, Colombia required a $5 million loan commitment. Hayward declined. At an impasse, Dillon Read enlisted Kemmerer as a consultant. Kemmerer immediately asked one of his friends in Bogotá to discuss the matter directly with the Colombian minister of treasury. The friend should vigorously lobby for Dillon Read to become Colombia's US banker.

Negotiations stalled. On November 30, 1923, Hayward wrote to Kemmerer asking if Dillon Read should send a cable directly to President Ospina. On December 1, 1923, Kemmerer replied: yes, sending a telegram directly to President Ospina would speed up the process. He even spelled out exactly how Hayward should word the telegram.

Ten months later, Dillon Read found itself successfully issuing a $6 million loan for the city of Bogotá. Throughout the decade's end, the firm retained Kemmerer on advisory missions in other Latin American countries where they had interests or sought opportunities. Kemmerer was always well-compensated for such advisory missions.

Clarence Dillon was not only seeking insider information that could shove aside his banking rivals, he also understood that highlighting Kemmerer's Princeton pedigree and his academic-sounding fiscal reforms would boost US consumer confidence and raise bond prices both on Main Street and among banking institutions.

Kemmerer played ball, persuasively pitching his expertise to Main Street investors:

"A country that appoints American financial advisers and follows their advice in reorganizing its finances, along what American investors consider to be the most successful modern lines, increases its chances of appealing to the American investor and of obtaining from him capital on favorable terms."

Why would Dr. Edwin Kemmerer, a distinguished Princeton economics professor, be willing to jeopardize his reputation and his status as a supposedly impartial advisor to foreign governments by accepting annual retainers from Dillon Read?

Dillon Read's confidential annual retainer of $3,000 was no doubt a major factor, considering that Kemmerer's Princeton salary was $4,000 per year—an amount which made him the highest paid professor at the university.

Of course, the Money Doctor's compensation from Dillon was further supplemented by his State Department fees and payments in cash from various governments in South America.

In 1927, eyes were raised when Professor Kemmerer began construction of a six-bedroom mansion at 161 Hodge Road, the most fashionable residential street in Princeton. (Homes today on Hodge Road are worth as much as $5 million—in 2001 actor Harrison Ford bought a $4 million estate on Hodge—and it's doubtful that any of the current Princeton faculty can afford to live as grandly as Professor Kemmerer did in the 1920s.)

Kemmerer's profitable brand still depended upon the Princeton association. But throughout the 1920s, the professor spent most of his time abroad, lining his pockets through government and private sector consultancies. The professor was rarely seen on campus.

Like James Forrestal, Kemmerer wasn't born rich and privileged; he had to pay his own way through prep school and university. Long before he'd read the works of Adam Smith or learned about the invisible hand in the free market—subjects he taught Princeton freshmen in introductory survey courses—Kemmerer had learned the lessons of economic self-interest.

At fourteen, financial hardship forced Kemmerer to leave his prep school. He worked as a newsboy and then, cleverly, doubled his income by selling eggs to these same newspaper customers. Paying his own way, he got back into prep school, then attended Wesleyan University, where he managed a frat house for free room and board while selling stereoscopic pictures. After completing graduate studies at Cornell, Kemmerer taught economics at Purdue University—but found the $600 annual salary rather paltry. When offered a $3,000 position to be an expert advisor on monetary policy in the Philippines, he quit his teaching job at Purdue.

From 1903 to 1906 in Manila, Kemmerer lived comfortably with his family and advocated for the gold standard as an anti-inflation measure—a strategy he'd later apply globally despite its mixed outcomes for struggling economies. Returning to the US, he joined Cornell as an assistant professor before moving to Princeton in 1912 with a negotiated $4,000 salary.

Kemmerer's academic reputation grew with his 1916 publication, *Modern Currency Reforms*, and in 1917, he advised Mexico on monetary matters, followed by Guatemala in 1919. By 1921, Kemmerer's expertise became highly sought after for central bank currency guidance and securing US loans for infrastructure projects like railroads and power plants through State Department referrals. By 1934, he had extended his advisory role to nine more countries.

"Why go through the State Department when you can approach a major investment bank directly?" Kemmerer's son once asked him.

Many companies sought Kemmerer's expertise, but he mainly

worked with Dillon Read. This firm often recommended that governments hire Kemmerer as an advisor, resulting in profitable contracts for him. In 1924, he charged a client $1,000 for expert testimony. When the client objected to the fee, Kemmerer explained that he had recently earned $10,000 (around $140,000 today), plus expenses and a contingent fee likely worth much more for a three-month job in Central America.

In 1925, Chile agreed to pay $20,300 for his six-member team; Kemmerer received $15,000 of that amount, plus expenses, for another three-month project. He also consulted with Dillon Read about their business opportunities in Chile.

He didn't see any conflict between these roles. In his diary, he noted that when someone from Wall Street inquired about rumors of his secret ties with Dillon Read, he replied, "I work with many banks and governments but have no connections that affect my work for Chile." However, others had different perspectives and informed opinions on the issue.

Kemmerer, unable to engage Dillon Read for an Ecuador loan, partnered with a rival securities firm, Kissel, Kinnicutt and Co. which offered him a profit of one half of 1% on any successful loan. In 1927 and 1928, Kemmerer worked hard to gain diplomatic recognition for Ecuador from the State Department, which was unaware that he had financial ties to Ecuador's bonds.

His pursuit of personal profit kept the Money Doctor away from Princeton for five years, most of 1922 through 1927, either by taking sabbaticals or various other leaves.

These long absences from campus—it was also no secret that Kemmerer was well remunerated during his world travels—led to growing complaints about Kemmerer within the economics department. The chairman of the department suggested Kemmerer go on "permanent sabbatical" from Princeton.

Sensing the danger of losing the firm's golden goose, Dean Mathey came up with an ingenious plan to maintain Kemmerer's ties with Princeton—without which he'd lose his cachet among investors—while still acting as Dillon Read's advisor. He suggested an endowed chair that would match or surpass Kemmerer's teaching salary, allowing Princeton to profit by hiring a less expensive replacement during Kemmerer's advisory missions. The estate of an alumnus pledged $400,000 for the chair if others contributed $200,000. Dillon Read donated $25,000 and helped raise the remaining funds. In 1928, Kemmerer became the first holder of Princeton's Chair of International Finance.

In 1927, Mathey rewarded Kemmerer by investing in the profitable Amerada stock syndicate. Kemmerer wrote from Bolivia on April 29, 1927: "I appreciate very much your letting me in the Amerada syndicate. The outcome was a real help to me in my house building plans." This cash injection allowed Kemmerer to finish building the elegant six-bedroom mansion on Hodge Road in Princeton and to acquire a lakeside retreat in New Hampshire.

Kemmerer was celebrated as a reliable doctor for nations needing economic cures, praised in reports like "Sick Nations Take the American Cure."

However, "by 1934, [Kemmerer] had treated thirteen patients on five continents, not all of whom recovered. Kemmerer's basic prescription: get on the gold standard," *Fortune* noted shortly after his death in 1945. And his ties with Dillon Read had catastrophic consequences for the Republic of Bolivia.

Dillon Read backed two high-risk loans that pushed Bolivia toward bankruptcy. Despite the country's debt, they issued a loan in 1927, relying on Kemmerer's reputation to sell Bolivian bonds in America. The $14 million loan was earmarked to build fifty miles of railway between Cochabamba and Santa Cruz, connecting regions previously reachable only by mule. Dillon

Read bought the bonds at 90.05 and sold them at 98.50 to Americans, making nearly an 8.50-point profit per bond while paying $10,000 as a finder's fee to an American engineer who introduced them to this project.

As in the case of the loan to Brazil for the demolition of Rio de Janeiro's Morro do Castelo, Robert Hayward handed off this project to his Yale classmate Leonard Kennedy, who received $70,000 for making studies for the proposed railroad. He later acquired a contract from the Bolivian government to construct the railroad.

After the embarrassing revelations in the Goodyear litigation in 1927, Dillon Read was more cautious about publicizing the Kennedy connection and did not stipulate the use of his company in the loan contract. Kennedy claimed to have been the low bidder for it. By then, Leonard Kennedy & Co. had been dissolved. Leonard Kennedy had formed Kennedy & Carey with an experienced contractor with no obvious financial connection to Dillon Read. Yet the firm had used the Kennedy & Carey engineering deal to gain an exclusive underwriting relationship with the Bolivian government. It was mutually beneficial.

In 1927, Professor Kemmerer and his economic advisory team visited Bolivia. Privately, he questioned whether Bolivia should take on more debt. His report advised against further borrowing, yet he remained silent when Dillon Read proposed a $23 million loan in 1928.

On August 3, 1928, Kemmerer wrote a warning letter to Dillon Read expressing his reservations about Bolivia's credit.

"I would not want to assume any responsibility with reference to the advisability of this loan, and personally I would not buy the bonds. . . .The financial burden they [the Bolivians] will be carrying, I think, will be very heavy, their eggs are largely in one basket, tin." Kemmerer continued: "They have dangerous neighbors, their ethical standards are not high and I do not think that they have yet proven themselves to be a people of much political capacity."

Yet, the loan prospectus issued by Dillon Read highlighted Kemmerer's mission to reassure American investors, noting Bolivia's clean record on foreign obligations—though they had few at the time. Kemmerer may have had grave reservations. He did not, however, ask to remove his name from the prospectus. He hoped that the loan would assist Bolivia in its financial reorganization. In his alternative role as a consultant to the Bolivian government, Kemmerer wrote a congratulatory letter on September 21, 1928, to J. Arturo Arguedas, the Bolivian vice consul: "I am very glad to know that the loan contract has been signed with Dillon Read, and I congratulate Bolivia on the success of her efforts to obtain funds to carry through her new program."

Dillon Read floated the 1928 Bolivian loan contingent on the Bolivian government's implementation of the Kemmerer reforms but with no contractual requirement to do so. The State Department issued its customary "no objection" to the 1928 loan. The new money was mostly intended to be used to pay off previous loans, including the $6 million to Vickers-Armstrongs, a British company, for armaments purchased by the Bolivian military in 1926. The State Department was by then concerned that the Kemmerer missions were being used to justify irresponsible lending and considered blocking Bolivia's continued borrowing. Despite the numerous red flags, the American public participated in the Bolivian bonds, lulled by the promise of security offered by the name of the highly esteemed Professor Kemmerer. The underwriters were skillful at making claims about the stability of countries whose bonds they were marketing at the time.

None of the nations were stable and almost all were corrupt.

During this period, Dillon Read's average gross spread on South American dollar government bonds was $6.07 per $100, notably higher than J.P. Morgan & Co.'s $3.35.

Analysts noted that Dillon Read and J. & W. Seligman vied for the poorest record in Latin American bond marketing at the time. One observer wrote that words like "shear" and "fleece" aptly described some of their operations "without exaggeration."

According to Ibsen Martinez, an award-winning journalist from Caracas, Venezuela: "The abandonment of gold standard rules after 1931 led to a series of debt defaults throughout the region. Depreciation of the exchange rate made the burden of the debt on the budget simply intolerable." In fact, by 1934, Martinez writes, "only Argentina, Honduras, Haiti, and the Dominican Republic had not defaulted. Having already paid off its debt, Venezuela did not need to default. That is only five countries out of twenty."

By early 1931, Dillon Read's South American bonanza collapsed, along with the entire house of cards that was the continent's economic system. In June 1931, Brazil defaulted on its loans. And in August 1931, Bolivia defaulted on its loans, as well. Main Street Americans who'd bought bonds based on Dillon Read's high-yield prospectuses, recommended by Princeton's famed economist, the Money Doctor, were left with worthless securities, deepening their losses during the Depression due to investments in South American junk bonds.

Although global economic conditions after October 1929 contributed to numerous bond defaults, the actions of Wall Street firms like Dillon Read, in particular, left a trail of bitterness and resentment in South America. President Franklin Roosevelt sought to redress these grievances by announcing, in March 1933, his Good Neighbor Policy, which promised "non-intervention and non-interference in the domestic affairs of Latin American nations," and vowing that United States henceforth would, indeed be a "good neighbor" to all nations in the hemisphere.

But in the collective consciousness of Latin Americans, the

damage of the roaring twenties bonanza was irreversible. Generations grew up with images of crooked gringo financiers, slick-talking men from esteemed Wall Street firms and their Ivy League–educated economics experts, crossing the equator to work out shady deals with utterly venal South American politicos. The result was the "fleecing" of the Spanish- and Portuguese-speaking republics. Nearly an entire continent—fifteen of its twenty nations—was left with worthless currencies and unfathomable levels of debt.

The "dance of the millions" in which Latin America's economies were manipulated based on US State Department policy objectives achieved in collusion with predatory Wall Street bankers would not soon be forgotten—nor forgiven.

"Kemmerer is Denounced" ran a *New York Times* headline on August 7, 1932. In a lecture at the National University in Quito, Ecuador, speaker Manuel Corona Cid, director general of the Spanish-American Union of Buenos Aires, charged Kemmerer "with being the agent of American bankers in their effort to dominate Latin America. The speaker was especially concerned with the apparent indifference of Spanish Americans to the policy of the 'Yankees designed to absorb Latin America by any possible means.' He called the Latin American financiers 'imbeciles,' and asserted that the present economic crisis in Latin America is the work of the 'Yankees, who do not desire better conditions in these countries.'"

This single article notwithstanding, Professor Edwin Kemmerer emerged unscathed from the entire chapter. He was noted as the first US academic economist to brand himself internationally, paving the way for experts advising foreign governments for fees.

Kemmerer remained a distinguished professor at Princeton until his retirement in 1943 when he became professor emeritus and was a member of American Philosophical Society and the American Academy of Arts and Sciences. In 1935, he received an honorary doctorate from Columbia University; throughout the 1930s, he was regularly quoted for his expertise on monetary policy in *The New York Times* and other leading US publications.

In an era before widespread investigative reporting, the press accounts through the 1930s and 1940s make no connection between Professor Edwin Kemmerer's contracts with the US State Department, his well-paid private sector advisory work with Dillon Read, and the catastrophic impact for American bondholders when both Bolivia and Brazil defaulted on their loans in 1931.

Thirty-two years after the Wall Street Crash, as a mild midwinter sun warmed the Uruguayan resort town of Punta del Este, sixty-five miles east of Montevideo, Clarence Dillon's fifty-two-year-old son, Douglas, held court in the blue and white assembly hall of Punta del Este's Cantegril Country Club. Dillon had come to address the economic ministers of twenty-one Western hemisphere nations gathered to launch a dramatic new program of massive aid for Latin America's underdeveloped nations known as "the Alliance for Progress."

It was August 11, 1961, and Douglas Dillon, who'd been appointed US Secretary of the Treasury in January of that year, vowed that the United States would take the lead in securing $20 billion in low-interest loans over the next ten years to help raise Latin America's standard of living.

"We welcome the revolution of rising expectations," Dillon said in a flat, almost expressionless voice, "and we intend to transform it into a revolution of rising satisfactions."

Across the table, clad in an open-necked army shirt and puffing on a Montecristo No. 4 cigar, sat a thirty-three-year-old

Argentine-born medical doctor, now a global icon of anticapitalism, described by *Time* magazine's reporter in the room as "Cuba's spinach-bearded economic commissar, Che Guevara."

As Secretary Douglas Dillon made the unprecedented offer of $20 billion in low-interest loans, the most generous US aid package to Latin America in history, Che Guevara continued puffing on his Montecristo, nonplussed, glaring at the tall, well-spoken capitalist-imperialist, the son of banker Clarence Dillon. When Douglas Dillon uttered the word "revolution," Che Guevara almost smiled, calmly exhaling a cloud of smoke.

Too much had transpired between Clarence Dillon's era and that of his only son. This was 1961, after all, not 1921. The Marxist revolution Che planned to spread from Cuba throughout Latin America had no time for patronizing double-talk about some "revolution of rising expectations" or "revolution of rising satisfactions." Guevara's brand of revolution wasn't concerned with US loans, high-interest or low-interest, no matter how many billions were dangled as bait to supposedly raise the standard of the proletariat of Latin America.

"While envisaging the destruction of imperialism," Che Guevara later wrote, "it is necessary to identify its head, which is no other than the United States of America."

Secretary Douglas Dillon of the Treasury Department represented the legacy of imperialist US policy and its tactic of using Wall Street "speculation" to gain control of the economies of emerging Latin American nations.

"American capitalism replaced some of the old colonial capitalisms in the countries that began their independent life," Guevara wrote. "There is no real security for its financial speculation in these new territories. The octopus cannot apply its suckers firmly. The claw of the imperial eagle is trimmed. Colonialism is dead or is dying a natural death."

Chapter Eight

PROFITS, PROFITS ÜBER ALLES

HAVING NOW MADE his mark as a financier to be reckoned with in the United States and South America, Clarence Dillon's last and greatest challenge was carving out a space for his firm in Europe's hugely unsettled bond markets.

In October 1919, Dillon attended a meeting with J.P. Morgan partners and leaders from other major banks to brainstorm postwar financing strategies. The J.P. Morgan team was obviously overconfident, and for good reason. The Morgan name carried weight even with snobbish Europeans accustomed to banking dynasties like Rothschild, Berenberg, and Warburg—French, Dutch, Italian, and German families whose histories in banking on the continent went back to the 1700s, if not longer.

Given its strong ties with Britain and France, J.P. Morgan assumed that no other bank could muscle in. Dillon dispatched his old Harvard classmate and editor of the *Crimson* Ralph Bollard to Europe. Bollard's first stop was England, where he met with executives at J. Henry Schroder & Co. The London-based firm, founded in 1818, was one of the UK's biggest investment banks; because its founder, Johann Heinrich Schröder, had come to London from Hamburg, the bank still maintained powerful business and banking ties in Germany.

In 1921, Dillon Read joined a $30 million loan syndicate in Belgium and managed $23 million in French bonds for Marseilles, Lyons, and Bordeaux. By February 1922, Dillon led a 150-million-guilder loan to the Netherlands government, which he'd innovatively insisted be made in Dutch currency.

J.P. Morgan was, to no one's surprise, displeased by Dillon's aggressive moves in Europe. So were the bankers at Kuhn, Loeb & Co., one of whom derided Dillon Read's moves abroad as reckless ventures made by "second-rate people."

In June 1922, Clarence Dillon was invited to attend a ceremony in Palermo celebrating the expensive harbor development that his firm was financing. To Dillon the Sicilian festivities were a lark. From his lavish hotel suite overlooking the harbor, Dillon wrote to Anne, calling the preparations for the ceremony "the most amusing party on record." The stifling heat added to his amusement. Dillon described the Sicilians as a "wild lot" who took themselves too seriously. Palermo was festooned with tricolor flags, its cobbled streets filled with soldiers in full ceremonial regalia marching behind a brass band and drummer.

Leonard Kennedy, the compliant, almost ludicrously unqualified frontman of the now-ubiquitous Leonard Kennedy & Co., had traveled to Sicily with Dillon—solely, it seems, to serve as an affable and entertaining sidekick, one so blue-blooded that he was a member of the Society of Mayflower Descendants.

"I wish you could see the smiles we all have in spite of the heat," Dillon wrote to Anne. "I'm now clad in my heavy cutaway, while the perspiration stands out even on my hands. Leonard is having his Sicilian-made Prince Albert coat and fancy waistcoat draped on him, and we are just about to sally forth to meet the king—the reception is to be held down at the harbor where his battleship lies in the full glare of this everlasting sun."

US Ambassador Richard Washburn Child, a fellow alumnus of Harvard College (class of 1903) and graduate of Harvard Law School, was one of the earliest American supporters of Italian Fascism. Child would soon become a paid propagandist for Benito Mussolini. Still, in Dillon's view, the ambassador was "not a bad sort." Child arrived at Dillon's hotel suite, overheated and out of breath, "dressed up like a plush horse and simply dripping wet." They were running late to join King Emmanuel III for the harbor expansion's groundbreaking ceremony. Dillon dashed a quick goodbye in his missive to Anne: "We're off!"

Officiating the ceremony was King Victor Emmanuel III, the Neapolitan-born monarch from the House of Savoy who'd ascended to Italy's throne at age thirty, following the murder of his father, King Umberto I, by an anarchist assassin in 1900. Alongside the king stood Ambassador Child, who made a point of urging more Americans to invest in Europe's postwar recovery efforts—emphasizing the potentially lucrative collaboration between American capital and Italian industry, like the harbor of Palermo which would, after the expansion and modernization, become the largest shipping port in the Mediterranean.

After the Palermo celebration, Dillon traveled to Rome by train with Ambassador Child, who must have talked Dillon's ear off about the glories of Italy's fast-rising fascist movement and the extraordinary "greatness" of the bald, burly former journalist, Benito Mussolini, leader of the *Partito Nazionale Fascista*. A few months later, Child would claim that he was one of the first men to urge Mussolini and his Blackshirts to march on Rome in the late October 1922 coup d'état that gave the fascists total power in the Kingdom of Italy.

If Dillon felt any repulsion to Child's extreme political views, he didn't write about them. On the contrary, he seemed to enjoy the company of this Massachusetts-born fellow Harvard man; Child had played varsity football for the Crimson and made witty contributions to the *Harvard Lampoon*. By the mid-1920s, Child began to churn out fascist propaganda masking itself as "journalism" in numerous articles for the Hearst newspapers in the US.

He used the notes of his conversations with Mussolini to ghostwrite Il Duce's autobiography, serialized in *The Saturday Evening Post*. *My Autobiography* by Benito Mussolini was published in 1928 by Charles Scribner's Sons, the same august house which published the 1920s novels by F. Scott Fitzgerald, Ernest Hemingway, and Thomas Wolfe.

"In our time it may be shrewdly forecast that no man will exhibit dimensions of permanent greatness equal to those of Mussolini," Child slavishly writes in the book's introduction.

Neither the reputations of Ambassador Richard Child nor of the book have aged well. The work is today dismissed as an elegantly designed—its cover is gilt-lettered on green cloth—but self-serving personal history mixed with turgid propaganda speeches, literally dictated by a brutal dictator to his useful Harvard-educated idiot. The autobiography was not even published in Italy until 1971.

While accompanied by Ambassador Child in the Italian capital, Clarence Dillon spoke about how commercial and financial transactions of US bankers could restore faith in European commerce. "Everyone, however, must think first of all of his own particular business," Dillon said, once again echoing his faith in Adam Smith's invisible hand. "In so doing he will render a service to himself and to others."

One such venture, Dillon noted, was the massive expansion

of the Port of Palermo. John R. MacArthur II, a New York-based engineer, had won the contract on February 14, 1922, with Ambassador Child assisting in his negotiations with the municipality of Palermo and the Italian government.

MacArthur, yet another Harvard College and Law School graduate—he was Child's classmate as an undergraduate in Cambridge—was vice president of the contracting firm MacArthur Brothers. To fulfill the Palermo contract, he'd formed a separate Italian company called Societa Anonima Italiana MacArthur.

MacArthur had been advised to approach Dillon, Read & Co. for financing. The engineer was ready to offer the investment bank a 6% interest on capital and a 15–20% share of profits. MacArthur tried to personally meet Dillon but was sent instead to confer with Edward Wilmer—the friend of Armin Schlesinger now acting as president of Goodyear Tire—in Akron, Ohio, in May 1922.

Wilmer told MacArthur to leave all the financial details up to Dillon. MacArthur traveled to Europe to meet with Clarence Dillon and Leonard Kennedy in Palermo and review the contract's terms.

As the date of the June ceremony fast approached, MacArthur was hanging around Palermo, still waiting for Dillon's response. When Dillon's counteroffer finally came, it was conveyed through frontman Leonard Kennedy, and it shocked MacArthur: Dillon wanted two-thirds of the profits and stock plus 6% interest on capital.

MacArthur told Kennedy that he'd expected to pay only 15% or at most 20% of the profits.

"Well, those are our terms," Kennedy said. "Take it or leave it."

MacArthur argued that he "must not lose control of the company. I'm responsible to the Italian government for the faithful fulfillment of the contract and the execution of the works."

"But you'll remain president," Kennedy said. "And no one will ever *know* that you have lost control of the company."

MacArthur felt trapped between a Sicilian rock and a hard place. He was forced to accept what he later called Clarence Dillon's "ruthless terms."

"According to an announcement yesterday," *The New York Times* reported on May 27, 1922, "Leonard Kennedy & Co. have acquired a large interest in Societa Anonima Italiana MacArthur which has Government contracts to develop the port of Palermo, Sicily, largely by Americans with American money. A celebration in which the King of Italy is expected to participate will be held June 6, when work starts."

Following the June 1922 celebration, MacArthur wrote to Clarence Dillon and to Leonard Kennedy, insisting that a "certain Italian" of questionable character be made a vice president of the company in Sicily.

Dillon was aware of how things operated in Sicily. Mafia shakedowns, payoffs, bribes—the crooked business climate was well-known. Equally well-known was the fact that most local politicians in Sicily expected their piece of the action. There's even a famous Sicilian proverb *Pesci fet d'a testa*, "the fish stinks from the head"—meaning, corruption starts at the very top. The island, long in the grip of various Mafia clans, was rife with graft—especially in massive construction projects like the Palermo Harbor revitalization. Dillon could only imagine the *real* powers behind this "certain Italian" MacArthur had proposed as vice president of the company.

Just as with the nearly simultaneous destruction of Morro do Castelo in Rio de Janeiro, little or no thought was given to the historical and cultural damage done by the Palermo Harbor development. A magnificent and remarkably intact fortress, Il Castello a Mare, in the Castellammare neighborhood of Palermo, stood in the way of "modernization and progress." The

Castello a Mare dated back more than one thousand years; but it was earmarked by engineers for dynamiting. The sort of crude and destructive expansion of the Port of Palermo which Clarence Dillon (through Leonard Kennedy) financed would be unthinkable today. The Castello a Mare would have been declared untouchable by developers—a UNESCO World Heritage Site.

But in 1922, the "Port Consortium" reached a deal with Palermo's city officials—one can only imagine the graft involved—which gave the builders permission to demolish the castle in order to create a larger deep-water harbor. Even today controversy swirls around the destruction of the Castello a Mare. Outraged citizens of Palermo, as well as historians and archeologists worldwide, protested right up until the last moments; but their voices were drowned out by the sound of dynamite blowing the majestic ancient castle to bits.

A few remnants can be seen by tourists in Italy's Castello a Mare Archaeological Park, but the true glory of the fortress exists only in black-and-white photographs taken before June 1922. "All that remains today is a gatehouse, a circular tower and the foundations of the moat," a travel writer recently bemoaned. "For short-sighted greed, one of the city's most historic treasures was destroyed."

MacArthur became an immediate thorn in Dillon's side—and the pain would only grow more painful in the coming years. MacArthur claimed Dillon provided only a small portion of the much-needed capital and that he'd demanded it back within a year. MacArthur was required to float a joint-stock company with €20 million fully paid in capital but opted instead to convert his registered shares to "bearer form" for resale, in direct violation of Italian law. An inquiry by Mussolini's Minister of Public Works confirmed the capital shortfall and declared forfeiture. Dillon may have been less than honest by promising MacArthur financing and then changing the terms. Dillon also insisted on owning control of the company. MacArthur had no choice and had to accept Dillon's re-trading of the deal.

By August 1922, Dillon was battling multiple lawsuits in Ohio challenging the legality of his Goodyear reorganization plan. Now he was being threatened with a breach-of-contract lawsuit in the Palermo Port expansion. George Franklin, Dillon's lawyer, eventually paid an out-of-court settlement to John MacArthur. The aggrieved engineer had been seeking $1 million, but Dillon shelled out $450,000 in what attorney Franklin called a "nuisance" settlement.

Yet even after the settlement, MacArthur, divorced and suffering financially during the Great Depression, continued to write bitter letters to Clarence Dillon until 1937. By the mid-1930s, he could no longer sue Leonard Kennedy & Co.—that dummy corporation was now defunct. The failure of his role in the Palermo Harbor redevelopment was, MacArthur claimed, an irreparable injury to his reputation in Italy. This reputational damage had hurt his ability to acquire other engineering contracts in Europe. If Dillon did not pay him an unspecified sum of money, MacArthur wrote in one letter, he'd go to the press and expose Dillon's "inordinate greed" and his "manipulations and falsifications."

Dillon called MacArthur's bluff. He never paid the troubled engineer another nickel.

Clarence Dillon had pursued exorbitant profits in the Goodyear restructuring, the Rio de Janeiro mountain removal loan, and in the Palermo Harbor works revitalization, most of which were funneled to him through the frontman Leonard Kennedy. In July 1922, Clarence Dillon returned to New York after two months investigating financial conditions in the rest of Europe, including examining German financing needs with the Schroders of London and with Max M. Warburg, director of the most important private bank in Hamburg, M.M. Warburg & Co. Max's brothers, Paul and Felix Warburg, were partners at Kuhn, Loeb on Wall Street.

Reporters asked Clarence Dillon, upon his arrival back in New York, to assess the international financial situation. Dillon said that the phase of massive loans from US banking institutions to European governments had ended.

"The next phase in international relations between the United States and Europe will be loans to industries, private arrangements between bankers here and industrial leaders abroad," Dillon said in *The New York Times* on July 18, 1922. "Our opportunity lies in industrial Europe, and I might say that all Europe looks to us for help in this direction. The railroad and public utility financing that is to be done in Europe is tremendous, and it is lucrative, too. We will lend, but we will lend with care."

He stressed that US bankers needed to put in the shoe-leather, as he'd been doing for two months in Europe, getting familiar with the players in different nations, their industries, and their individual needs. "It must not be forgotten that England has been doing this financing abroad for two generations or more and that we became lenders abroad almost overnight."

The instability of Germany's economy and the issue of its war reparations payments, Dillon assessed, still hindered Europe's economic recovery. "A German loan is almost a certainty, but when it comes depends entirely upon when the political situation is adjusted," he told *The Baltimore Sun*, adding ominously: "It does not seem to me that relief can be arranged before Germany collapses."

Dillon was one of the first American bankers to realize that solving the German reparations crisis could open new opportunities for US enterprise. The United States needed a prosperous Europe for its own self-interest in trade, and the European Allies required Germany's billions in reparations to repay their own war debts.

Germany had suspended the gold standard when World War I broke out in 1914, opting to finance the conflict through borrowing instead of taxes. Believing, of course, that they'd win the war, they'd pay off debts through postwar reparations from defeated nations.

Germany had gambled—and lost. Now, under the Treaty of Versailles, Germany was required to pay restitution of 132 billion gold marks, almost $600 billion in current dollars.

This staggering burden of reparations quickly brought down Germany's entire economic system. The Weimar Republic kept printing money and the mark's value tumbled. When Germany was unable to make good on its reparations, the crisis reached its peak in the Ruhr Valley.

On January 11, 1923, 60,000 French and Belgian troops reoccupied the Ruhr region—Germany's industrial heartland. Due to the Weimar Republic's failure to meet its obligations under the Treaty of Versailles, France took over civil administration from the Germans, seized factories, smelters, and coal mines to fulfill the reparations.

The economic crisis only deepened. Hyperinflation soon rocked Germany and by November 1923, 42 billion marks were worth about one American penny. Leaders around the world realized they needed to act decisively resulting in the Dawes Plan of 1924 which successfully restructured Germany's war reparations.

Charles G. Dawes, a banker, diplomat, and Republican politician from Ohio—later the thirtieth vice president of the United States under Calvin Coolidge—led a committee to address Germany's inability to pay reparations.

The Dawes Plan, led by the US and British governments, also involved experts from France, Belgium, Italy, Britain, and the US. Meeting in Paris from January to April 1924, the committee formed a plan to stabilize the mark and reorganize Germany's budget. The Dawes Plan began by propping up the Reichsbank with an initial loan of 800 million marks from foreign banks. On August 16, both the Allies and Germany accepted the terms.

Germany would not complete paying off its World War I reparations for an astonishing ninety-one years. The Federal Republic of Germany made its final First World War reparations payment on October 3, 2010—the twentieth anniversary of German reunification—under Chancellor Angela Merkel.

By late 1924, Clarence Dillon saw a chance to overtake his establishment rival J.P. Morgan & Co. by seeking exclusive ties with Poland—a nation recovering from political collapse post–World War I.

Despite Poland's weak loan prospects due to economic instability, Dillon saw potential. In 1922, Samuel Vauclain of Baldwin Locomotive Works piqued Dillon's interest in financing Polish railways; however, Dillon hesitated due to Europe's uncertain conditions then. By November 1924, under the Dawes Plan, the landscape had shifted. Recognizing Poland's urgent need for loans, Dillon empowered Trowbridge Callaway and Robert Hayward from his team to negotiate terms in Warsaw.

J.P. Morgan also saw the profitable opportunity, but they were too slow—unable to match Dillon's pace. By January 1925, Dillon Read agreed to issue a $50 million loan—with provisions allowing adjustments against unforeseen risks—and secured future exclusivity as Poland's banker.

This deal elevated Clarence Dillon's standing against competitors like Otto Kahn at Kuhn Loeb & Co. Kahn privately lamented how his slower-paced firm had been beaten to the punch by aggressive players like Dillon.

In February 1925, however, Dillon Read's loan to Poland hit a snag due to longstanding frictions with Germany. Tensions between the two nations had long been simmering over numerous issues, the most grave of which was the so-called Polish Corridor—also known as the "Danzig Corridor"—the narrow strip created after World War I to give Poland access to the Baltic Sea. Yet another humiliation of the Treaty of Versailles, to many German eyes, the Polish Corridor included West Prussia and most of Poznań, separating East Prussia from Germany and creating a large landlocked German-speaking exclave.

The Treaty of Versailles also created, within the corridor, the Free City of Danzig, an independent city-state under the protection of the League of Nations. For centuries the Poles had called the city Gdańsk (its current name). When he came to power in 1933, Adolf Hitler demanded the return of Danzig, a 95% German city, and the Polish Corridor, leading to the Danzig Crisis of 1939 and, ultimately, to Hitler's invasion of Poland in September 1939—starting the Second World War.

But in February 1925, the war between Germany and Poland was still being fought with words. The German Foreign Office cast doubt on Poland's creditworthiness, aiming to isolate it financially and pressure it to relinquish its claims on the Danzig corridor. This negative campaign by the Germans worked.

Other New York firms shied away from joining Dillon Read in supporting the loan. Clarence Dillon now backtracked, adjusted his firm's terms, initially transferring only $35 million and secretly arranging for Poland to buy back up to $7.5 million of unsold bonds. A second transfer of $15 million was planned for August 1, 1925—but only if market conditions improved.

Dillon Read's efforts aligned with a US-Poland trade agreement under the most-favored-nation clause. Yet when Dillon

Read's Polish bonds went public on February 15, subscriptions lagged far behind expectations.

Clarence Dillon's overweening ambition to overtake J.P. Morgan by financing a major European government had led him, uncharacteristically, to misjudge the marketplace. There wasn't a demand for Polish bonds in Main Street America. By April, Robert Hayward expressed frustration over selling difficulties amid rumors of potential Polish territorial losses to Germany. Moody's analysts rated the Dillon Read bond issue poorly due to political instability.

The Polish government was in a bind, grappling with financial troubles and desperate for Dillon Read to release the next loan installment. Dillon was cagey, publicly repeating his eagerness to be Poland's exclusive banker, but behind the scenes, Dillon held back the funds. He wanted to travel to Poland and assess the political and economic situation firsthand.

To navigate European politics, he hired Colonel James A. Logan as his representative. Logan had strong ties with leaders across Europe and America—connections that could be crucial for a banker like Dillon still making his mark in Europe. Clarence Dillon then boarded a train in Paris's Gare du Nord in June 1925, en route to Poland, Czechoslovakia, Germany, and Hungary.

Arriving in Warsaw, Dillon was given the red-carpet treatment, for obvious reasons. Poland was now a teetering nation with a shaky economy further weakened by a trade war with Germany; the nation badly needed loans from US bankers. Prime Minister Wladyslaw Grabski gave a lavish dinner for the Dillon Read partners. He then provided private luxury railcars to tour the rest of Poland.

"The government will furnish me with a special train to go over the country," Dillon wrote to Anne and, for one of the first times in his life, he let down his guard, openly recalling his father's Jewish roots in Poland. "They want me to take over their railroad situation," he continued, "interesting and rather romantic when you think father left there only fifty-five years ago."

Dillon may have sounded privately a bit nostalgic in his prose—uncharacteristically using the word "romantic"—but he publicly wanted nothing to do with his father's Polish past.

The *Lodzer Tageblatt*, one of the country's most widely circulated Yiddish daily papers, published a short piece in 1927 about Dillon's Polish-Jewish origins on his father's side. It mentioned Samuel Lapowski's childhood in the small town of Vizne and the years that he lived and worked in Lodz; the Yiddish paper also revealed that one of Sam's sisters had never left the city. "Clarence Dillon's aunt who still lives in Lodz has an envelope factory on Podlunowa Street," the *Tageblatt* reported. "Dillon also has a cousin in Lodz who is a well-known attorney."

The *Lodzer Tageblatt* added that "when Dillon was in Lodz on a visit, however, he refused to receive any of his relatives. He did not even pay a visit to the graves of his [grand]parents."

The minister of foreign affairs, Count Aleksander Skrzynski, hosted a palace ball for the visitors, attended by Warsaw's elite. Count Alfred Antoni Potocki invited the American bankers to his family's castle which included dinner "in a different dining room every evening," since "in the twilight of their centuries-old prominence, the Potocki family were still living more or less as they had always lived."

Despite the extravagant wooing, Dillon left Poland without making any commitment on the loan's second transfer to the struggling nation.

On their way back from Poland, Dillon and his partners stopped in Prague to have lunch with US Ambassador Lewis Einstein. Dillon took a shine to Einstein when he learned that the ambassador was a fellow art connoisseur. Einstein told Dillon about a magnificent Buddha head statue, once part of the Hermitage Museum collection in Saint Petersburg; it was now on the market, but the asking price was far beyond his means. Clarence Dillon, already a keen collector of antiques, was beginning to get a taste for fine art as well—especially while doing business in the great capitals of Europe. In Prague, he snapped up the Buddha statue Lewis Einstein had coveted. He shipped it back to the US and the Buddha head was soon prominently displayed in Dillon's New Jersey estate, Dunwalke.

In July 1925, Poland's foreign minister, Count Skrzynski, traveled to the US, hoping to speed up the second tranche of the Dillon Read bonds and improve Polish-American relations, which had been strained by allegations of Polish repression of Jewish and German minorities.

On August 4, Clarence Dillon hosted a luncheon for the minister, attended by Otto Kahn and other leading Wall Street bankers. At the luncheon, Dillon and Robert Hayward were both given the Grand Cross of the Order of Polonia Restituta, a high honor bestowed on foreigners for distinguished service.

During his American tour, Skrzynski told the Jewish Telegraphic Agency about his government's agreement with the General Jewish Labor Bund in Poland that would open "a new chapter in the Polish-Jewish relations." *The American Israelite* newspaper, in describing the Polish-Jewish parliamentary agreement, noted that, "Clarence Dillon of Dillon, Read & Co., the firm which floated the last Polish loan, is believed to be of Jewish descent."

Despite the red-carpet welcome in Warsaw, the extravagant hospitality of Polish nobility, and the receipt of the Grand Cross of the Order of Polonia Restituta, Clarence Dillon had now soured on the nation. He recognized his mistake now, his misreading of the marketplace. Yes, bankrolling Poland had the *potential* to prove profitable, but when? And at what risk? Poland's credit was shaky, its currency falling, and a new government led by Count Skrzynski had taken over. He not only postponed the second loan transfer, but he also gave up his exclusive role as Poland's banker.

But what about Dillon Read's Polish bonds already on the market? Dillon needed to change the narrative somehow—and quickly. He needed to generate some positive publicity for Poland to counteract the campaign of negative press coming from the German Foreign Office.

But facts were facts. If Poland was politically unstable, its currency weak, and deemed a bad credit risk by Moody's, how could Dillon possibly reassure investors?

Dillon returned to a tried-and-true strategy, the same template he'd used to such a profitable—if destructive—effect in South America's emerging economies struggling with bond sales. Indeed, the situation in Poland was not much different than that of Bolivia or Brazil.

Dillon told the new Skrzynski government in Warsaw to invite Princeton economics professor Edwin W. Kemmerer to review its finances and suggest reforms. If the Money Doctor gave his stamp of approval, a new Dillon Read loan might follow.

In early December 1925, the Polish government invited Professor Kemmerer for a twelve-day "investigation." He arrived in Warsaw on December 31, 1925, "met at the railway station by high Polish officials," according to the next day's *New York Times*. Kemmerer assured the Poles of his neutrality in promoting Polish interests without preexisting ties to any Wall Street banking house. Dillon, Read & Co., for its part, issued a public statement denying *any* connection between the firm and Kemmerer's mission.

This was not only false but farcically so.

Kemmerer received his usual exorbitant payments—his "retainer"—from Dillon Read before and after the trip. All his travel expenses, his first-class tickets aboard luxury passenger liners to and from Europe, were covered by Dillon Read. Dillon Read even negotiated his remuneration with Polish officials.

And what were the results of the Money Doctor's report?

Professor Kemmerer advised the Polish government to proceed solely with Dillon Read as its bankers and recommended against accepting loans from any other Wall Street firms such as Bankers Trust.

To improve the US market for Polish bonds, Kemmerer made sophisticated-sounding economic predictions about Poland's future, including a speech before the Council on Foreign Relations in New York City. Based on Kemmerer's initial recommendations, Dillon Read and Benjamin Strong of the Federal Reserve Bank planned a second "advisory mission" to Poland to establish terms for a new "supervised stabilization loan."

The Poles saw American advisors as more neutral than those from European powers such as the United Kingdom or France. British officials, however, openly distrusted Kemmerer, who'd upset them by pushing for the immediate gold standard during his time with the Dawes Committee in 1922. They also disapproved of his ties with Dillon Read, which was known in the UK as a "maverick" firm—perhaps a more genteel British manner of saying "something of a pirate ship roaming the market for booty." The Bank of Poland, of course, backed Kemmerer's stabilization plan, though one official hinted that it was all just a "facade" to promote Poland in the US.

Kemmerer's report and speeches did make Poland more attractive for US investors. An unrelated boost came during Britain's

1926 coalminers' strike, when there was an increased demand for Polish coal exports. Bankers Trust and Blair & Company proposed a $62 million loan to Poland with minimal oversight by a US advisor who would join the Bank of Poland's board. Clarence Dillon refused to play second fiddle to Bankers Trust—or to any other US bank, for that matter.

Then, in November 1926, Germany's foreign minister Gustav Stresemann warned that Dillon Read's standing in Germany would suffer great damage if it issued more loans to Poland.

Dillon was caught up now in a much larger geopolitical battle. The warning from Stresemann was, for him, the tipping point in Poland. Weimar Germany had made a remarkable recovery in the past three years from the depths of Ruhr Valley reoccupation and the hyperinflation crisis. Unlike Poland, Germany had a tremendously profitable industrial sector, world-renowned companies like Krupp, Siemens, and Thyssen Iron & Steel Works, all of which were now seeking foreign capital.

Reporters covering Wall Street predicted more industrial loans as American banks explored opportunities in Germany: "Practically every large banking institution," *The New York Times* reported, "has scouts in Germany looking over the field."

Despite Dillon's sentimental-sounding letter to Anne about traveling by rail through the country of his father's birth, he remained unemotional in financial matters.

After two years of an uneasy partnership, Dillon, Read & Co. and the Polish government parted ways. Dillon turned his sights across the border to the west, to Poland's fiercest political and economic enemy.

In November 1924, Dillon began negotiations with Thyssen Iron & Steel Works, among Germany's industrial giants after World War I. August Thyssen, dubbed "the German Andrew Carnegie," struggled with lost facilities and hyperinflation-induced capital shortages. In November 1924, he dispatched two of his executives, Carl Rabes and Walter Barth, to New York to negotiate loans with Dillon, Read & Co.

In their diaries, Carl Rabes and Walter Barth described the American banker in detail: "Herr Dillon ruled his firm as an autocrat. The deal interested him from the beginning." But the Americans' focus on formal financial figures and ratios, along with their need to reconcile national differences in legal and accounting procedures, disappointed the Germans.

"Dillon came across to us as an excellent jobber in the good sense of the word, as a man with an exceptional flair. It was questionable to us whether he could pioneer a truly great idea, whose fruit might ripen slowly."

This partly reflected a conflict between the long-term perspectives of industry and the short-term perspectives of finance. Dillon was asked by Thyssen for a $100 million loan to a consortium of the "Big Six" heavy industrial companies, including Krupp, Deutsche Luxemburgische, Phoenix, Klockner, and the GBAG. Thyssen Iron & Steel Works owned mines supplying about 10% of Germany's coal. They also exported 30% of their product and were the leading German source of foreign currencies.

Thyssen Iron & Steel Works had always relied on its assets and reputation in Germany. Dillon Read, however, wanted full financial transparency. For about a month, Clarence Dillon stalled, seeking more data and insisting on property mortgages as collateral. Thyssen resisted these terms and the extremely high 8% interest rate. The deal faltered when Krupp secured a $10 million bond at 7% through Goldman Sachs & Co.

To avoid losing prestige, Dillon proposed a $20 million bond at 7%, using raw materials as collateral instead of mortgages. Rabes's persistence led to an agreement without public financial disclosure. Dillon reduced the loan to $12 million after further negotiations focused on Thyssen's assets rather than goods mortgages. A Chicago firm praised Thyssen's modern facilities in a report: "They are the most efficient steel manufacturers in Europe." Dillon sought exclusive future deals with Thyssen but settled for an option of first refusal.

In late 1924, Ferdinand Eberstadt, a brilliant thirty-four-year-old lawyer, arrived in Europe to become Dillon Read's point man in Germany. Eberstadt was a partner at the white-shoe legal firm Cotton and Franklin, and a man known for his keen insight into European affairs. He'd crafted the Dawes Investment Brochure for Dillon Read. Half-Jewish though raised Presbyterian, Eberstadt had longstanding connections at the highest levels of European financial circles. His German father was related to the Paris Rothschilds and had moved to America in the late 1800s. Eberstadt was also a cousin of Otto Kahn, head of Kuhn Loeb.

Fluent in German and French, Eberstadt had excelled at Princeton where he became close friends with James Forrestal. He studied economics and politics at Berlin University and the Sorbonne before earning his law degree from Columbia University. While working in Germany for Cotton and Franklin on legal matters for the firm's American clients, he identified investment banking opportunities that earned him finder's fees from Dillon Read—a practice not typically expected of law firms, then or now.

Dillon and Eberstadt sought German companies with strong export businesses capable of making payments on loans in US dollars, not Reichsmarks.

Siemens & Halske stood out immediately. The company was one of the world's largest electrical manufacturers with products like radio equipment and telephones but had lost much during the war including patents abroad. Carl Friedrich von Siemens aimed not only to restore but also expand its global reach postwar. In January 1925, Dillon secured the company a $10 million bond at 7%, marking Siemens as Dillon Read's second prestigious long-term client in Germany. (Today, Siemens AG is the largest industrial manufacturing company in Europe.)

In July 1925, Ferdinand Eberstadt led Dillon Read and J. Henry Schroder & Co. of London to acquire half of the coal mining giant Deutsche Luxemburgische company for $4 million. The firm was part of Germany's largest producer of coal, coke, iron, and steel. *The New York Times* noted this as the first joint American-British venture in German industry postwar. It strengthened Dillon Read's presence in Germany and led to a $25 million bond for Rheinelbe Union in January 1926. Eberstadt also arranged a $3 million bond for Rudolf Karstadt, Inc., Germany's largest department store chain, and facilitated investments in Disconto-Gesellschaft Bank through share purchases.

Clarence Dillon rewarded Ferdinand Eberstadt for all these dogged efforts by making him a full partner in Dillon Read and tripling his previous salary with Cotton and Franklin.

Eberstadt transitioned from lawyer to investment banker smoothly and nearly tripled Dillon Read's German underwritings from $39 million in 1925 to $117 million in 1926 while coordinating efforts between Paris and Berlin's Hotel Adlon.

Clarence Dillon, of course, had the final word, but he made financing decisions based on Eberstadt's groundwork.

In the experimental atmosphere after the First World War, Weimar Germany led a worldwide artistic revolution. The theater was transformed by Brecht and Weill's *Threepenny Opera*; architecture by the Bauhaus School, led by Walter Gropius; and the visual arts by Max Ernst, George Grosz, Hans Richter, and Kurt Schwitters of the Dada movement.

The accompanying decadence of the nightlife in Berlin's glittering cabarets and bars earned the city the sobriquet, "Sin Capital of Europe." The Hotel Adlon, a short walk from the Brandenburg Gate, was home to the most fashionable salon of the 1920s. Guests ranged from Benito Mussolini to Albert Einstein. In the Hotel Adlon, Eberstadt met with hundreds of European leaders in finance, industry, and the government. These included Gustav Stresemann, foreign minister of the Weimar Republic, Hjalmar Schacht, the president of the Reichsbank, and Albert Voegler, the director general of the mining conglomerate, Rheinelbe Union.

While living at the hotel, Eberstadt's typical schedule, combining work and play, was "a half dozen or more important business meetings during the day, followed by a dinner and perhaps a performance at the opera with important clients." Then: the nightlife. Eberstadt enjoyed partying late at cabarets and managed to get by on only a few hours of sleep.

In June 1926, Dillon Read led a major European industrial financing on Wall Street, facilitating a $30 million loan at 6½% for the formation of Vereinigte Stahlwerke AG (United Steelworks Co.), which would soon become the world's largest mining and steel cartel.

Vereinigte Stahlwerke unified multiple firms to streamline production and secure larger financings. Before his death in 1926, August Thyssen decided to merge his firm into Germany's leading steelworks. International media called him the "great Americanizer," while *The New York Times* dubbed him the "Rockefeller of the Ruhr." His son, Fritz Thyssen, was now chairman of Vereinigte Stahlwerke's board.

"The new trust controls one-quarter of Rhenish-Westphalian coal, one-fifth of coke, and half of all iron and steel produced in Germany," *The Wall Street Journal* reported on June 15, 1926. Between 1926 and 1928, Dillon Read underwrote about $100 million worth of bonds for Vereinigte Stahlwerke. Although no Americans served on its board, Dillon Read now had more influence than any single German bank over Germany's second-largest corporation.

Clarence Dillon returned from Europe on the SS *Olympic* in June 1926 after completing the financing for the consolidation of Germany's leading steel companies. The financing and creation of Vereinigte Stahlwerke, often called Germany's "steel cartel," would stand as Clarence Dillon's crowning achievement as a banker in Europe.

Eberstadt continuously highlighted favorable US markets for German securities, noting improved interest rates from two years ago when they were at 10¼% to bonds now trading above par at 6¾%. The main obstacle was uncertainty over Germany's reparation payments. Parker Gilbert and the State Department warned against Germany's excessive borrowing.

In an October 31 letter to Clarence Dillon from the Hotel Adlon, Eberstadt described the obvious tensions between German Foreign Minister Gustav Stresemann and Reichsbank President Hjalmar Schacht. Despite the personal respect between Stresemann and Schacht, the two men clashed, philosophically, over the all-important issue of Germany's war reparations.

The Prussian-born Schacht was a staunch and outspoken opponent of Germany's reparations obligations. He would later urge Chancellor Hindenburg to appoint the first Nazi-led government. A right-wing ultranationalist, he served as Minister of Economics under Adolf Hitler and then as head of the

Reichsbank until 1939, hailed as the architect of the Third Reich's "economic miracle." Although Schacht remained a minister until 1943, he was implicated in the July 1944 assassination attempt on Hitler and was lucky not to end up hanged by piano wire or summarily shot by the Gestapo. Schacht instead ended World War II as a prisoner in the Dachau concentration camp.

Schacht had gone along with the Dawes Plan begrudgingly. He despised the "war guilt clause" in the Treaty of Versailles which laid sole responsibility on Germany and forced the Weimar Republic to pay unfathomable reparations. Like most Germans, Schacht adamantly believed the assigning of "war guilt" was a great injustice—as if *one* nation alone was responsible for the Great War.

By contrast, the far more statesmanlike Gustav Stresemann viewed the fulfillment of Germany's financial obligations under the Versailles Treaty to be a matter of national honor. The Berlin-born Stresemann was the founder and leader of the Deutsche Volkspartei ("German People's Party"), a moderate centrist who served as chancellor of Germany in 1923 and as foreign minister until his sudden death in 1929. His life's achievement was the 1920s political reconciliation between Germany and France, for which he received the Nobel Peace Prize in 1926.

His first major diplomatic success was working on the 1924 Dawes Plan, which reduced Germany's overall reparations commitment. Stresemann felt that honoring the war reparations would "demonstrate that Germany was once more a valuable partner in the community of nations."

Eberstadt's ambition, meanwhile, was nothing less than to make Dillon Read the leading American bank in Germany. To achieve this, he needed the backing of both Stresemann and Schacht. The latter was cautious about upsetting J.P. Morgan due to its political and financial clout in Washington and with the Federal Reserve. During a meeting with Eberstadt, Schacht criticized Dillon Read for making tough deals with German companies, a point Eberstadt initially disputed but was eventually forced to admit was true.

In October 1926, Eberstadt wrote to Dillon about Germany's improving business climate in the Weimar Republic: the population seemed more confident, optimistic and, as was to be expected of Germans, showed a tireless work ethic. Personal wealth was rising and consumer spending had increased since spring. Eberstadt believed he was surpassing American banks in securing industrial loans in Germany. By year's end, they expected to issue over $100 million in German industrial obligations—a feat that impressed local Germans.

"From the cables I have sent over, it is evident there is still a good deal of first-class business lying around here," Eberstadt wrote. "I refer particularly to the Berlin Electricity and the Gas Central, which the Steel Trust is proposing to organize shortly."

Dillon Read led a deal for Disconto-Gesellschaft Bank in August 1926, and in December, the firm would underwrite $20 million at 6½% bonds for the Berlin City Electric Company. In November 1926, Eberstadt continued to solicit business with the German government and reported to Dillon about his "amiable" personal meeting with the Reichsbank president. Eberstadt believed that "Schacht is awake to the possibilities of improving his position by cooperating with us." But, Eberstadt added, "I don't think he will do it out of any love for us."

Eberstadt was absolutely convinced that without Hjalmar Schacht's backing "we can do nothing toward getting the German national financing unless his current strong position becomes seriously undermined."

Gustav Stresemann, on the other hand, seemed to be an easier sell; he was extraordinarily interested in Eberstadt's idea of forming a group "which would take over the German obligations at a rate fast enough to clean up Germany's debts to the creditor nations in ten to fifteen years." Stresemann, however, was concerned about whether J.P. Morgan would do the financing jointly with Dillon Read.

Tradition was so important in European business that many Germans like Stresemann and Schacht regarded Dillon, Read & Co.—a firm they'd scarcely heard of—as a newcomer on Wall Street playing second fiddle to the great House of Morgan.

Eberstadt took only a few days to come up with an effective solution. He would simply lie. Or at least, be quite flexible regarding the facts. He stopped using the name Dillon Read. He began to refer to the firm in which he was a new partner as Vermilye & Co.—even if the Germans hadn't heard the name, it was easy enough to check that Vermilye & Co.'s history as a banking institution in New York went back to the mid-1800s.

He could also provide the numbers to the German foreign minister. Eberstadt showed Stresemann the comparative figures of J.P. Morgan and Dillon Read—or rather Vermilye & Co.—issues in the last twenty months. "The aggregate was about 818,000,000 against Morgan's 770,000,000." In Weimar Germany, in Dawes Loan financing alone, Eberstadt's firm had to date done $160 million and it was, in fact, J.P. Morgan playing second fiddle, with $110 million, and National City Bank, at distant third place, had $79 million.

Eberstadt lunched with Jakob Goldschmidt, the chairman of the Danatbank, who'd been in charge of liquidating the huge holdings of industrialist Hugo Stinnes after his death.

As one of Germany's wealthiest Jewish bankers, Goldschmidt would soon become a favorite target of Nazi propaganda about the "unwarranted power" and "sinister influence" of Jews in Weimar Germany. Clarence Dillon would also find himself being pilloried in a series of articles in the Nazi press about the American Jewish bankers who were part of the same vast global conspiracy.

In November 1926, Eberstadt reported to Dillon that Goldschmidt "had made some nice remarks about our position here saying that he thought we undoubtedly had taken the leading position for foreign financing in Germany." These words carried a lot of weight since, "Goldschmidt has clearly become the recognized leader among the German bankers. He concretely suggested that we join with him in the organization of a large company to finance German business abroad," Eberstadt wrote Dillon, concluding that "it will be profitable to work with him."

Ferdinand Eberstadt's work in Germany was suddenly interrupted by a cable from his boss in New York. Clarence Dillon had an urgent need for Eberstadt's legal mind to coordinate Dillon's defense in the Goodyear lawsuits from December 1926 to May 1927. Once the Goodyear bankruptcy fiasco was resolved, in the summer of 1927 Eberstadt returned to Germany to wrap up the biggest achievement Dillon, Read & Co. would have in Europe.

Eberstadt often needed to reassure US investors, through the media, about Germany's economic stability, telling *The New York Times* that 1927 had been Germany's best business year since adopting the Dawes Plan. Eberstadt supported a fixed total on German debt to encourage cooperation for solutions. By January 1928, Eberstadt highlighted these achievements in Germany to motivate bond salesmen at Dillon Read's general sales meeting:

"We have in the iron, coal, and steel industry, the United Steel Works, which is approximately the size of Bethlehem Steel, and second only to the United States Steel Corporation," Eberstadt said. "In the electrical industry we took Siemens, which is recognized as a rival only to the United States's General Electric . . . And in the banking field, we selected the Disconto and Deutsche Banks," roughly the size of the First National and the National City banks in the United States.

In 1928, Dillon Read expanded its German ventures still further. That March, they issued a $15 million loan at 6% to the Gelsenkirchen Coal Mining Company and underwrote $20.6 million for various Ruhr corporations. They also provided a $15 million loan at 6% to Rudolf Karstadt, Inc., a large department store chain.

Ferdinand Eberstadt's nights, spent in Weimar Berlin's cabarets and restaurants, led to an affair with Greta Mosheim, a famous stage actress. He took a bigger risk by sleeping with Kathe Kleefeld, the wife of Gustav Stresemann. Foreign Minister Stresemann, the Nobel Peace Prize winner who'd supported most of Dillon Read's efforts in Germany, was in failing health. His wife was one of Berlin's most renowned hostesses, her home was a hub for international businessmen and diplomats seeking connections beyond mere conversation.

But Eberstadt's months as a married playboy in Berlin had by now exhausted him. He missed his wife and children in New York.

Eberstadt was also alarmed by the direction in which Weimar Germany was moving. Extreme nationalism was rampant. The violent antisemitism of members of the Sturmabteilung ("Storm Troopers")—Hitler's Brownshirts—was becoming more violent, more routine, and more openly expressed.

In the summer of 1929, Clarence Dillon provided letters of introduction for Paul H. Nitze, a brilliant Harvard graduate, to several German bankers and industrialists. Nitze, the twenty-two-year-old son of a University of Chicago professor, was working at a small investment bank in Chicago. The firm aimed to capture a share of the profitable market for German securities that Dillon Read had enjoyed. They sent Nitze to assess the situation in Germany and report back. Nitze was perfectly suited for the job. His grandfather had emigrated from Germany in 1867 and served as the German consul in Baltimore.

In September 1929, when Nitze returned to the US, Clarence Dillon requested to read and hear the young banker's report. Nitze told Dillon that stock and bond prices in Germany were seriously inflated and industrial earnings and profits prospects were poor.

Like Eberstadt, Nitze was alarmed by the increasing political turmoil in the streets, the growing popularity of the Nazi Party, which would likely lead to extreme solutions to Germany's economic issues. The death of Gustav Stresemann in 1929 removed one key obstacle to Hitler's rise. Right-wing nationalists, not only the Nazi Party, had long despised Stresemann's compliance with war reparation payments and the Dawes Plan.

After the Wall Street Crash in October 1929, Clarence Dillon faced a critical moment in his relationship with the German government. In December, Rudolf Hilferding, the Weimar Republic's new finance minister, reached out to Dillon in utter desperation. The Weimar Republic was on the verge of a total financial collapse. Hilferding asked Dillon for an immediate $75 million credit line for six to nine months. He promised that this would strengthen future ties between Dillon's bank and the Reich.

But Reichsbank President Hjalmar Schacht blocked any such bailout from Dillon Read. As a right-wing ultranationalist, his agenda was to see yet more economic chaos—the failure to pay further war reparations would accelerate the collapse of the Weimar Republic. "Dillon Read [is] a second-class firm," Schacht scoffed when told about the prospective $75 million loan. Without Schacht's approval, as one German Foreign Ministry official put it, "the Dillon Read loan is as good as dead," adding that "a direct demand on the foreign market by the Reich government for either long- or short-term funds is no longer a possibility."

Under extreme pressure, Hilferding was forced to resign as finance minister on December 21. Dillon Read had lost its last link with the German government.

Meanwhile, the Weimar Republic was teetering on a platform built on foreign credit. Damaged already by the crash of US financial markets, Germany's credit pyramid collapsed during the global banking crisis in the summer of 1931.

On January 30, 1933, Adolf Hitler became the chancellor of what he now called the Third Reich. The Weimar Republic was dead. One of Hitler's first actions was to fulfill his oft-stated promise about the Versailles Treaty. To the approval of most Germans, even those who didn't support the Nazis, Hitler canceled all reparations payments on May 17, 1933, in a speech to the Reichstag.

Leading German-Jewish bankers with whom Dillon Read had done business like Jakob Goldschmidt of the Danatbank and Oscar Wassermann, who sat on the executive boards of both the Deutsche Bank and the Disconto-Gesellschaft Bank, were forced to retire. Most German-Jewish bankers who could escape Nazi Germany immediately did so.

During the 1920s, Clarence Dillon and his firm earned tens of millions by floating German securities, making Dillon Read the third-largest American underwriter of international securities. Even after Hitler came to power in 1933, it was difficult for many American companies, Dillon Read included, to abandon their lucrative German business interests.

Clarence Dillon left us no record of how he personally felt when he was being attacked in the pro-Nazi newspapers. He wrote nothing about it to Anne, nor to any of his partners.

Yet he'd certainly read or heard what was written about him, even before the Weimar Republic collapsed. Numerous articles stressed that the headquarters of an alleged "international conspiracy" of Jewish financiers was in America—centered on Wall Street—and singled out "Clarence Dillon of New York" as being one of the leading bankers at the head of "the world-wide Jewish conspiracy." This alleged global conspiracy aimed to give the Jews "supreme power and undermine Christendom."

The Jew-baiting press once referred to Clarence Dillon as "the man who controls Wall Street" and the greatest rival today of J.P. Morgan. The Nazi Party's official daily paper, *Völkischer Beobachter*, even claimed that Clarence Dillon was second only to Henry Ford as a financial genius in America.

Throughout the 1920s and early 1930s, the pro-Nazi press hadn't just been railing against this supposed sinister financial cabal, it had been naming names. *Der Weltkampf* published a long denunciation of Jewish—and a few non-Jewish—bankers worldwide, listing firms and individuals with the headline:

THE ORGANIZATION OF THE
STOCK EXCHANGE PIRATES

Under the subheading "America," the journal listed, among others: J.W. Seligman & Co., Hallgarten & Co., Kuhn, Loeb & Co., Mortimer L. Schiff, Otto H. Kahn, Speyer & Co., Lazard Brothers, Ladenburg, Thalmann & Co., Knauth, Rachob & Kuehne, Stosz, Levy-Gerstle, Lewinson Brothers, the Guggenheim Brothers, Untermeyer, Meyer, Strauss, Hellman and Neumarkts, Bernard M. Baruch, Paul and Felix Warburg, Morgan &

Co., Peabody & Co., Lee Higginson & Co., Brown Brothers & Co.—as well as Dillon, Read & Co. and its head.

The Nazi press had already explained to German readers that the head of Dillon Read was a Polish Jew whose birth name was Clarence Lapowski not Clarence Dillon.

Throughout his rise to power Hitler would refer to Jewish bankers as *Internationalen Finanzjudentum*—or "international Jewish financiers." His (Hitler's) denunciations turned increasingly ominous and threatening, culminating on January 30, 1939, during his infamous "prophecy" speech to the Reichstag:

"If international Jewish financiers inside and outside Europe should succeed in plunging the nations once more into a world war," Hitler declaimed to applause and shouts of approval, "the result will be not the Bolshevization of the earth and thereby the victory of Jewry, but the annihilation of the Jewish race in Europe."

Once World War II did break out in September 1939, Dillon Read faced widespread criticism for having financed the building of Hitler's war machine. Dillon Read's bonds had, indeed, financed much of prewar German industrial production, especially of the steel cartel, Vereinigte Stahlwerke, which had many Nazi supporters among its executives.

America had maintained an isolationist stance toward European political affairs, while a few Wall Street bankers and lawyers arranged deals to rebuild Weimar Germany for profit. Between 1924 and 1930, German industrial firms issued $214,419,000 in bonds in the United States, with Dillon Read handling the largest share.

During this period, American financiers earned $50 million in profits on German loans, many of which were never repaid. Before Hitler's rise in 1933, American businesses were already linked with many German industries. Major US banks dealing with Germany knew about the steel cartels' ties to the Nazis and to Hitler's remilitarization beginning in 1933.

The German chemical conglomerate I.G. Farbenindustrie (or "I.G. Farben") was formed from a merger of companies in Germany and the United States to produce drugs, synthetic gasoline, rubber, dyes, film, high-octane aviation fuel, plastics, and insecticides. The I.G. Farben "cartel"—once the largest corporation in all of Europe—included reputable companies like Bayer, Sterling, and BASF. As Farben's investment banker, Dillon Read used its experience in creating a gypsum monopoly and sold bonds to the unsuspecting American public.

In 1929, I.G. Farben formed a partnership with Standard Oil in the US, a connection which helped the Third Reich in the 1930s as it illegally built up the Luftwaffe. During the early years of World War II, while the US remained neutral, Standard Oil supplied Germany with critical high-grade aviation fuel, while the British were denied it. James Forrestal served on the Standard Oil board before and after World War II and, from 1938, sat on I.G. Farben's international subsidiary board.

Declassified CIA files cite hundreds of millions in financing by Dillon, Read & Co. for businesses in Nazi Germany and even include allegations *never* substantiated—that some I.G. Farben plants were not bombed in World War II because James Forrestal, the secretary of the navy, remained a shareholder of the company. After hearing a radio report about these claims in 1948, Forrestal vehemently denied this accusation.

In the summer of 1947, the "I.G. Farben Trial" began at Nuremberg. Twenty-three senior executives were charged with war crimes, crimes against humanity, and the abuse and murder of slave laborers in Farben's factories. In 1948, ten of the I.G.

Farben defendants were acquitted completely. Thirteen Farben defendants were found guilty, receiving prison terms ranging from one and a half years to eight years, including time already served.

For Clarence Dillon found it profitable to maintain his firm's German business ties, regardless of how he felt about Adolf Hitler and his goose-stepping hordes. Though there's no disputing that Clarence Dillon was a patriotic American, there's also no disputing that Dillon, Read & Co. continued refinancing loans for its clients in the Third Reich, Siemens & Halske and Vereinigte Stahlwerke, until late 1937.

For over a decade doing business with powerful German industrialists, Dillon Read placed the pursuit of profits above any moral and ethical concerns.

Chapter Nine

THE BUYOUT WIZARD

THE FIRST DAY of May 1925 dawned overcast and unseasonably cool in the gray stone canyons of Lower Manhattan. Heavy rains were in the forecast, but at 8:00 a.m. the leaden skies over Wall Street remained tranquil. Hordes of young bond salesmen and teenaged messengers hustled toward the stock exchange.

The headlines splashed across the copies of *The New York Times* and *The Wall Street Journal* hawked at the newsstand on the corner of Nassau and Wall Streets were about the mass influenza vaccinations in Washington, DC, and Field Marshal von Hindenburg forgoing "all military trappings" as he was inaugurated the new president of Weimar Germany. The sports pages were abuzz about the upcoming Kentucky Derby—the first Triple Crown race to ever be broadcast live on national radio. Gene Tunney, the Shakespeare-loving heavyweight champion of the world, was gearing up to take on a tough contender named Tommy Gibbons in the Polo Grounds, home to the New York Giants.

Half a mile west across the Harlem River, the New York Yankees were in an early season slump, largely attributed to the absence from the lineup of slugger Babe Ruth who'd been hospitalized in St. Vincent's for over a month. Yankees' third baseman Joe Dugan succinctly summed up the cause of Ruth's hospital stay.

"Day and night, broads and booze, booze and broads," he said.

The same could be said for life in much of freewheeling America in the mid-twenties.

"Fifty Drinks a Day on His Job," ran one headline in *The New York Times*. It was a brief account of a Federal Prohibition Department agent named Don Okle who'd resigned his position in San Francisco claiming that, while simply doing his work as "an undercover man," he had to "consume on average fifty drinks a day," the *Times* reported, "or 36,400 in two years to gather evidence as an agent of San Francisco's 'Dry Forces.'"

Meanwhile, on April 10, Scribner's Sons had published F. Scott Fitzgerald's third novel, *The Great Gatsby*—a very short book for which Fitzgerald had set the grandest aspirations. He felt he'd captured the very essence of the Jazz Age in perhaps the best prose he'd ever put on paper.

At 10:00 a.m. on that May 1, on the fourth floor of his book-lined office at 28 Nassau Street, Clarence Dillon sat in a Queen Anne armchair, engrossed in the morning's papers.

Dillon had dressed for the day: a navy blue pinstriped suit, tailored in the Savile Row style and a starched white shirt. He folded his morning copies of the *Times* and *The Wall Street Journal*, hiked up his left cufflinked sleeve, rolled his wrist, and glanced at the minute hand of his Patek Philippe Tonneau.

He walked over to his mahogany desk—uncluttered by anything other than a simple lined notebook and two well-sharpened pencils—opened the top drawer and pulled out an oversized checkbook from the Central Union Trust Company of New York.

Dillon uncapped his fountain pen and began to write a check that seemed to have an inordinate number of zeros.

But the figure was no mistake.

Dillon neatly wrote out the amount in flowing script.

One hundred forty-six million dollars.

Below that, he penned the name of his firm—Dillon, Read & Co. His face showed no emotion—not even a hint of excitement—despite the unprecedented events that were about to unfold on Wall Street and beyond. The payment for Dodge Brothers, Inc. was then the largest cash transaction in history.

Dillon slipped the check into a plain white envelope, left the flap unsealed, and carrying nothing else but a rolled-up umbrella, descended in the creaking elevator to the ground floor. Accompanied by his two most trusted partners, Dean Mathey and James Forrestal, he exited through the doors to the bustle of Nassau Street.

The three men rounded the corner and passed the neoclassical J.P. Morgan building at 23 Wall Street. Compared to the rather pedestrian building which housed Dillon Read, Morgan's was like a limestone fortress—indeed, it was such a formidable symbol of American capitalism that it had been bombed by an anarchist five years earlier, an act of terrorism that killed thirty-eight people.

As they walked to the Central Union Trust Company at 80 Broadway, Clarence Dillon remained in stoic silence, his gait unhurried, his face inscrutable. As was their habit, Mathey and Forrestal followed a few strides behind the boss.

Behind the placid demeanor, Dillon may have reflected on the past nine months of negotiations and bidding in the high-stakes game of poker he'd played against the House of Morgan to acquire Dodge Brothers, Inc. Dillon knew that his acquisition of Dodge was the deal of the decade.

At the start of the First World War, the fledgling auto company founded by John and Horace Dodge—two former employees of Henry Ford—was one of the country's most esteemed and profitable businesses. By 1916, the new Dodge touring car was considered so reliable and rugged that the US Army placed a special order for General Pershing's campaign to capture Pancho Villa in Mexico.

The car industry was still in its infancy, but by 1919, the Dodge factories were rolling out five hundred new cars daily and couldn't keep up with consumer demand. In 1920, Dodge built 141,000 cars—behind only Ford and Chevrolet.

But at the pinnacle of success, catastrophe struck the Dodge family. John, the elder of the brothers, died suddenly on January 14, 1920, at age fifty-five. On December 10, 1920, Horace fell gravely ill and died at age fifty-two. The nation was in the grip of the "Fourth Wave" of the Spanish Influenza that year, and the Dodge brothers' deaths were quickly blamed on the epidemic. But both Horace and John were hard-drinking Midwesterners. In addition to pneumonia, Horace's physician listed cirrhosis of the liver as a cause of his premature death.

Rumors spread throughout financial circles that it wasn't influenza that killed the Dodge brothers. Rather, two premature deaths fit the wildly risk-taking Prohibition era. Bernard Baruch recalled an encounter on January 2, 1920, when the brothers were in Manhattan for the weeklong National Automobile Show. Baruch ran into John Dodge in the lobby of The Ritz-Carlton and Dodge invited Baruch to his room for a drink, likely "wood alcohol"—industrial methanol—passed off as smuggled Scotch.

It was the bootleg booze consumed in their suite at the Ritz, said Baruch, that killed the two Detroit millionaires.

In any event, the Dodge brothers were dead, and their widows, Matilda and Anna, grew weary of the day-to-day grind involved in running the company. They were approached by a pair of ambitious young speculators from Kentucky. Charles Schwartz and his brother Morton, first-generation Jewish-Americans, offered to help the widows sell the corporation.

Charles Schwartz was as quick on his feet as he was with his words. He was an articulate street hustler who moved in all the right social circles. A former amateur boxer, Schwartz liked to claim that he'd held his own while sparring with Jack Dempsey. As a star on his Long Island polo team, he played alongside World War I ace Tommy Hitchcock Jr., a Harvard man who Scott Fitzgerald idolized and used as the inspiration for the Tom Buchanan character in *Gatsby*.

When the Schwartz brothers sent out feelers that Dodge was for sale, many buyers were interested. Yet when push came to shove, only two banks had both the financial muscle and the liquidity to remain in the game. The back-and-forth between Dillon Read and the House of Morgan was heated, and often pushed the limits of 1920s transportation, technology, and acceptable business practices. Both sides chartered high-speed trains to carry their financial envoys to Detroit. At one point, Clarence Dillon went so far as to charter airplanes so that his men could outrace Morgan's trains. Bankers and lawyers worked long nights on Wall Street. Private telephone lines and telegraph wires buzzed for days on end.

To observers it seemed like a spirited but fair competition. Like the Kentucky Derby, or a heavyweight championship bout between Tunney and Dempsey. The fight seemed on the up-and-up. But it wasn't. Clarence Dillon had taken no risks. He never did—even with lesser sums than over $100 million dollars. He'd offered Charlie Schwartz a sizable cut of the eventual sale price for his "assistance." In other words: for inside information.

Throughout the bidding process Schwartz kept giving Dillon up-to-date news about Morgan. Clarence Dillon seemed to know J.P. Morgan's next move before he did.

The House of Morgan was expected to acquire Dodge on behalf of the General Motors Corporation. Morgan had never previously been bettered on a deal of this scale. Morgan thought he'd won with an offer of $59 million cash and $90 million of non-interest-bearing installment notes.

At the eleventh hour, as if drawing an inside straight on the final card—"On the river," in Texas Hold'em terms—Dillon sealed the purchase of Dodge with an all-cash bid of $146 million by a certified check.

Inside the echoing marble halls of the Central Trust Company, Clarence Dillon shook hands with Charles Spicer, the vice president of the Detroit Trust Company, who was representing the Dodge Brothers estate. They stalled by making small talk as they waited for two telephone operators to connect a long-distance line to Detroit.

In 1925, the simultaneous closing in two cities separated by more than six hundred miles was without precedent.

At 10:30 a.m., Arthur Ballantine, counsel for Dillon Read in New York, lowered the phone receiver.

"Everything is ready," Ballentine said.

Dillon opened the envelope. Spicer immediately took the receiver.

"I have the check," he said, and the deed to Dodge Motors was handed over to Dean Mathey.

One hundred forty-six million dollars in current value is almost three billion dollars, an unthinkable amount of cash to pay up front for the purchase of any corporation. And all this done without extensive due diligence.

With the Dodge Brothers deal consummated, Dillon walked calmly back to 28 Nassau Street, saying nothing to Dean Mathey or James Forrestal along the way. Exiting the still creaking elevator on the fourth floor of Dillon Read, he crossed the green carpet and glanced at the other partners at their rolltop desks, before shutting the door of his office behind him. He slipped into his leather armchair again—and became engrossed in a book of history. At the moment, he was fascinated by the Medicis.

Outside, shortly after 11:00 a.m., the downpour was so relentless that the gutters of Nassau and Wall Street swelled with prodigious puddles that flooded the sidewalks, sending traders darting into the dark taverns serving pork sausages and cheap pints of ale throughout the day.

The thunderheads swept swiftly north over Central Park and Harlem, over the Polo Grounds and Yankee Stadium, in the heart of the Bronx. The electricity unleashed itself with a destructive fury that was described on the front page of the next morning's *Times*:

"A terrific clap of thunder that followed when lightning struck the copper ball atop the central unit of Conservatory Range 1, in the New York Botanical Gardens, Bronx Park, during the shower yesterday afternoon, shook buildings within a radius of many blocks, breaking several hundred windowpanes and leading many people to believe that that section of the city had been visited by an earthquake."

The only earthquake in New York City on May 1, 1925, was the financial one on Wall Street, and the aftershocks would be felt for years to come.

In the days after the Dodge deal, it was the name "Clarence Dillon" flashing across the front pages of newspapers—not just in America, but around the world.

To Americans who would never understand the intricacies of Wall Street financial dealings, the $146 million check was a concrete embodiment of unattainable—unimaginable—wealth. Photographs of the check appeared on newspapers' front pages and the details, the very play-by-play of the handover at 80 Broadway breathlessly recounted as if it had been a World Series game between the Yankees and the Giants.

The public was enthralled by the mysterious Harvard graduate from Texas who, according to an account in *The New Yorker*, "appeared to buy Dodge Brothers as casually as a housewife purchases a peck of potatoes."

Clarence Dillon had already achieved recognition with his innovative financial restructuring that rescued the Goodyear Tire Company from bankruptcy. He was viewed as a bright young banker, certainly—but to have outmaneuvered, outsmarted, and outbid the great J.P. Morgan? Unthinkable.

Bertie C. Forbes, the former Hearst newspaper reporter who eight years earlier had founded his own magazine, offered up an "exclusive" and intimate profile of Dillon that ran in *Forbes* on May 15, 1925.

"Has a second J.P. Morgan arisen in the financial world?" he wrote. "Clarence Dillon is the very antithesis of the public's conception of the typical mercenary, money-grabbing, ceaselessly scheming, boorish, beefy, gross, blustering Wall Street magnate, interested in nothing higher than his moneybags," Forbes wrote. The "sharp-featured, refined, cultured" man with long, sensitive, tapering fingers, and the slight Southern drawl from his Texas upbringing, had an artistic approach to work and life. Courteous and elegantly groomed, Dillon is a perfect host, "equally at home discussing art with artists, cattle with farmers" as he was analyzing complicated financial transactions.

Dillon was not a second J.P. Morgan. No, as an investor, a financial innovator, as a man—for good or ill—Dillon was unique. By

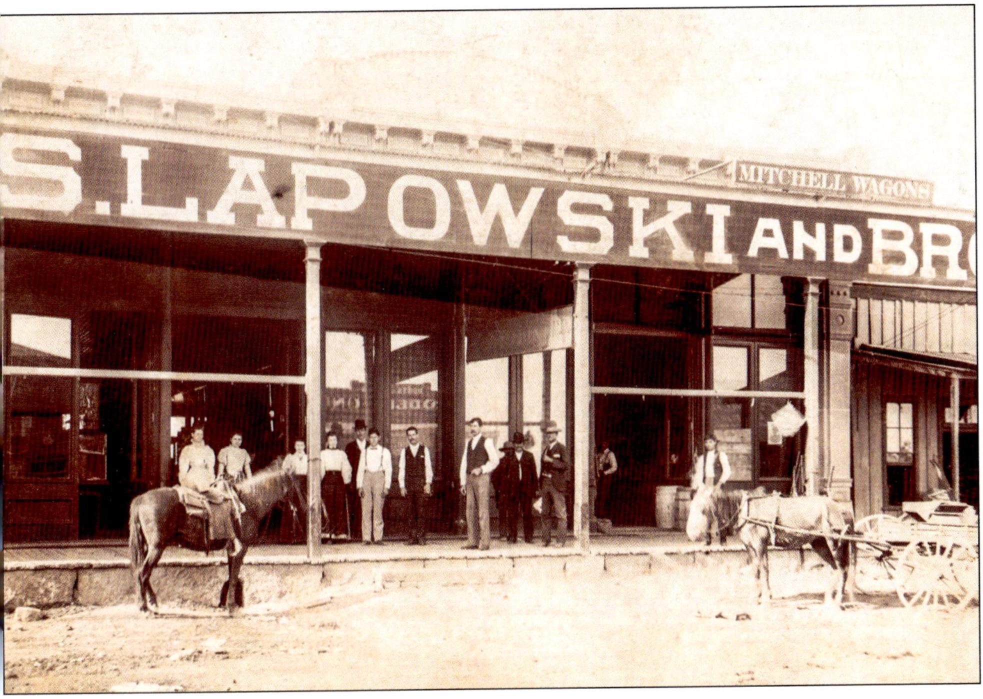
S. LAPOWSKI AND BR
MITCHELL WAGONS

Clarence Dillon's father, Samuel Lapowski, built one of the largest dry goods stores in Texas, called S. Lapowski and Brother.

Photo credit: Courtesy West Texas Collection, Angelo State University

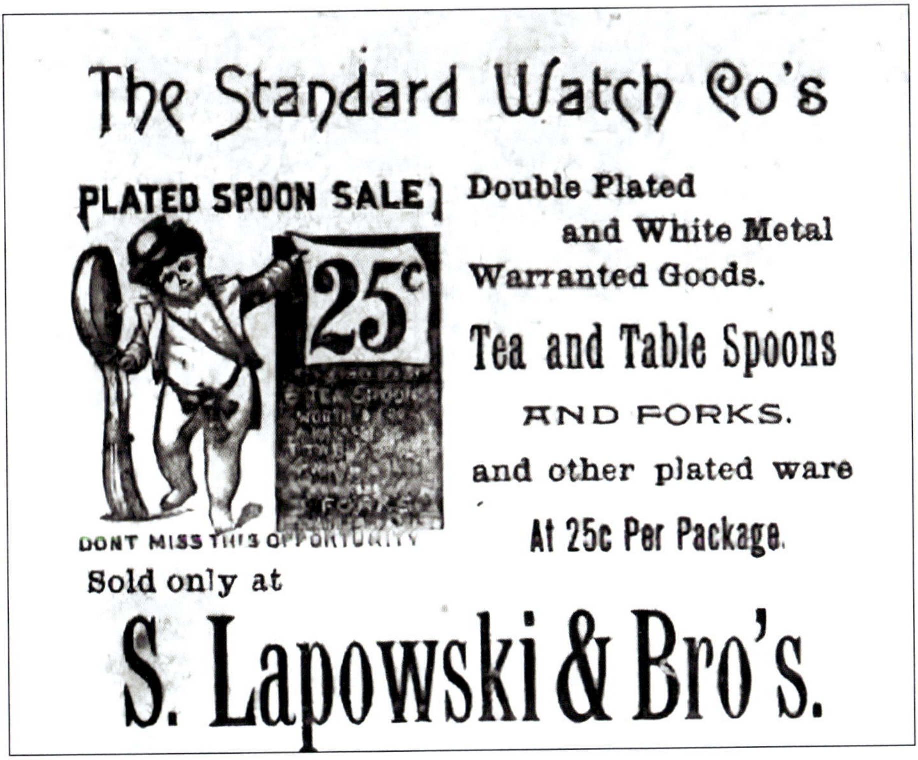
The Standard Watch Co's
PLATED SPOON SALE
25c
Double Plated
and White Metal
Warranted Goods.
Tea and Table Spoons
AND FORKS.
and other plated ware
At 25c Per Package.
DONT MISS THIS OPPORTUNITY
Sold only at
S. Lapowski & Bro's.

An ad for Samuel Lapowski's dry goods store, offering "double-plated" tea and tablespoons for 25 cents.

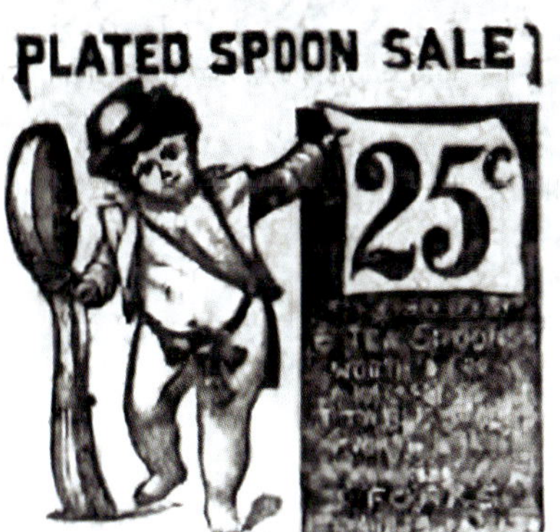

Samuel Lapowski. An impoverished Jewish immigrant from Poland, he arrived in Texas in 1869 and first worked as a peddler.

Photo credit: Family of Sam Lapowski's brother, Nathan, with permission

Clarence Lapowski as a young boy. By age nine, he was already joining his father on twice-yearly buying trips to New York City, where Sam purchased inventory for the Lapowski stores and arranged financing.

Photo credit: Courtesy of Dillon family

Clarence Dillon managed the track team at Worcester Academy. A teacher observed that Dillon "leads his fellows naturally," but warned that accepting so many school positions left him overextended for his studies.

Photo credit: Worcester Academy

Clarence Dillon from his 1905 Harvard yearbook. Clarence managed both the junior and senior crew teams at Harvard.

Photo credit: Courtesy of Dillon family

Dillon with the Sigma Zeta Kappa debating society at Worcester Academy. Dillon proved to be a brilliant debater, captaining the Sigma team to victory over the rival Legomathenian Society.

Photo credit: Worcester Academy

Clarence and Anne Dillon in 1907 in Wisconsin, just months before announcing their engagement; they would marry the following February.

Photo credit: Courtesy of the Dillon family

Anne Douglass Dillon, the youngest child of a leading Milwaukee business family and one of the city's most sought-after young women. Dillon first met her in 1905 and was, by his own account, immediately smitten.

Photo credit: Courtesy of the Dillon family

Anne Dillon in 1910 with her first child, Douglas. To celebrate his grandson's birth, Sam Lapowski sent a small American flag for the nursery, asking that it hang "where the future President of the United States will first see the light." Douglas would later become Secretary of the Treasury.

Photo credit: Courtesy of Dillon family

Cable Address "Edison, New York"

From the Laboratory of Thomas A. Edison, Orange, N.J. April 21st. 1915.

Clarence Dillon, Esq.,
% William A. Read & Co.,
Nassau & Cedar Streets,
New York City.

Dear Mr. Dillon:

Confirming the telephone conversation between you and Mr. Meadowcroft, I beg to say that I will take four hundred (400) gallons per day of your pure Benzol for one year at sixty-five (65) cents per gallon, provided you can commence making regular deliveries by May 15th, 1915. I will furnish the tank car to move it to my works. This pure Benzol should distill at 1/2 degree of 80 Centigrade, and the 90% Benzol from which the pure is made should be well washed with acid and alkali before distillation. There is no trouble in doing this, and it is essential in order to make your Toluol meet specifications. This washing is done in a lead lined tank specially made for the purpose. If you have not already got one at your plant I could probably put you in the way of getting one in twelve or fourteen days.

At my Chemical Works in Silver Lake, I have a still but have no acid washer at present, but I have ordered one, which I expect will be ready in about twelve days. In that event I could take some crude Benzol and fractionate it. At what price, or on what terms would you let me have crude for this purpose.

I would add for your information that you will find the fractionating of the Benzol into pure Benzol and pure Toluol attended with some difficulties, as there is considerable Paraffene Hydrocarbons to contend with.

Yours very truly,

Thos A Edison

A letter from Thomas Edison to Dillon, April 21, 1915, ordering 400 gallons of benzol per day for Edison's new phenol plant—the deal that launched Dillon's first fortune.

Telephone Rector 7335

1:3:6 Acid
(Naphthylamin Disulphonic acid)
(25-30%)

Tolidin (98%)

Para Amido Phenol (97%)

Alpha Naphthylamin (99%)

Para Nitro Phenol

"American Made and Actually Available" for Immediate Shipment

Ortho-Toluidin 98%
Para-Toluidin 99%

Ortho-Nitro Toluol 98%
Para-Nitro Toluol 100%

NEWPORT CHEMICAL WORKS, Inc.

Works: Carrollville, Wis.

New York Office: 120 Broadway

General Offices: First National Bank Bldg., Milwaukee, Wis.

1916 trade ad for Newport Chemical Works, the phenol plant cofounded by Dillon and the Schlesingers for Thomas Edison. Its runaway success convinced William Read to make Dillon a partner at his firm that same year.

William A. Read was a patrician banker who sponsored Dillon's early career, but died a week after Dillon became a partner in his firm, allowing Dillon to take control.

James Forrestal, America's first Secretary of Defense, began his career at Dillon Read, where his relentless work ethic quickly made him Dillon's protégé.

Photo credit: Princeton Papers

Clarence Dillon with his wife, Anne; his son, Douglas; and his daughter, Dorothy, in New Jersey, 1919.

Anne and Dorothy Dillon at the beach in the 1920s.

Photo credit: Getty Images

$6,000,000
City of Bogota
(REPUBLIC OF COLOMBIA)

8% External Sinking Fund Gold Bonds of 1924

Dated October 1, 1924 **Due October 1, 1945**

Interest payable April 1 and October 1

Total authorized issue $10,000,000. Coupon bonds in denomination of $1,000 and $500, registerable as to principal only. Principal and interest payable in United States gold coin free of all Colombian governmental and municipal taxes, present or future, at the office of Dillon, Read & Co., New York, Fiscal Agents for this loan.

A Cumulative Sinking Fund of 2% per annum is provided to redeem bonds by purchase semi-annually in the market at or below the then current call price or, if not so obtainable, by call by lot. Interest on bonds so acquired is to be added to the Sinking Fund which, applied against the present issue, is calculated to redeem practically the entire amount by maturity.

Callable for the Sinking Fund at 105 and interest on any interest date to and including October 1, 1934, and thereafter callable on any interest date as a whole or in part by lot at 102 and interest.

Upon retirement of 2,250,000 Pesos internal bonds from the proceeds of this issue, these bonds will constitute the only funded debt of the City

Application will be made in due course to list these bonds on the New York Stock Exchange

Central Union Trust Company of New York, Countersigning Agent

---

The following information is summarized from statements furnished us by the President of the Municipal Council of Bogota:

BOGOTA

Bogota is the capital and the largest city of the Republic of Colombia, having a population of approximately 160,000. It is situated in the interior plateau region at an altitude of 8600 feet with a healthful climate, and is adjacent to the large coffee producing areas, and the emerald and salt mines. The city has manufacturing industries of importance, and is a growing commercial centre.

SECURITY

These bonds will be the direct general obligation of the City of Bogota, the full faith and credit of which is pledged to the payment of principal, interest and sinking fund. In addition, this loan ($10,000,000 authorized) will be secured by a first lien on the gross receipts obtained by the City from the Real Estate Taxes (Impuesto Predial, including Servicio de Aseo, Servicio de Alumbrado, Servicio de Vigilancia), and also from all municipal tramways, water works, electric power plants, and other specified sources, now owned or to be constructed with the proceeds of this issue. For the four years ended December 31, 1923, gross revenues from these sources averaged approximately twice the interest and sinking fund requirements of the present issue. The City has covenanted to deposit each month, with a depositary in Bogota for transmission to Dillon, Read & Co. as Sinking Fund Agent, all pledged revenues until the proportionate amount required for service of this issue has been provided for. The City furthermore covenants that it will at all times maintain the revenue from pledged sources at 150% of the requirements of this issue.

FINANCIAL CONDITION

The financial condition of the City is sound and payments of interest on funded debt always have been made promptly. During each of the five years ended December 31, 1923, the revenues of the City exceeded expenditures by a substantial margin.

PURPOSE OF ISSUE

This loan is issued to refund the outstanding funded debt of the City of Bogota amounting to the equivalent of $2,250,000. The balance of the proceeds of this issue will be employed in the construction of and improvements to municipal enterprises, including extension of the City water works, extension of the municipal tramways and construction of an electric power plant, the improvement of sanitation works, extension and improvement of a public market, the construction of workmen's houses and school buildings. All engineering and construction work in connection with the above will be carried out under the direction of American engineers and contractors.

COLOMBIA

The Republic of Colombia has an extensive seaboard on both the Pacific Ocean and the Caribbean Sea. Its area approximately equals that of New England and the Middle and South Atlantic States, while in point of population it ranks third in South America. Colombia is the world's largest producer of platinum and emeralds, and the second largest producer of coffee; over 60% of its foreign trade is with the United States. The Colombian Government has reorganized its banking and fiscal system under the direction of an American Financial Mission which inaugurated a banking system modelled on the United States Federal Reserve System, and the Colombian Peso is now quoted in New York at a premium over the dollar. The United States has agreed to pay to Colombia the sum of $25,000,000 in connection with the establishment of Panama as a separate republic, and annual instalments of five million dollars each are now being paid.

(Colombian Peso at Par equals 97.33 cents. The conversion in the above statements has been made at the approximate present exchange rate of $1 per Colombian Peso.)

We offer these bonds for delivery when, as and if issued and received by us, subject to approval of legal matters by our counsel, Messrs. Root, Clark, Buckner & Howland, of New York, and Dr. Esteban Jaramillo of Bogota.

Price 98 and interest. To Yield 8.20%

Dillon, Read & Co.

The statements herein have been accepted by us as accurate but are in no event to be construed as representations by us.
October, 1924.

An example of a bond offering to finance the city of Bogotá, Colombia, offering an attractive interest rate. Colombia agreed to the financing only after Princeton's "Money Doctor" drafted a persuasive cable.

Princeton economics professor Edwin Kemmerer appeared to be an independent advisor to nations but was secretly paid by Dillon Read to recommend the firm to South American governments.

Photo credit: Harris & Ewing Collection—Library of Congress

Clarence Dillon as a young investment banker.

Photo credit: Courtesy of the Dillon family

Dodge Brothers factory in 1925. At the time of Dillon's purchase, it was comparable in size to Ford Motors.

Photo credit: Library of Congress

An illustration from a 1926 advertisement for Dodge Brothers.

Dodge Brothers Motor Car Company Plant, Wayne County, Michigan.

Photo credit: Alamy

A Dillon, Read & Co. check for $146 million to purchase Dodge Brothers, the largest transaction for an automaker up to that time.

Film mogul William Fox, who turned to Dillon Read for refinancing after the 1929 crash threatened his film empire. He soon found himself in tense, difficult negotiations with Clarence Dillon, which ultimately cost him control of all his companies.

Photo credit: Getty Images

The Dillon town house on East 80th St., where Dillon lived in Manhattan when not a "summer bachelor" at a nearby hotel.

Clarence Dillon's Dunwalke estate in New Jersey.

Photo credit: Courtesy of photographer David Gruol

Douglas Dillon with President John F. Kennedy, August 1961.

J. P. Morgan Jr. and Lya Graf, 1933, at the Pecora hearings.

Photo credit: Alamy

A crowd gathering in anger on Wall Street after the stock market crash in 1929. Dillon's high-yield bonds contributed to the crash, but he anticipated it, closed his bond offices around the country and entered October with zero margin debt and plenty of cash.

Ferdinand Pecora's investigation led to the Securities and Exchange Commission that made many of Dillon's prior dealings illegal.

FIFTEEN CENTS (IN CANADA, 20¢ Reason: Tariff) June 12, 1933

TIME

The Weekly Newsmagazine

Keystone

Volume XXI

FERDINAND PECORA

A Roland for an Untermyer.

(See BUSINESS)

Number 24

Circulation Office, 330 East 22nd Street, Chicago. (Reg. U. S. Pat. Off.) Editorial and Advertising Offices, 135 East 42nd Street, New York.

Circulation this issue more than 400,000

Clarence Dillon with Douglas Dillon and Paul Nitze at the Pecora Hearings in 1933.

Photo credit: Harris & Ewing Collection—Library of Congress

Clarence Dillon became a philanthropist in his later years. This portrait hangs in the Clarence Dillon Library in Bedminster, New Jersey.

Photo credit: Used with permission of the Clarence Dillon Public Library. David R. Surks Creative Eye Photography

French wine estate Château Haut-Brion was purchased in 1935 for $160,000. Thomas Jefferson had purchased wine there.

Portrait of Clarence Dillon by Philip Alexius de László, 1926.

Photo credit: Harvard University Portrait Collection, Gift of C. Douglas Dillon for the Dillon Field House, 1977

May 1925, his star was in its ascendency; he was a man who'd successfully refashioned himself, Gatsby-like, into a figure of his own imagination. In his telling of the tale, he was the scion of European gentry. He was an investor of "inherent honesty, unfailing dependability," a new financial heavyweight on Wall Street, but one for whom—at least according to *Forbes*, "the piling up of a fortune of a Rockefeller or a Ford [had] no place in his ambitions" because his "aspirations flowed toward the simpler things of life, toward art rather than the mart."

Similarly fawning portraits of Dillon followed in *The New York Times* and *The Wall Street Journal*. Dillon's financial acumen was likened to "smooth ball bearings running in clean oil."

A man descended from European nobility? A financier unconcerned with the vulgarity of acquiring wealth for its own sake? A businessman of uncommon integrity and honesty, devoted solely to "justice and fairness"?

A skeptical reader—or anyone who personally knew Clarence Dillon—might be forgiven for thinking that these articles had been written not by experienced financial reporters, but by publicists being paid by Dillon, Read & Co.

This was precisely the case.

Nothing surrounding the Dodge Brothers transaction was left to chance.

Bernard Baruch had steered Charlie Schwartz to his friend and public relations advisor, Arthur Krock—a Kentucky-born son of German-Jewish immigrants who was making a name for himself as a newsman in New York. While officially writing for the *New York World*, Krock began moonlighting for Dillon Read, giving private counsel on public relations. Clarence Dillon was not only touted as a financial virtuoso in the newspapers, but the Dodge purchase was also portrayed as a "titanic struggle between the old warrior, Morgan, and the new challenger," Dillon.

Krock later insisted that he'd offered Dillon advice "on a

friendly basis" that in no way impacted his journalistic integrity at the *New York World*.

The esteemed newsman Walter Lippmann, editor of the *World*, strongly disagreed. One day, Lippmann walked by Krock's office and overheard the journalist on the phone with Charles Schwartz. Krock was discussing an upcoming *World* editorial Lippmann had written but which hadn't yet gone to press, that would affect stock prices because it condemned the Dodge acquisition.

It's unclear if Lippmann fired Krock or if Krock quit the *World*. But Bernard Baruch quickly helped Krock land a job at *The New York Times*, where he became the Washington correspondent and bureau chief.

Krock's behavior working for both Dillon Read and the *New York World* was not as shocking as it now seems; in the freewheeling 1920s—when the sale of liquor in New York was strictly illegal yet booze could be found on virtually every block of the city—it wasn't uncommon for journalists, even respected men like Krock, to promote influential friends in exchange for insider stock market tips.

And within a few years, all was forgotten.

Krock went on to have a distinguished career at the *Times*, writing his "In the Nation" political column for decades, winning the Pulitzer Prize three times (1935, 1938, 1951), and receiving the Presidential Medal of Freedom in 1970. During his storied sixty-year career, covering eleven presidential administrations, Krock was so widely respected he was called: "The Dean of Washington Newsmen."

Shortly after the formal contract for the Dodge Brothers purchase was signed on April 7, 1925, in a suite in Detroit's Book-Cadillac Hotel, the syndicate sales operation under James Forrestal's direction sold $160 million of new Dodge securities. Dillon Read retained 650,000 shares of the Class A stock in exchange for managing the offering and all of the 500,000 Class B common shares, the only shares that carried voting rights.

Dillon maintained complete control of Dodge Brothers. The retained holdings had a face value of $34.5 million which, when added to the $14 million profits on the underwriting, brought a total profit of $48.5 million to Dillon and his syndicate.

With the leviathan deal now landed, Charles Schwartz expected to receive $10 million for his role. He'd done more than assist Dillon in the buyout of Dodge. In Schwartz's view, without his inside tips, Dillon wouldn't have had a chance against Morgan.

When Schwartz arrived at 28 Nassau to collect his finder's fee, he found Dillon calmly seated at his uncluttered desk, making a note on his lined pad in pencil.

"Charlie," Dillon said, "it strikes me that that amount is far in excess of what you're really entitled to."

The typically verbose Schwartz was, momentarily, stunned into silence.

"Wait, we've got a deal on that."

Dillon was unfazed. "I know we have a memorandum agreement but I'm talking reality now and, Charlie, this is *real* money."

Dillon was speaking the truth: $10 million in 1925 is worth more than $180 million in 2025. But Dillon knew he had the upper hand. He knew that Schwartz—a supposedly neutral broker—couldn't sue him, or even go to the press, without revealing his own duplicity while representing the Dodge widows.

Schwartz took the Dillon Read memorandum from his pocket, tore it up, and threw the pieces like confetti on Dillon's pristine desk.

"If that's what your word means," he shouted, "then this is what I think of your written contracts!"

Dillon frowned. It wasn't clear if he was more displeased by Schwartz's histrionics or the way that he'd needlessly made such a mess of Dillon's immaculate desktop.

"Calm down, Charlie," Dillon said.

"Calm *down*?"

"You'll get your money."

To this day, it's unclear how Dillon did it, but he clearly paid Schwartz off. He may simply have transferred part of the Dodge shares that he'd received.

On May 5, 1925, Dillon Read recorded a receipt from Schwartz for $410,652, which was clearly only partial payment for his services.

It's doubtful that Schwartz received the full ten million he felt was due him, but he was soon living a Gatsbyesque life on Long Island. Schwartz invested in racehorses and frequented lavish parties on Long Island.

When Schwartz later hosted a luxurious dinner staffed by liveried servants, he invited Clarence Dillon among other rich and powerful guests to celebrate his newfound wealth. Dillon returned his RSVP, politely declining, and sent Ferdinand Eberstadt to attend in his place.

The Dodge Brothers buyout victory was a signature Clarence Dillon deal. Audacious and imaginative but coldly calculated to succeed with minimal financial risk. The financial press was deeply impressed with "the ease with which Dillon seemed to direct such vast undertakings," and a mystique developed around the investment banker.

Each of the Dodge widows received the equivalent of approximately $1 billion in today's value. Matilda Dodge, a former secretary who had married her employer, built a 110-room Tudor Revival mansion in Rochester, Michigan, after the Dodge sale. She then got remarried, to an independently wealthy lumber baron.

Of the two widows, Anna Dodge, a former piano teacher from Scotland, was particularly astute. Investing $594 million in tax-free bonds, she was never obliged to pay federal income taxes. Anna married a handsome actor, fourteen years her junior. He was known to be a playboy and they divorced, but Anna recalled that he'd "taught me how to have fun with my money." She owned a seventy-five-room mansion in Grosse Pointe, Michigan, modeled after the Château de Versailles and a hundred-room showplace in Palm Beach, Florida. When she died at the age of 103, despite the years of wild spending, her estate was still worth more than $110 million.

The Dodge deal turned Clarence Dillon into a national celebrity. His name was known even by people who had no interest in Wall Street, who'd rather read the baseball box scores than stare at the percentage point of an underwriting banking deal.

To a large degree this was because the public looked at the automobile industry as dazzlingly modern. The newer models coming out of Detroit, with their whitewall tires and candy-colored paint, seemed to epitomize Jazz Age glamor. In the 1920s, the automobile was the single most sought-after possession on the American market.

Most of the major car companies' founders: Henry Ford, Walter Chrysler, Ransom Olds, and James Packard, were still alive. The activities of these heroes were closely followed in newspapers and watched on newsreels. Some editorial writers bemoaned the transfer of the Dodge Brothers company from the widows of the men who had created it to Wall Street bankers. They feared that Wall Street was "swallowing" all of American business and believed that financiers like Dillon could never develop Dodge as the founders had done.

Clarence Dillon demonstrated this to be balefully true. Success in banking, he soon learned, doesn't translate into success in running an industrial enterprise. He was great at making business deals, but he had no idea about the business of making *things*.

Dillon decided to manage the enterprise through his firm. Starting in May 1925, Dodge Brothers directors' meetings were held at Dillon Read's New York offices, with Clarence Dillon participating as a board member.

He made Edward Wilmer the new Dodge president. Wilmer had held vice presidential positions at the Milwaukee Coke and Gas Company, Newport Mining Company, and the Steel & Tube Company before Dillon had appointed him president of Goodyear.

Goodyear Tire had been a fine business, simply having liquidity issues, and didn't rely on Wilmer in any way. Nonetheless, Dillon gave full credit to the Milwaukee lawyer: "Wilmer's rehabilitation of the Goodyear Rubber Co. is almost the greatest feat in the history of American industry," Dillon told reporters with a straight face.

At Dodge Brothers, Dillon planned to replace the top management team with his own men. Initially, he made Wilmer the chairman of the Dodge board of directors.

In contrast to Goodyear, Dodge was solvent at the time of its sale, and the funds raised through the recapitalization provided the company with ample cash.

Wilmer resigned his Goodyear chairmanship and moved from New York to Detroit. As Dodge's chief executive, Wilmer now received an annual base salary of $250,000, 1% of Dodge Brothers profits between $15 million and $20 million, 2% of all profits above $20 million, and $50,000 to cover his moving expenses. The quiet new Dodge president was described by associates in words often used to describe Dillon:

"No one really knows what Wilmer really thinks behind his reserve," one said. "We get the feeling that there is always more behind the quiet power of his personality. He would have been as good a general or statesman as he is a businessman."

A general? Like Ulysses S. Grant or John Pershing? It's more apt to say that Edward Wilmer, an otherwise undistinguished lawyer from Milwaukee, is a case study of a business theory first popularized in the late 1960s: The Peter Principle. An employee rises through the hierarchy until they reach the level of their own incompetence.

Wilmer had no more expertise in the car industry than he did in the tire and rubber business. And at just thirty-eight, as *The New York Times* noted, he was one of the youngest chief executives in American industry.

Dillon also rewarded Wilmer by making him a partner at Dillon, Read & Co. The *Times* claimed that Wilmer had been selected to run Goodyear "after a country-wide search for the man the stockholders felt could lead the company out of the wilderness." A more accurate line in the same article states that: "Wilmer's acquaintance with Mr. Dillon dated back to the time that Mr. Dillon first entered business" in "1915, when Dillon was with the Milwaukee Coke & Gas Company and Mr. Wilmer was a representative in its legal department."

In an interview with *Automotive Industries* in April 1926, Wilmer said that the previous management had been "competent, but conservative," and that he intended to aggressively grow the business. The Dodge Brothers board of directors had approved "a plan to expand production from 1,100 cars per day to 1,500 and to spend $5,873,400 on new plants."

The one management holdover from the pre–Dillon Read days was Arthur Waterfall, who stayed on as a Dodge Brothers vice president. Without experienced auto industry men surrounding him, Wilmer largely listened only to Dillon's ideas, which did not take into account the complexity of manufacturing operations in automobile production.

Dillon was, at heart, a salesman. He believed that retail car dealers, not the assembly line managers, were the key to improving Dodge's profitability. In early 1926, Dillon arranged for the appointment of two Dodge retail dealers to the board of directors—a move which raised eyebrows since it was unprecedented in the automobile industry.

Dodge cars, powered by rugged, economical four-cylinder engines, had an industry-wide reputation for reliability. But, for reasons still unknown, Wilmer decided to tinker with design, style, and retail prices. Wilmer believed that Dodge needed to produce a lighter, faster, lower-priced four-cylinder car as well as simultaneously introduce two lines of superior six-cylinder motor cars, one priced in the $1,000 range and the other in the $1,500 price range. Wilmer didn't foresee—or even comprehend—the inherent production difficulties of introducing so many new lines of cars at the same time.

The rollout began with the most expensive new model, the Senior Six, with prices ranging from $1,495 for a two-door coupe to $1,595 for a four-door sedan, introduced in May 1927, and "a completely reworked four-cylinder car called the Fast Four (base price of $855)" in August 1927.

Better roads and technology plus a strong economy created a booming market for cars in America. Successful general sales managers of the car companies were "treated with more deference and respect than Napoleon." Advertising firms were given huge budgets to publicize the latest models. The presidents of the major automobile companies built manorial palaces at Grosse Pointe, Michigan, trying to constantly one-up each other.

Dodge Brothers, while under Dillon's ownership, introduced major innovations in publicity and marketing. Dodge was one of the first companies to make full use of new mass communication technology and employ social science experts to shape public opinion. This is the lasting legacy of Dillon's Dodge Deal.

Foremost among these experts was Edward L. Bernays, considered the creator of modern public relations, who'd been retained to scientifically promote, publicize, and sell the new Dodge models.

Born in Vienna, raised in New York, Bernays was, by the mid-1920s, famed for his understanding of crowd psychology. He drew heavily on the psychoanalytic work of Sigmund Freud—not surprising, since he was Freud's nephew. His mother was Freud's sister, Anna.

By the mid-1920s, observed author Ann Douglas, "Freud was the chosen mentor of Madison Avenue," and "Edward Bernays, often called the 'father of public relations,' who orchestrated the commercialization of a culture, was Freud's nephew and a self-conscious popularizer of his thought."

In the late summer of 1927, Bernays came to Detroit to meet with Dodge executives as the company was about to launch its new six-cylinder car on the American market. Years later, Bernays recalled arriving at the Book-Cadillac Hotel in Detroit. The lobby was packed with buyers and sellers, excitedly milling around at a "jazz tempo." Bernays was startled by their all-night manic activity: "the doors of many of the hotel rooms were wide open . . . with drinking parties going on inside," and women "kept ducking from one room to another."

The first job Bernays had was to come up with a catchy name for a new mid-priced Dodge six-cylinder car that the Company believed would soon dominate the market.

This vehicle was a technological marvel, engineered with "a steel body unit and a low center of gravity—for safety, health, and comfort." Bernays accepted the assignment. He contacted a longtime advertising friend, Frank Fletcher, who demanded $15,000 for research and submission of a list of names that connoted "stability, power, dignity—status." Fletcher combed encyclopedias, dictionaries, and books on ancient mythology, then sent Dodge hundreds of names "in a beautiful tan presentation folder, tied by a red silk ribbon."

For all the expertise that Bernays and Fletcher used—crowd manipulation, unconscious psychological associations—the tan presentation folder went untouched. Dodge had come up with a name on its own: Victory. A name chosen to honor American soldiers on the tenth anniversary of the ending of World War I.

Whatever the appellation, Bernays now needed to change public opinion about the Victory Six. Luxury? Comfort? Status? No, the route he chose to go with was *safety*. He lined up engineers and health officers to "educate" the public about the safety benefits of a car with a solid steel body and lower center of gravity. The Victory Six's most significant innovation was "its monopiece or unit body design."

Newspaper ads were old hat, as were roadside billboards. An innovative car needed an innovative publicity strategy.

What Bernays came up with next was a stroke of genius: he created an event with the highest possible public visibility, using the newest mass mediums: radio and film. The National Broadcasting Company, a subsidiary of the Radio Corporation of America, was still only two years old. Bernays arranged a "Victory" Hour broadcast to promote the new Dodge six-cylinder model in January 1928 for the unheard-of cost of more than

$60,000. Nothing like the "Victory" Hour had ever been attempted; so much so, that *The New York Times* covered the event on the next day's front page:

ALL AMERICA USED AS A RADIO STATION
47 STATIONS IN A HUGE CHAIN
MILLIONS THROUGHOUT THE NATION
LISTEN IN ON UNIQUE DODGE
"VICTORY" BROADCAST

The live coast-to-coast broadcast was, indeed, revolutionary. The nation's most-beloved humorist, Will Rogers, emceed from his Beverly Hills home:

"Hello, folks," Rogers said into the microphone, in the relaxed tone of an old buddy sitting next to you on your living room sofa. "I'm the town crier. This is a cinch of a job Dodge Brothers is givin' me. All I gotta do is stand here and talk. I got all the movie folks around me here—all of 'em. There's Ben Turpin, Jack Barrymore, Mary Pickford, Douglas Fairbanks, and fifteen others—they're all right around me here, within fifteen blocks, and if I only knew their telephone numbers they'd all be sitting right here at the fire with me. Say I oughtn't to mention fires. They don't need any fires in California. By the way, all the movie stars out here are making New Year's resolutions and taking new wives. It's a question which they're going to drop first."

Rogers began to do an imitation of the president—"This is Cal Coolidge"—plausibly sounding like the Republican president, then the millions of listeners heard the Paul Whiteman Orchestra in New York City playing George Gershwin's "Rhapsody in Blue."

Then it was back to Will Rogers joking in Beverly Hills, next to Fred and Dorothy Stone singing in a dressing room between the acts of *Criss Cross* in the Erlanger Theatre in Chicago, and to Al Jolson in a room at the Roosevelt Hotel in New Orleans, belting out "Mammy" and "California Here I Come."

Sandwiched between the entertainment acts, Rogers threw the microphone to Detroit, where Dodge president Edward Wilmer described the wonders of the Victory Six—earnestly and stiffly—and invited listeners to view the new model in Dodge dealers' showrooms.

He had a rapt audience; an estimated thirty-five million people were listening live to the broadcast.

After ad-libbing about the flowers on the floats in the recent Rose Bowl parade, Rogers irreverently took a jab at the ludicrous expense his sponsors had laid out for the broadcast.

"Folks, I'm not here to tell you about the flowers in the California hills. I'm here to tell you about that new Dodge sedan so that the Dodge Brothers can get back some of that jack they're spending on this program. I'm not asking you to buy a car, mind you, I'm just tellin' you about it. After a company extends you the courtesy of giving you a great big, splendid program, the least you can do is to give their car a trial."

Americans loved the homespun humor of Will Rogers and trusted his commonsense delivery. In the following days, consumers flocked to Dodge dealerships nationwide to see this new Victory Six sedan—often telling showroom salesmen they'd come down solely at the recommendation of Will Rogers.

Bernays organized a second nationwide radio broadcast in the spring to launch the Dodge Standard Six, a quick replacement for the Fast Four sedan which had immediately bombed. Joseph Schenck of United Artists offered a $25,000 package of top film talent, John Barrymore, Charlie Chaplin, Douglas Fairbanks, Norma Talmadge, and D.W. Griffith, for Dodge's March 29, 1928, radio program.

In the meantime, Bernays created a five-story-high, half-block-long neon sign on Broadway advertising Dodge Brothers.

To publicize the unveiling of the sign—the biggest advertisement Times Square had yet seen—Dodge hosted a VIP black-tie dinner at the Hotel Astor. Instead of six courses, the meal featured "six cylinders," including "Chassis of Lamb with Mushroom Rivets" and "Alternating Current Jelly."

Despite all the ingenuity—the five-story-neon sign flashing DODGE BROTHERS on Broadway; Will Rogers, Charlie Chaplin, Douglas Fairbanks, and John Barrymore shilling for the Victory Six on national airwaves—the new Dodge models weren't selling.

Wilmer should perhaps have allotted more money to research and development in Detroit than he did to superstar endorsements from Beverly Hills and six-course public relations dinners in Manhattan.

The new Dodge models didn't need better publicity.

They needed better designs.

The Victory Six sedan did, indeed, have a "low center of gravity" but it was so low that the car didn't have, in contemporary terms, "good clearance," making it useless in much of Middle America, where roads were often unpaved, littered with large rocks. During wintertime, the Victory Six would get "high centered" (that is, hopelessly stuck) in deep snow. In the brutal honesty of the car industry, the Victory Six was a lemon.

Then, as now, that label is the kiss of death. Once a car's known as a lemon by car dealers and consumers, no amount of PR spin can turn it into a peach. Victory Six sales were abysmal. As were those of the Standard Six. All the new models were plagued by mechanical problems, a surprise to loyal consumers who were accustomed to the reliability of Dodge products.

Despite being poorly designed and unreliable, the new models came with higher sticker prices than Dodge's classic four-cylinder cars. By trying to go upmarket, Dodge lost many of its longtime customers.

In 1927, Dodge Brothers' sales revenues declined by one

third. Over the same year, the combined stock value of Dodge fell from $190 million to $176 million—this during a period when the prices of other major automakers' stock shares significantly increased.

Although Clarence Dillon, clearly trying to save face, kept publicly defending his Dillon Read partner and handpicked choice for the Dodge presidency, even Edward Wilmer seemed to realize the jig was up.

He was simply a Milwaukee-born lawyer who, through business connections and loyalty to friends, had been shoved into industrial managerial positions—first at Goodyear Tire and now at Dodge Brothers—far beyond his expertise or abilities.

"Mr. Wilmer did not follow the usual success pattern," *The New York Times* dryly observed later. Wilmer told the paper that "he started out in life with no clear idea of where he was going, that he changed his ambition several times, and that he was a poor hand at detailed paperwork. He did, however, work at odd jobs from the time he was thirteen or fourteen. He changed jobs frequently" in the early years of his career.

"Most young men shift about considerably," Wilmer continued. "The most any one can do is to be ready for the opportunity—or accident—when it turns up."

With Edward Wilmer thrust—by opportunity or by accident—into the driver's seat of Dodge, the company's sales had not only plummeted, but the brand's value was at risk of being irreparably damaged. Wilmer was forced to admit "that after spending close to fifteen million dollars converting the Dodge Brothers plants for the new six-cylinder models, they had produced new cars they could not sell."

Clarence Dillon had had enough; he wanted out of the automobile business and began angling for a buyer. He hoped he could unload the Dodge Brothers franchise with more success than Wilmer had selling the company's six-cylinder lemons.

In mid-April 1928, Dillon approached Walter Chrysler about selling Dodge, casually suggesting some "trading might be on the table." Chrysler feigned disinterest at first. But this was all part of the high-stakes negotiating game. Chrysler was just as eager to acquire Dodge as Dillon was to sell it.

Clarence Dillon was a wizard at engineering banking deals; Walter Chrysler was a wizard at engineering automobiles. Born in Wamego, Kansas, in 1875, Chrysler had been a machinist apprentice at eighteen and then worked on both the Santa Fe Railroad and the Chicago Great Western Railroad. By 1911, he was Buick's production chief at General Motors, where Chrysler cut costs and eventually became president. Chrysler built his first car under his own name in 1924.

Chrysler and Dillon spent over a month in some kind of strange staredown-tango, trying to get the upper hand. Dillon may have understood investment banking better than any young financier on Wall Street, but Walter Chrysler knew the car business. He knew cars as only a man who'd gotten his elbows and knees dirty as a teenager, disassembling an entire Ford by hand, then putting it meticulously back together could. He'd transformed Buick into General Motors' powerhouse brand and revived Maxwell Motor Company as the thriving Chrysler Corporation.

Walter Chrysler knew exactly what he wanted from Dillon: he needed more manufacturing capacity to expand his own automobile production. He couldn't build factories quickly or inexpensively enough to stay ahead in an increasingly competitive industry.

Chrysler aimed at producing new models such as the low-priced Plymouth and the mid-priced DeSoto. Dodge Brothers had the large, modern factories and foundries that Chrysler lacked. Dodge Brothers also had one of the best dealer-distributor networks in the country.

An important attraction for Walter Chrysler was the fact that a merger with Dodge Brothers wouldn't require cash. Which was a good thing, because Chrysler had none.

Clarence Dillon and Walter Chrysler found themselves in adjoining suites at The Ritz-Carlton, the Madison Avenue hotel where Otto Kahn kept an apartment year-round, the scene of some legendary show business parties.

For five days, the two men were deep in negotiations over a Chrysler-Dodge merger. Each brought along teams of financial experts and attorneys.

Finally, Dillon and Chrysler felt they'd reached an agreement—a handshake deal.

Dillon Read would sell Dodge Brothers for $170 million in Chrysler stock plus the assumption of the Dodge debt, approximately $60 million. Each Dodge Brothers stockholder would receive one share of Chrysler common stock in exchange for one share of Dodge preferred stock, five shares of Dodge common stock Class A, or ten shares of Dodge common stock Class B—with voting rights.

Walter Chrysler, wary of minority stockholders' opposition, demanded that Dillon secure 90% approval from each class of Dodge stockholders before proceeding with the merger. Despite extending the deadline three times, Dillon was still struggling to meet this condition. Just days before the offer's expiration, Dillon had secured 86% of the preferred shares and 76% of Class A common shares, along with nearly all Class B common shares.

Dillon phoned Walter Chrysler to inform him about the sticking point—he wasn't sure he'd have the full 90% approval by the fast-approaching deadline. Chrysler flew into a rage, shouting that Dillon would either live up to his end of their agreed-upon terms or the deal was off. Before slamming down the receiver, Chrysler said he'd be at Dillon Read's office in a couple of hours.

Dillon called Chrysler's bluff.

He gave James Forrestal a strange-sounding order.

"Get all the reporters you can to come down to our office as soon as possible—tell them we've got some important news to announce."

When Walter Chrysler made his way through the crowded reception area filled with men in fedoras and some photographers, then got out of the elevator at Dillon's fourth-floor office, he did not appear pleased.

"Downstairs—what's all that about?"

Dillon shrugged. "They're reporters."

"And what're they doing here?"

"You and I are going to announce that our deal is off."

"No, we aren't! Listen, Dillon, we'll walk out of here and tell the reporters there's been a slight delay, but we still have an agreement."

Then Ferdinand Eberstadt and James Forrestal employed a bold strategy: they bought necessary Dodge shares on the open market while short selling the exact same amount. This maneuver allowed them to achieve the crucial 90% proxy without full payment upfront. The Chrysler-Dodge deal was finalized.

On Monday afternoon, July 30, 1928, Chrysler executives assumed control of Dodge Brothers facilities and displayed signs reading "Dodge Division, Chrysler Corporation." Many industry analysts believed that Walter Chrysler had overpaid for Dodge and that he'd been outmaneuvered by Dillon.

But Walter Chrysler was resolute. "Buying Dodge Brothers

was one of the soundest acts of my life. I say sincerely that nothing we have done for the organization compares with that transaction."

By merging with Dodge, Chrysler became one of Detroit's Big Three, the world's third-largest automobile company, and a worthy rival of General Motors.

Clarence Dillon, who had made spectacular profits by purchasing Dodge, quickly extricated his firm from a situation of industrial mismanagement by selling Dodge.

The Dodge division of Chrysler would not surpass its 1926 earnings until 1938. The hapless-seeming Edward Wilmer returned to his position as a partner at Dillon Read and was never again given the role of running a major corporation, industrial or otherwise. Wilmer retired from his career in finance in the mid-1930s and died at age seventy-five in 1962.

Today, Dodge remains a household name—though the brand is now part of the Stellantis multinational conglomerate.

Dodge buyers still swear by the brand's quality and reliability. Car aficionados consider the 1969 Dodge Charger R/T one of the greatest muscle cars that Detroit ever turned out. In recent years, the Dodge Ram has consistently ranked among the second- or third-bestselling pickup trucks in the United States.

Despite a few hiccups, Clarence Dillon could look back at the 1925 Dodge deal as an unqualified success—both in business and in personal terms.

He'd turned a tidy profit of over $48 million—$700 million in today's currency.

And he'd turned himself into the biggest new star that Wall Street had seen in a generation.

Chapter Ten

HOLLYWOOD PLAYER

ON A CHILLY Tuesday evening in April 1929, over two hundred attendees—wealthy men in single-breasted dinner jackets and bow ties, much younger women in sable coats and cloche hats—packed the Motion Picture Club on the sixth floor of 1560 Broadway in the heart of New York's Theater District. The occasion was a testimonial gala dinner to honor the founder of Universal Pictures, Carl Laemmle.

Laemmle, a former stationer's apprentice, had transformed Hollywood. Short, balding, bespectacled, the sixty-two-year-old Jewish immigrant from Laupheim in Southern Germany, looked more like a physics professor than a Hollywood powerhouse. But by 1929 Laemmle had become an entertainment legend. Having founded Universal City in 1915, he produced over four hundred pictures, including early silent hits like *The Hunchback of Notre Dame* and *The Phantom of the Opera*, both starring Lon Chaney. Laemmle was a master showman and innovator—the creator of the Hollywood star system. Over the past two decades, he'd been one of the moguls most responsible for making movies a major industry, with $2 billion in annual investments, employing more men and women than Ford and General Motors combined.

The night was a perfect snapshot of New York in the roaring twenties, Gotham at the height of wild excess six months before the Crash. As soon as the event was announced, one newspaper reported, "the two-hundred and twenty-five tickets were snapped up like a flash. You couldn't get near the dining room for love or money."

Jimmy Walker, the flamboyantly corrupt mayor of New York was seated at the speaker's table with his young mistress, a Ziegfeld Follies girl. Next to the mayor was Florenz Ziegfeld himself, the Chicago-born impresario known for discovering some of the most beautiful chorus girls in the country. Ziegfeld was instrumental in setting the standard for beauty in the age of the flapper, and the dapper, devil-may-care mayor was seen as the epitome of the Jazz Age.

Walker, who vocally opposed the Eighteenth Amendment, had fired one overly scrupulous NYPD commissioner and replaced him with another clearly instructed not to enforce the dry laws. Bootleggers and gangsters openly ran hundreds of speakeasies, beer halls, and burlesque clubs throughout the city. Tall, good-looking and stylish, often referred to as "Beau James," Walker's more fitting nickname was "The Night Mayor," because he skipped most mornings at city hall after a hard night of carousing and boozing.

The testimonial dinner's guest list, according to one reporter, looked "like a 'Who's Who in the Motion Picture industry,'" the most powerful men in the business gathered to celebrate Carl Laemmle's twenty-third year in the industry and his twentieth as a producer.

Seated at the speaker's table were David and Arthur Loew, the sons of the late Marcus Loew, who'd founded Loew's Theatres and Metro-Goldwyn-Mayer. Nathan Burkan, the Romanian-

Jewish entertainment attorney whose high-profile clients included Ziegfeld, Charlie Chaplin, and Mae West, was one of the night's featured speakers. Harry Reichenbach, the press agent for Chaplin, Rudolph Valentino, Gloria Swanson, and Ethel Barrymore, served as the jocular toastmaster.

Also dining at the speaker's table—elegantly dressed, smiling, but of course having no intention of *speaking* on the microphone—was Clarence Dillon, the puppet master financier behind the scenes. By April 1929, Dillon Read had been bankrolling Laemmle's Universal Pictures for almost five years.

All the speeches were broadcast live on the radio, and Laemmle, whose English resounded with a rich German accent, gave the concluding address, thanking all the attendees for the warm tribute. Then the *real* party began: "The affair terminated with a great display of gaiety. Dancing and general hilarity held sway until almost one o'clock."

Wall Street financiers like Clarence Dillon had discovered the Hollywood party relatively late—not until the middle of the 1920s. By then, they realized that there was glamour to this "moving pictures business." The film industry offered opportunities to make enormous profits—and to meet starlets—in both New York and California.

To an investor like Dillon, the earliest ventures into cinema, the nickelodeons associated with carnivals and penny arcades, seemed hardly worth his time. They were down-market, the earliest silent short films a frivolous novelty. Certainly, there was no serious money to be made for an investment bank like Dillon Read in the first nickelodeon.

Dillon may also have felt a sense of personal embarrassment: the motion picture industry had been started, virtually from scratch, by a group of men who hailed from the same background and social class as himself. The original Hollywood moguls, almost to a man, came from shtetls in the Russian Pale of Settlement much like Sam Lapowski's hometown, Vizne.

Will Hays, president of the original Motion Picture Producers and Distributors of America, called Hollywood "the quintessence of what we mean by America." But as film historian Neal Gabler observes in his definitive *An Empire of Their Own*, the great paradox is "that the film industry was founded and for more than thirty years operated by Eastern European Jews who themselves seemed to be anything but the quintessence of America."

Almost all the entrepreneurs who created the American film industry—Samuel Goldwyn, Marcus Loew, William Fox, Carl Laemmle, Jesse Lasky, Adolph Zukor—were Jewish immigrants from Russia, Poland, and the Austro-Hungarian Empire. They self-financed their ventures from early profits with nickelodeons and amusement arcades. They very quickly created an alternative to the East Coast industrial and financial realms dominated by WASP elites. With so many employment opportunities closed to them, as Gabler put it, impoverished Eastern European Jewish immigrants "invented Hollywood."

It was actually Dillon's former partner in the phenol business, Thomas Edison, who pioneered—and tried mightily to monopolize—the motion picture trade. Edison held numerous film-related patents, including for the first motion picture camera, which he patented as "the Kinetograph" in 1891. Though little remembered today, Edison's film studio produced nearly twelve hundred films, almost all of them silent shorts: black-and-white moving images of routine things like parades, fire engines, and even a man sneezing. Edison also produced Edwin S. Porter's twelve-minute silent single reel *The Great Train Robbery* (1903) which experts consider a seminal work in the history of the art form.

Before the industry moved to Hollywood, California, the motion picture business was centered in Fort Lee, New Jersey. Considered the birthplace of American cinema, the town on the Palisades gave us the film terms "cliff-hanger" and "seat of your pants." Edison's Black Maria studio was located in nearby West Orange, but he shot most of his pictures in Fort Lee. By 1914, Fort Lee housed more than a dozen working studios, including Victor Film Company, Fox Film Corporation and Goldwyn Picture Corporation.

All left their imprints, but it was the Independent Moving Pictures Company (IMP) founded in Fort Lee in 1909 by Carl Laemmle that revolutionized early cinema. Before Laemmle, there was no such thing as a movie star. Actors on nickelodeon screens were recognized as brands—"The Vitagraph Girl" or "The Biograph Girl." Laemmle was a master showman who'd used his savings to open a nickelodeon in 1906, before establishing his first film company three years later. In 1909, Laemmle ended the anonymity of silent screen actors by hiring the "Biograph Girl" and putting her name, Florence Lawrence, in bright lights and in advertisements in the new fan magazines like *Photoplay* and *Motion Picture Story*. Laemmle created an even bigger star in young Mary Pickford, who became the best-known silent film actress and—despite being born Gladys Smith in Toronto, Canada—was soon billed as "America's Sweetheart."

The reason for the explosion of motion pictures as a glamorous, billion-dollar industry in the US was multifactorial. In large part, it was due to the Eighteenth Amendment—which made illegal the manufacture, transportation, and sale of alcohol—first passed by the US Congress in 1917 and on January 16, 1919, ratified by three-quarters of the nation's states. Men and women across the US, accustomed to spending a weekend evening over cocktails, now found that a night at the movies was the next best thing.

"Prohibition has proven a big boon to picture theaters," *The Wall Street Journal* reported in 1919, "the business doubling in one western city of 450,000 population when the dry law closed 2,700 saloons."

At the same time, a pair of Jewish brothers in Chicago made an innovation that changed the moviegoing experience forever. One of the drawbacks of the first nickelodeons and vaudeville-style theaters was the oppressive heat in summertime. In cities like New York and Chicago, many theaters simply closed their doors in the stifling heat of July and August, not just because the audience was uncomfortable, but because the live vaudevillian acts could not perform without passing out.

Barney and A.J. Balaban, born in Chicago's rough Maxwell Street ghetto, resolved to find a solution so that nickelodeons and theaters didn't have to shut their doors and lose business for two months of the year. Barney Balaban, who'd worked in the Chicago stockyards at Western Cold Storage Co., saw no reason why meat-freezing technology couldn't be used to cool a 1,700-seat theater, like the one he and A.J. envisioned building on Roosevelt Road.

At first, the air conditioning was provided by blocks of ice delivered in the early morning. Massive fans would blow the cool, moist air into the theater, but it was a crude and messy system that would often drench moviegoers with sprays of water. The Balabans hired an engineer to refine the process, and crowds began to flock to the movies to escape the heat during the summer months. Doctors would sometimes prescribe a day or two at the movie theater for patients suffering from heat exhaustion.

Since movies were all about fantasy, the Balabans believed the magic should start the moment patrons paid their admission fee of twenty-five cents. In a Balaban movie palace, audiences entered a world of ornate Gothic cathedrals, Egyptian pyramids and Venetian palazzos. With all legal bars and nightclubs shuttered, air-conditioned movie palaces became the nation's favorite form of nightlife. Most opened at noon and dimmed their lights at 11:00 p.m. or midnight. From Chicago, the vogue spread nationwide: the glamorous, air-conditioned movie palace experience attracted middle-class and wealthy patrons who would never have set foot inside filthy overheated nickelodeons.

But the true inflection point came with the realization that the *real* money was to be made, not in owning nickelodeons and theaters, but in creating a much higher-quality product shown on their screens.

Though William Fox's run at the top was relatively short—he's often called "the forgotten mogul"—his name has endured as one of the best-known brands in entertainment: Twentieth Century Fox pictures and the Fox television empire.

Born Wilhelm Fried Fuchs on January 1, 1879, in Tolesva in the Austro-Hungarian empire, Fox grew up on New York City's Lower East Side, the eldest of a family of thirteen children; only six of his siblings survived childhood. Fox quit school at eleven and, like so many recent Jewish immigrants on the Lower East Side, went to work in the *schmatte* trade—the garment business. He put in eleven-hour days in a sweatshop, pressing pants, to earn just eight dollars a week.

But he saved those dollars and by the time he was twenty, Fox invested in his own company, preparing bolts of cloth for garment manufacturers. By 1904, Fox had enough savings to purchase a penny arcade in Brooklyn; on the second floor, he installed a 150-seat theater showing silent movies, charging a nickel admission—hence the name "nickelodeon." Recognizing opportunity in the burgeoning film business, Fox purchased more theaters, developing a chain and building a small fortune.

His next step was to begin producing his own films. In 1915, he founded Fox Film Corporation with the financial backing of several New Jersey investors and leased his first studio in Fort Lee. The studio raked in millions for Fox, who gave his personal attention to every production. Fox also oversaw the construction of Fox theaters in major cities throughout the country; his theaters emphasized comfort and elaborate design.

Fox features were hits and very profitable. A series of silent movies starring cowboy actor Thomas Mix popularized the genre of the Western. Tom Mix became an international celebrity, grossing almost $1 million per film for Fox.

In 1923, Fox began to build the famed Fox Hills Studio on one hundred acres just outside Hollywood, California. The eccentric mogul refused to wear a watch or have any clocks in his office. "The day ends when the work is done," he liked to say. Fox ultimately owned a third of all the movie theaters in the world. "No second of every twenty-four hours passes but that the name of William Fox is on the screen in some part of the world," he boasted.

Fox wasn't the first of the early producers to move his operations from Fort Lee to Hollywood. In 1914, Carl Laemmle paid $165,000 for 230-acres of farmland in the San Fernando Valley and, by March 1915, opened the world's largest motion picture production facility, Universal Studios Hollywood. Southern California's sunny climate allowed for year-round outdoor filming, which cut production costs. The state offered diverse landscapes—beaches, deserts, mountains—ideal for shooting various genres like Westerns. Southern California also provided affordable land for expansive studio lots.

However, the pivotal reason that the pioneering Jewish moviemakers like William Fox and Carl Laemmle moved west was Edison's aggressive attempt at patent enforcement to control the entire film business. Holding numerous film-related patents, he filed lawsuits against all competition.

While the court cases dragged on, Edison resorted to hiring thugs to sabotage competitors' sets, breaking cameras and shutting down productions. Many fled to California to escape his "patent police."

The quickest solution for producers not willing to play ball with Edison's Trust? Simply relocate—as far away from Edison as possible, three thousand miles to the west, in the era before commercial airlines, when transcontinental travel was costly and onerous. (In 1910, even the fastest train from New York to Los Angeles took around 70 hours.)

For years, William Fox fought against the movie monopoly of the Motion Picture Patents Company owned by Edison, eventually winning a landmark Supreme Court case. By then most independent filmmakers were thriving in Southern California, free from Edison's reach, and Hollywood emerged as the global hub of filmmaking.

The first link between Wall Street and Hollywood was the German-born investment banker Otto Kahn, the senior partner of Kuhn, Loeb & Co. and a devoted patron of the opera and theater in Manhattan. Kahn was the first to see Hollywood's potential as what he called "an investor's El Dorado." Kahn was also one of the first financiers whose interest in show business profits was exceeded by his interest in the "beautiful women who constituted their products."

Kahn was both an inveterate womanizer and a shrewd businessman. He sent Harris De Haven Connick, a Stanford-educated engineer, to investigate Famous Players-Lasky, which would later become Paramount Pictures, when he was considering a possible underwriting. Adolph Zukor sought $10 million from Kuhn, Loeb for stock issuance; Kahn secured profitable financing for the studio on Wall Street.

Clarence Dillon's own interest in Hollywood was piqued when his former Harvard classmate, lawyer Carl Ehlermann, stopped by his New York office one cold December day in 1923 to tell Dillon that he had formed an account with a few other colleagues who were looking into the motion picture business.

Although Dillon chose not to proceed with Ehlermann's proposal, he was approached again in late 1924 by United Artists president Joseph Schenck. Schenck was a tough Russian-born Jewish immigrant who'd come to New York City in 1892, under the name Ossip Schenker.

United Artists was unique among all the early film studios, founded in 1919 by four of the most important film artists: Charlie Chaplin, Mary Pickford, Douglas Fairbanks and D.W. Griffith. Chaplin, Pickford, Fairbanks, and Griffith incorporated United Artists as a joint venture company on February 5, 1919. Each held a 25% stake in the preferred shares and a 20% stake in the common shares of the joint venture.

They were spurred on by established Hollywood producers and distributors who were tightening their control over actor salaries and creative decisions, a process that would become known as "the studio system."

When Griffith dropped out in 1924, Joseph Schenck assumed the presidency of United Artists. Mary Pickford, "America's Sweetheart," announced at an emergency meeting called by Schenck that "she was alarmed at what was going on in the industry . . . theatre circuits were merging," and unless measures were taken to counteract these moves, "the future of United Artists would be in jeopardy." Schenck disagreed. He warned the United Artists partners that "although the company was fundamentally healthy," they should ensure their future by not taking all the risks themselves but allowing others to "participate a little" in their profits.

"Joseph Schenck approached Dillon, Read and Company, of Wall Street, who were willing to put up $40,000,000 for an issue of stock and an interest in our company," Charlie Chaplin later wrote in his autobiography. "I said frankly that I was opposed to Wall Street having anything to do with my work and again contended we had nothing to fear from mergers as long as we made good pictures."

In the heated discussion that ensued, Chaplin threatened to leave United Artists if the company accepted even a dime from investment bankers, which "brought about a solemn avowal of loyalty" from his partners and "the matter of Wall Street was dropped."

Despite the Little Tramp's insistence on refusing Dillon Read's financial backing, Clarence Dillon's interest was now piqued. In December 1924, he was contacted by Carl Laemmle of Universal Pictures for "new financing amounting to $30,000,000." This Universal Pictures deal was the beginning of Dillon Read's financing of the movie business.

Dillon could see that the film industry was now a viable business opportunity—a chance to invest with the promise of high returns. Dillon's firm, along with Shields & Co., agreed to offer Universal preferred stock for public subscription. Paul Shields, the founder of Shields & Co., was an Irish American friend of James Forrestal. His small brokerage firm was a reliable distributor of Dillon Read's securities.

On Wall Street, Shields had a reputation as a "tough, cold operator" who'd made many smart deals. In early December 1925, Shields & Co. prepared an investment booklet titled *The Development of Motion Picture Theatre Chains*, in which Shields noted: "A year and a half ago, it would have been rather difficult to market an issue of securities of a motion picture company or a chain of picture theatres, whereas today there is a well-defined demand for securities of this character."

Motion Picture News announced on December 12, 1925, that "Universal and Dillon, Read & Co., of New York, are forming a corporation to take over the present Universal theatre holdings and to acquire, if necessary, as many as one thousand more in cities and towns where Universal is not being given what it considers a 'fair break' in the matter of showings."

Universal followed the lead of Famous Players, Fox, Metro-Goldwyn, and Warner Bros. by forming a subsidiary for its theaters. Dillon Read managed the stock issue for this new corporation in exchange for a majority share.

From a banking perspective, it was still risky to finance an expansion of theater holdings for film exhibitions. Yet in 1926, Clarence Dillon increased his firm's involvement in the growth industry by forging a relationship with Loew's/MGM, the most profitable studio in the movie business. At the time, the Big Three Hollywood film companies were, in order of profitability, Loew's/MGM, First National, and Famous Players-Lasky/Paramount.

Marcus Loew, born on the Lower East Side of Manhattan on May 7, 1870, was the most financially astute and well-liked of all the original Jewish studio moguls. Will Rogers once quipped that Loew "made more money out of [motion pictures] than anybody. But he always said, 'I don't know what they are all about, and the more I learn about them, the less I know.'"

"The biggest financial news of last week was the issue of $15,000,000 worth of 15-year 6-percent debentures by Loew's, Inc.," *Variety* reported on April 21, 1926. "The issue, handled through Dillon Read and the National City Company, was entirely sold by 11:00 a.m. last Thursday morning when it was first issued."

Loew's operated over a hundred theaters nationwide and owned Metro-Goldwyn Pictures Corporation. MGM produced higher-quality films than competing studios to extend their theater runs. Clarence Dillon saw instantly that Marcus Loew and his key advisor, Nicholas Schenck, ran Loew's "as coolly and conservatively as other men might run a bank."

Loew also had a keen eye for real estate when expanding his theater chain. Dillon and Loew liked each other and, from an investing perspective, saw eye to eye. In the volatile movie business, Dillon Read became known for its stability as Loew's longstanding bankers.

Hollywood was not exclusively an "empire" created by Eastern European Jewish immigrants shut out from traditionally WASP-dominated business. Although almost all the pioneering moguls were Yiddish-speaking newcomers to America, the new industry was wide open enough that a few outsiders were able to set up business operations—and two Wall Street men profited handsomely.

The most high-profile was an Irish Catholic financier from Boston, Joseph P. Kennedy, father of the future thirty-fifth president of the United States. Two months before Clarence Dillon became the banker for Loew's/MGM, in February 1926, Joe Kennedy became "the first outsider to simply purchase a studio outright," paying $1 million for the Film Booking Offices of America (or "FBO").

FBO was considered a second-tier film company, its productions low-budget silent reels aimed toward small-town America. Still, Joe Kennedy, a partner at Hayden, Stone & Co., a venerable investment bank located at 1 Wall Street, was convinced that motion pictures could be a gold mine—perhaps even that El Dorado of which Otto Kahn had prophesied in 1919.

Before venturing out to California, according to historian Janet Wasko's *Movies and Money: Financing the American Film Industry*, Kennedy once commented to a fellow banker at Hayden, Stone: "Look at that bunch of pants pressers in Hollywood making themselves millions. I could take the whole business away from them."

"Pants pressers" was Joe Kennedy's own coinage, in keeping with his well-documented antisemitism. Jews in the 1920s were so dominant in the *schmatte* trade in cities like New York, Chicago, and Boston that no listener, certainly not a fellow New York banker, could have misunderstood Kennedy's ugly reference to the Jewishness and humble origins of the major studio moguls.

When he showed up in Hollywood in 1926, no one had heard of Joseph P. Kennedy. He was not yet the patriarch of the nation's leading political dynasty. Nonetheless, he took Hollywood by storm. Always meticulously dressed, chauffeured in his Rolls-Royce Silver Ghost, he was already rich—with rumors that before becoming a legitimate Wall Street banker, back in Boston he'd done very well for himself in the bootlegging rackets.

Despite the widespread lore, most historians today think that Joe Kennedy was never truly a bootlegger, although bosses like Frank Costello, Owney Madden, Joe Bonanno, and Meyer Lansky all later claimed to have had profitable ties to Kennedy during Prohibition. Arriving in Hollywood with an estimated net of one million dollars, Kennedy would "increase that tenfold over the five years he was immersed in the film industry."

If Dillon approached all business deals with the mind of a no-limit stud poker player, Joe Kennedy's strategy in Hollywood came from the "Game of Kings." In 1937, *Fortune* magazine ran a cover story which likened Kennedy's Hollywood years to chess: he first captured "small pawns like Robertson-Cole and F.B.O., while toppling knights and bishops such as Pathé and KAO, and within four years, forming his 'queen'—RKO Pictures." Kennedy moved so rapidly "that opinions still differ as to whether he left behind reorganized companies or merely wreckage," *Fortune* reported.

Much like Dillon—whom he knew from Wall Street—Kennedy could be utterly coldblooded: "tracing his path from Boston to Hollywood leads you into the ruins of vanished corporations . . . from which there arise whiffs of an atmosphere distinctly gamey."

Kennedy's quite calculating Hollywood agenda was not only to wrest the entire movie business away from a bunch of low-class, Yiddish-speaking pants pressers; it also involved liaisons with some of the most beautiful young women in America.

Historian Doris Kearns Goodwin encapsulates Kennedy's outlook: "He viewed the world as an endless battlefield and could scheme and exploit people without hesitation."

Even before arriving in California, where he bought a mansion on Rodeo Drive in Beverly Hills, Kennedy had become smitten with Hollywood's reigning golden girl, Gloria Swanson. Twenty-eight years old when they met, Swanson was barely five feet tall with "huge sapphire blue eyes and dazzling white teeth." Lenore Coffee, one of the pioneering female Hollywood screenwriters, described Swanson as "tiny and almost bird-boned." But by the end of 1927, due to a series of horrendous business decisions, the petite, fragile-looking bombshell was in dire financial straits, by her own admission having only $65 in the bank.

Joe Kennedy was recommended to Swanson as a wily financier who could sort out her financial mess. They met for lunch in Manhattan, during which he "bombarded her with questions about budgets, grosses, and distribution figures, most of which she couldn't answer."

Kennedy returned to his office at 1 Wall Street starstruck, his ego puffed at the thought he'd had lunch alone with "the best-known woman in the world." He began strategizing how he could see her again. The answer lay not in his roguish Irish charm, but in dollar signs and deal points. In Swanson's financial desperation, Kennedy swept down like some bird of prey—becoming first her business advisor and then her manager.

Swanson had an offer on the table from Paramount to pay her $1 million a year for four films. The deal would have made her the highest paid woman in the world. Joe Kennedy advised her to walk away from Paramount and shutter her own production company. With Kennedy as her Svengali, they could together make far more than a million a year. Or so he promised. In a matter of weeks, Kennedy had complete control over Swanson's finances and her artistic future.

Though both were married—Swanson to French nobleman Henry de La Falaise—their attraction was immediate and intense. Swanson first slept with Kennedy in his Palm Beach home, according to Jerry Oppenheimer's *The Other Mrs. Kennedy*. "He moved so quickly that his mouth was on mine before either of us could speak," Swanson recalled. "With one hand he held the back of my head. With the other he stroked my body and pulled at my kimono. He was like a roped horse, rough, arduous, rearing to be free. After a hasty climax, he lay beside me, stroking my hair."

Initially discreet—communicating in code by telegraph messages—the lovers began sleeping together regularly at Kennedy's Rodeo Drive mansion. As a devout Roman Catholic with a devoted wife and large family, Kennedy tried to avoid scandal, but the affair soon became the talk of Hollywood and, according to Oppenheimer, "a rumor even surfaced that Kennedy was the father of one of Gloria's children, a son whom she named Joe."

Later, after the year-long fiery passion had turned to ice, Swanson compared her lover to another egomaniacal Joe.

"Joe Kennedy operated just like Joe Stalin," Swanson recalled. "Their system was to write a letter to the files saying one thing and then order the exact reverse on the phone."

The silent feature film *Queen Kelly* was Gloria Swanson's passion project, bankrolled and produced by Joe Kennedy for United Artists and directed by Erich von Stroheim. Shot in 1928, production ran far over budget, and the film proved to be a disaster. It bombed in theaters, souring the public on Swanson and saddling her with the kiss of death label in the world of Hollywood: "box-office poison."

Overnight, Kennedy decided he was done with her. He cut off their affair, leaving Swanson's career, reputation, and personal finances in shambles.

The original Jewish studio moguls were hardly known for their business ethics or personal morality, but according to Neal Gabler, "they *did* take seriously their roles as leaders in the community; how they were perceived by that community was a vital part of their self-image. Kennedy alone was untethered by any sense of obligation to anything larger than himself."

Joe Kennedy's pursuit, conquest, and cruel abandonment of Gloria Swanson is perhaps the best example of one key motivation for Wall Street titans to invest in Hollywood productions. Here was a brand-new industry in which they could not only profit; they could bed the most stunning women in the world.

Otto Kahn, the senior partner at Kuhn, Loeb, never missed an opening night at the Ziegfeld Follies on Broadway. Much of the financial backing for Flo Ziegfeld's theatrical spectacles came from men like Kahn. Some investors funded a show simply out of infatuation with one particularly beautiful—and scantily clad—showgirl.

The Jewish comedienne Fanny Brice mocked the poorly kept secret of the sex-for-fame quid pro quo. In one of her earliest films, she sang, with an exaggerated Yiddish accent:

Is something the matter with Otto Kahn?
Or is something wrong with me?
I wrote a note and told him what a star I would make.
He sent it back and marked it "Opened by mistake."

The epicenter of all these sexual escapades was not Beverly Hills or Hollywood but rather The Ritz-Carlton Hotel on Madison Avenue and 46th Street in Midtown Manhattan.

Louise Brooks, silent film star and iconic flapper, the woman who popularized the bob hair style, started her career as an eighteen-year-old Broadway chorus girl straight from Kansas.

Dancing seminude in the Follies, by early 1925 Brooks drew the attention of Walter Wanger, a Paramount Pictures production executive. By one account, during the interview in his office, "Wanger asked Brooks what made her think she had what it took to make it in the movies. She promptly took off her clothes, lay down on the couch, and showed him." Wanger signed Brooks to a five-year contract with Paramount Pictures.

Wanger, a close friend of Otto Kahn's, was in charge of screening what Brooks described as "a hand-picked group of beautiful girls who were invited to parties given for great men in finance and government."

Brooks later wrote: "We had to be fairly well bred and of absolute integrity—never endangering the great men with threats of publicity or blackmail. At these parties we were not required, like common whores, to go to bed with any man who asked us, but if we did the profits were great. Money, jewels, mink coats, a film job—name it."

Brooks was invited to numerous parties at Kahn's apartment with some of the other girls from *George White's Scandals*, a hit Broadway revue in which she again appeared seminude.

"Naturally all the girls looked forward to becoming movie stars, and in The Ritz Hotel, most of the very famous, very rich men about town in New York kept apartments year-round where they would give parties. One of these belonged to Otto Kahn, though of course they would lend them to each other.

"I was invited to a party one night with some of the girls from *Scandals*," Brooks recalled. There they saw myriad Hollywood heavyweights drinking alongside Lord Beaverbrook—William Maxwell Aitken, the Canadian newspaper baron and future minister in Prime Minister Winston Churchill's wartime cabinet.

"All of us—all the girls—went up to this little grey suite in the Ritz and we were introduced and had drinks. I saw that Lord Beaverbrook was very, very interested in the girl I liked most in *Scandals*. She was a darling girl from the South—a darling girl. They became very cozy. I watched very discreetly as they disappeared into the little grey bedroom in the little grey suite in the Ritz," Brooks wrote. A few days after the tryst, Brooks recalled that her friend from *Scandals* "told me that she had a contract at MGM." Brooks said she was thrilled. "Hooray for Lord Beaverbrook!" she said.

At this same time, Brooks and Beaverbrook were, in fact, conducting their own flagrant affair, an arrangement in which Brooks was the Lord's "kept woman." She lived luxuriously at the Algonquin Hotel and Beaverbrook picked up the tab. "He was crazy about her," one of her fellow Ziegfeld girls recalled. "He covered her with jewels and gifts." But Brooks never liked or even cared about Beaverbrook. "She described him as an ugly monkey who had no manners."

Adding insult to injury, while Beaverbrook was footing all her extravagant bills, Brooks was also seeing "a fleet of men," and a chambermaid at the Algonquin described her room as "a bordello."

As the quintessential flapper, Louise Brooks embodied the free love movement of the roaring twenties, a groundbreaking era of sexual liberation for young women. Throughout the twenties, Brooks had a dizzying number of lovers of both sexes. Lord Beaverbrook was hardly the most famous. Soon after Walter Wanger discovered her dancing in the Follies, Brooks was introduced to Charlie Chaplin at a Wanger cocktail party. Chaplin was in Manhattan for the premiere of his film *The Gold Rush* on August 16, 1925, at the Strand Theatre on Broadway.

Brooks was still an eighteen-year-old chorus girl, yet to make her film debut, while Chaplin—thirty-six and married to American actress Lita Grey—was the biggest sensation that the silent film world ever produced.

With the release of *The Gold Rush*, Chaplin was, in the later (and perhaps slightly hyperbolic) estimation of British director Ricky Leacock, "infinitely more famous than Jesus Christ ever was—China, Africa, every continent, and corner of the world. In 1925, he was the most famous man who'd ever lived."

Chaplin and Brooks had an intense and very indiscreet two-month affair that summer in New York. When their affair ended, Chaplin sent Brooks a check. She accepted Chaplin's money, but declined to write him a thank-you note.

As a Wall Street powerhouse well acquainted with Otto Kahn, Joe Schenck, and Joe Kennedy, Clarence Dillon almost certainly attended his share of louche parties at The Ritz-Carlton. He also—

again, almost certainly—spent nights in the private company of Follies showgirls aspiring to be film starlets. Yet he did so with such discretion that there's virtually no record of his dalliances.

In 1926, Dillon purchased an apartment at the forty-one-story Ritz Tower on Park Avenue, the world's first residential skyscraper, strictly for his use in the July and August months when Wall Street business prevented him from joining Anne and his two children at their summertime Maine retreat.

Wealthy businessmen like Dillon who stayed in Manhattan apartments while their families were vacationing were called "summer bachelors," and their fidelity to their wives was assumed to be rather flexible.

The Saturnalia of nascent Hollywood was, for self-made millionaires like Joe Kennedy and Clarence Dillon, about more than mere womanizing. With the advent of movies as a multibillion-dollar business, a select group of financiers in Manhattan found that they had the power to create a glamorous screen goddess from a penniless small-town nobody. And not only to create her, but to *possess* her—physically and emotionally.

Wielding such power was clearly more intoxicating than the initial sexual spark. Because he also held the power to throw her away as quickly as he'd ensnared her, without a twinge of regret, as Joe Kennedy coldly ditched Gloria Swanson after the *Queen Kelly* fiasco—ending their relationship with no more thought than he'd give to tossing yesterday's edition of *The Wall Street Journal* in the waste bin.

Despite the fact Kennedy was a fellow Harvard man, Dillon didn't finance any of his film projects.

While Joe Kennedy wanted to produce films and run three studios—over one hundred films were released under the "Joseph P. Kennedy Presents" banner—Clarence Dillon had no desire to be in the spotlight. As always, he preferred to be offstage, directing quietly from the wings, keeping a keen focus on issuing film securities.

When Carl Laemmle nearly died of appendicitis in 1926 on his annual trip to Germany, two Dillon Read partners, Karl Behr and Dean Mathey, were part of the official committee greeting Laemmle's return to New York. The welcome included confetti, banners, and flowers.

In July 1927, Dillon Read and Shields & Co. offered a $2.5 million issue of Universal Pictures notes for general corporate purposes. Universal's films were distributed weekly to about ten thousand theaters in the US and Canada. Its affiliate, Universal Chain Theatre Corporation, leased or held a substantial interest in over three hundred theaters across the US. Although most films in 1927 and 1928 were silent, Warner Bros. Pictures' release of the first successful sound film, *The Jazz Singer* starring Al Jolson in October 1927, ushered in a new age for Hollywood: the beginning of the "talkies" and the end of the silent era.

Laemmle, the visionary creator of Hollywood's star system, badly misjudged the latest innovation, believing that "talking pictures" wouldn't replace silent ones, and began divesting some theaters from the Universal chain after deciding that the expense of wiring theaters for sound films was not worth it.

In the 1920s, Educational Pictures used an Aladdin's lamp logo with the slogan "The Spice of the Program" on short film title cards. Founded by Earle Hammons in 1915 to produce shorts, it soon distributed travelogues, cartoons, and comedies. By the mid-1920s, it was distributing Felix the Cat cartoons and comedies. In November 1926, Dillon Read began refinancing talks for Educational Pictures.

By February 1927, they offered $2 million in preferred stock as part of a $3.5 million plan to merge production units and exchanges, aiming to expand from distribution to production-distribution. Educational was a top independent short-subject distributor by the late silent era's peak year in 1927. Competing with companies like Paramount led them into feature-length productions. In November 1928, Hammons bought a stake in World Wide Pictures to distribute foreign films across North America using funds from stock issued by Dillon Read.

Marcus Loew died suddenly on Labor Day, 1927, of heart failure in his country home in Glen Cove, NY. He was only fifty-seven. Tributes to Loew's charm, influence, and affability overflowed. In its obituary, *Variety* called him "the most beloved man of all show business of all time."

In Hollywood, "memorial services for the motion picture business's first trailblazer were held on a studio stage" according to Samuel Goldwyn's biographer A. Scott Berg, with Rabbi Edgar Magnin of Congregation B'nai B'rith on Wilshire Boulevard, the oldest Jewish synagogue in Los Angeles, eulogizing Loew and reciting kaddish. "Louis B. Mayer fought back tears in describing Loew as 'Christ-like,'" Berg writes, before he "introduced Rabbi Magnin."

After Marcus Loew's death, Nicholas Schenck, a hard-driving, Yiddish-speaking immigrant from the town of Rybinsk in Czarist Russia, became president of Loew's, Inc.

He commuted to the sixteen-story Loew's building in Manhattan from his English country-style estate next to Walter Chrysler's property on Long Island. Schenck had "an uncanny eye for profitable pictures, and a genius for building theaters in the correct places." To continue Loew's expansion program, a new $15 million issue of preferred stock was offered by a group consisting of Dillon Read, Blyth, Witter & Co., and A.G. Becker &

Co. in December 1927. Dillon Read's closed-end investment trust, United States and Foreign Securities Corporation, owned 12,500 shares of Loew's common stock by January 1928.

In early 1929, however, Loew's independence was suddenly thrown into jeopardy. William Fox, perhaps the most flamboyant and volatile of the movie moguls, bought a 45% interest in the company by purchasing stock from Nicholas Schenck and a large block from the late Marcus Loew's estate.

Fox acquired West Coast Theatres in 1925, hoping to merge his corporation with Loew's. Schenck made an $8 million profit by selling his stock, valued at $47,000,000, to Fox at a 15% premium. Dillon, Read & Co. vehemently complained when Fox acquired Loew's shares because the Wall Street firm was Loew's banker. The firm believed Schenck had "double-crossed" them by selling the shares without allowing them to profit.

A young Dillon Read associate named Clifton Miller phoned Fox and made a "strenuous protest" about the Loew's purchase. Then Dillon's right-hand man and old Harvard roommate, Bill Phillips, made a follow-up call to Fox hammering home the firm's displeasure. Fox, who'd dealt occasionally with Dillon Read previously, tried to explain that he wasn't to blame for Schenck's "double-cross." He also promised that when he was ready to do the new financing, Dillon Read would "be in the picture."

Before William Fox could have any real impact on Loew's management, however, he suffered a series of devastating blows. On July 19, 1929, he was nearly killed. While driving in Westbury, Long Island, Fox's sedan was in a head-on collision. His chauffeur died instantly and Fox, fifty years old, survived only because some Good Samaritans rushed him to Nassau County Hospital to receive a blood transfusion. Fox also suffered a fractured skull, and it would be three months before he fully recovered.

Unfortunately for Fox, *Forbes* later wrote, the near-fatal car wreck was just the beginning of his troubles. "The stock market crash in late 1929 annihilated Fox's wealth. The crash eliminated not only his savings, but also any hope of the merger with MGM he had initially hoped for."

Next came a legal attack from the federal government. In November 1929, the US Department of Justice filed an antitrust suit against Fox's acquisition of Loew's.

In the economic turmoil of November 1929, Fox realized that his previously highly profitable corporation would be thrown into bankruptcy. He had to refinance his acquisitions quickly. To pay for the Loew's shares and an interest in the Gaumont-British Picture Corporation, Fox had borrowed over $40 million. The loans needed to be repaid within a few months.

Fox began to make the rounds of the usual New York banks and later said that he perceived "some mysterious influence was at work" against him. Fox's mind reeled with conspiracy theories: the one he settled on was that powerful forces in Wall Street had colluded to destroy him. The film mogul decided he needed to find a different investment bank that would offer a new issue of Fox securities to the public. He decided to go with Dillon Read.

We know what transpired next, or at least Fox's version of events, due to a lengthy, detailed account in a curious book published in 1933, *Upton Sinclair Presents William Fox.*

The Baltimore-born Sinclair, a prolific novelist and advocate of socialism and workers' rights, first made his mark in 1906 with his bestselling novel *The Jungle,* considered a classic in muckraking proletarian literature. (Jack London called it "the *Uncle Tom's Cabin* of wage slavery.") In 1933, the novelist and the former film mogul teamed up to publish a collaborative book; Sinclair writes in the third person about Fox—always referring to him as "W.F."—and includes long interviews with the former studio head describing the "cabal" that destroyed him.

Early in his career, it's worth noting, Sinclair made his distaste for Wall Street bankers clear. In *The Moneychangers*, a fictionalized account of the 1907 financial panic, he writes: "Wall Street had been doing business with pieces of paper; and now someone asked for a dollar, and it was discovered that the dollar had been mislaid."

Still, even factoring in this bias, Sinclair's rendering of Clarence Dillon offers perhaps the most revealing portrait of the investment banker's personality and professional behavior during his time as a Hollywood player.

In Sinclair's version of events, Fox requested a conference with Clarence Dillon. The following day, Dillon and other members of his firm met with Fox for a business lunch.

"Now we make the acquaintance of another big investment house," Sinclair writes. "Dillon, Read & Company had shot to the front in the past few years, among the new crop of wizards who were creating millions upon millions overnight. They bought the Dodge Company from the widows of the owners for $146,000,000, and they waved their wizard hands and overnight there was a new corporation, and a profit of $34,000,000 for the financiers. From that time on the Dodge Company began to slide, and in the end Dillon Read put it off on Chrysler. Wall Street men now point to the Chrysler Building and remark: 'That was Chrysler's commission on the Dodge Deal.'"

Sinclair reserved his most scathing prose for this character sketch:

"Clarence Dillon is one of those Jews who have forgotten the fact. He is tall, good-looking, egotistical, a rapid talker, and you get the impression that he knows what he is talking about. W.F. [William Fox] says it is hard not to believe that he is a kind man; which, of course, is a useful impression to give in Wall Street. I happen to know someone whom he employed in a confidential capacity, and I asked this person about his character, and the answer took only two words: 'Wholly unmoral.'"

At the conference Fox had requested, Dillon seemed conspicuously nervous. "The lunch was an elaborate one, and everybody had enough to eat, including Dillon; but in the center of the table was a massive bunch of grapes—there for an ornament, which, as a rule, nobody bothers." But all during the conference, which lasted for more than an hour after the luncheon, Dillon kept picking at the ornamental grapes, and by the time the conference was over he had gobbled up the massive bunch. Fox watched him closely and with curiosity, trying to figure out what was behind Dillon's nervousness.

"Dillon hadn't come there to negotiate a business deal with a new and valuable customer," Sinclair concluded. "Dillon had come under orders from somebody higher up, to tell W.F. that he must part with his voting shares. And Dillon perhaps didn't like that job so much; he might have preferred to be a financier, instead of an errand boy for a conspiracy."

To be sure, Clarence Dillon was nobody's errand boy, though Fox was right in deducing that Dillon *was* also representing the interests of somebody else: Albert H. Wiggin, chairman of Chase National Bank.

Dillon told Fox that he "would be glad to do the Fox financing," since Halsey, Stuart & Co. had relinquished their preferential contract. One issue stood in the way of the deal, however: Dillon demanded that Fox voluntarily dissolve his majority of voting shares. Dillon said that if Fox refused to do so, he might find his company controlled by someone outside the movie business.

Fox was shocked; he knew full well that when Clarence Dillon had bought Dodge, he had kept control by owning the majority of shares of voting stock. After rejecting Dillon's conditions, Fox ran to John E. Otterson at AT&T to explain "how the banking world had closed its doors to him."

Fox then returned to Dillon Read for a meeting with the young associate Clifton Miller. Miller prepared a plan for financing the film corporation by which Dillon Read would issue $75 million in preferred stock. Fox felt that all his troubles "had vanished" until he asked for a smaller loan of $500,000 to pay a debt that was due the next day for one of Fox's subsidiary companies. Miller and Fox argued over the collateral for this small loan. Miller wanted all six notes Fox had in his pocket even though two of the notes alone had a face value of $500,000.

Fox believed that the $75 million financing plan had only been a ploy to delay him until all his obligations fell due. This was—and remains to this day—a ruthless tactic on Wall Street.

Fox figured he'd only narrowly escaped from a trap when he met Clarence Dillon two months later. According to Fox, Dillon expressed great sympathy for his woes and denied that he'd heard about Clifton Miller's offer. He "laughed at the very idea that Dillon Read [had ever] contemplated the issuing of $75,000,000 worth of securities." (Miller left the firm a few months later.)

Fox was now desperate. In January 1930, Elisha Walker, president of the Bancamerica-Blair Corporation, approached Fox "to discuss the proposition of doing the Fox financing for a very high fee." Lehman Brothers wanted to also participate in the underwriting. Fox agreed, but insisted on including Loew's bankers, Dillon Read, as the third party in the financing group, which offered to sell $65 million of Fox securities.

As all the financing details were being worked out, it was agreed that three trustees would control the Fox voting shares: one selected by Bancamerica-Blair, one by Lehman Brothers, and one by Dillon Read. Clarence Dillon, however, now demanded that two more trustees be added: John Otterson of AT&T and Harold L. Stuart of Halsey, Stuart & Co., Fox's creditors. William Fox suspected that Dillon was conspiring with the two financiers, AT&T and Halsey, Stuart, intent on wresting control of his corporations by "steering me back into the spider's web."

After a long-drawn-out negotiating session at Dillon's estate in Rye, Fox was exhausted and ready to give in, but said he first needed to discuss this all with Eva, his wife of more than twenty years, who'd need to consent before he signed off on the deal.

When Fox asked to telephone Eva and bring her to Rye, Dillon nixed the suggestion—"This is kind of a stag party," he said—so instead Fox drove to his home, Fox Hall, in Woodmere, Long Island and explained Dillon's insistence on adding two more trustees who would bring about what Fox called his "ruination."

"The scene that followed was just as though a volcano had burst forth," Fox said. His wife "ran into her room and put her hat and coat on. When she came back again, nothing would do but to take her to Clarence Dillon's home." It was already one a.m. but Eva insisted on personally having a word with these supposedly "honorable bankers and lawyers."

After begging Eva to stay put, Fox returned to Dillon's house in Rye, where the intensity of his wife's "volcanic" rage was conveyed in no uncertain terms.

"A few minutes later Clarence Dillon came from the upper floor downstairs to where I was waiting, and took me into a separate room," Fox told Sinclair.

Dillon was no longer the same nervous-seeming banker Fox had watched compulsively munching ornamental grapes at the lunch conference. His brown eyes were now piercing, his expression calm and confident; he seemed grudgingly impressed.

"Fox," Dillon said, "I've seen all kinds of deals here on Wall Street. But I've never seen one just like this. You and your wife display more courage and more nerve than I've ever seen expressed before in a Wall Street transaction. Your courage deserves great consideration on the part of your bankers, and now that we know the true sentiment [of] you and Mrs. Fox, we'll manage to go forward and just leave three trustees."

Hard as it may be to believe, things became even more complicated for William Fox. As he was fighting the US Justice Department antitrust suit, he was slapped with another major court case. Halsey, Stuart & Co. and AT&T claimed that Fox could not have his financing done by any other group because of their own preferential contracts. They went to court trying to get Fox's companies placed into receivership.

Bancamerica-Blair, Lehman Brothers, and Dillon Read still wanted to proceed with their plan of issuing $65 million of new Fox securities for their 9% underwriting commission and receiving 135,000 shares of stock. Fox had no alternative: he saw this as the only way he could retain control of his businesses. Otto Kahn of Kuhn, Loeb & Co. was brought in by the judge as a mediator in an attempt to avoid protracted litigation. They settled on each company in the group receiving $1,600,000 "in cash without performing any further service."

But in the end, Fox did lose control of all his companies. Fox Film Corporation had to divest itself of Loew's after losing the Department of Justice's antitrust suit, and he was forced to sell all his other holdings to Harley L. Clarke of General Theatres Equipment, a company financed by none other than Albert Wiggin of Chase.

"In 1930 Fox collapsed and the ruins were left in the hands of Chase Bank," *Fortune* reported. "During the corporate turmoil which followed, the Law took action [with the antitrust suit] which delighted the hearts of Mr. [Nicholas] Schenck and his MGM partners."

How the mighty had fallen: William Fox, once the richest and most powerful of the original moguls, was forced into a grueling seven-year legal battle to avoid bankruptcy. He failed. Then at his bankruptcy hearing in 1936, he tried to bribe Judge John Warren Davis and also committed perjury. He was charged and tried for both crimes. In 1943, Fox served almost six months in prison for conspiring to obstruct justice and defraud the United States of America. President Truman granted him a full and unconditional pardon in 1947.

Loew's/MGM, meanwhile, was able to continue to run its corporation for its own profit. After the Crash, for about two years, the film industry suffered less than many other businesses; the anxious American public sought escape from grim reality in the fantasyland of air-conditioned movie palaces. By 1931, however, Fox Film, Paramount, RKO, and Warner Bros. had severe cash flow problems. Most of the major studios were forced into short-term debt.

Loew's, Inc., by contrast, "thrived through it all." Alone among the five vertically integrated major film companies, Loew's owned their production, distribution, and exhibition facilities, making the company able "to weather the Depression without bankruptcy, reorganization, or shake-up of any kind." Only Loew's paid regular dividends and never reported a loss during the Great Depression. Clarence Dillon's acumen was the primary reason that Loew's not only weathered the storm but prospered.

Educational Pictures' fortunes were soon in decline because of the transition to sound and Depression-era theaters' new policy of double features to boost attendance. This didn't allow time for Educational Pictures' two-reel shorts. In 1933, its creditors restructured the company and forced it into a merger with Fox Film Corporation.

In 1930, Carl Laemmle, still president of Universal Pictures, hit his artistic peak with the Academy Award–winning film, *All Quiet on the Western Front.* The movie was banned in Germany where it was regarded as traitorous. By 1934, a Nazi-controlled company had taken over Universal's office in Berlin and Laemmle, as one of the most famous Jewish movie moguls in America, was unable to ever again enter his country of birth.

In 1936, the indebtedness of Universal Pictures forced Carl Laemmle to sell his controlling interest to Cowdin of Standard Capital Corporation. In that year, Dillon Read headed a syndicate underwriting a new Loew's, Inc. issue of $15 million at 3½%, the lowest interest "ever carried by the obligation of an amusement company." Loew's profitability was due to Nicholas Schenck's cautious restraint in purchasing new theaters as well as by the consistent success of the high-quality MGM-released films such as *Mutiny on the Bounty*, a hit in 1935.

After the Nazis' rise to power, Laemmle retired from Universal Pictures and devoted himself to helping many German Jews flee to America, primarily by issuing affidavits.

In the early days of the Third Reich, many Jewish producers still tried to do business in Germany. That all changed after *Kristallnacht* on November 9, 1938, when synagogues all over Germany were torched, and Jewish businesses had their windows shattered—hence the English name of the pogrom, "The Night of Broken Glass." Early reports placed the number of Jews murdered at ninety-one, though it was probably much higher. More than thirty thousand Jewish men were rounded up and taken to concentration camps.

Nicholas Schenck sponsored a special showing of *Pygmalion*

at the Astor Theatre in Manhattan in December, with all proceeds going to aid Jewish victims of the Nazis.

Although Dillon Read was still doing business in Nazi Germany, refinancing German industrial companies including I.G. Farben as late as 1937, Clarence Dillon was listed by *The New York Times* as one of the "society notables and industry leaders" in attendance at Schenck's Astor Theatre benefit for German-Jewish relief.

Many Wall Street financiers and Hollywood studios were badly hurt or ruined by the Crash of 1929 and the Great Depression. Two businessmen walked away unscathed and personally enriched: Joseph P. Kennedy and Clarence L. Dillon.

Though Kennedy and Dillon had little personal interaction in the movie business during the 1920s, in something of an historical irony their sons, John Fitzgerald Kennedy and Clarence Douglas Dillon, would work closely together decades later when the former, a Democrat, was elected president of the United States and he chose the latter, a Republican, to be the nation's fifty-seventh Secretary of the Treasury.

Joseph Kennedy and Clarence represented vastly divergent approaches to the motion picture business. No one else from Wall Street had "simply bought himself the presidency of a studio," as Kennedy had in 1926 with the million-dollar acquisition of FBO. Kennedy's departure from Hollywood was perfectly timed. He'd sold all three of his companies, FBO, First National, and Pathé, by the end of January 1931 before the full impact of the Great Depression finally affected the movie business.

After less than five years, Kennedy left Hollywood roughly ten million dollars richer than when he arrived. According to Betty Lasky, daughter of Paramount founder Jesse Lasky, "Joseph Kennedy was the first and only outsider to fleece Hollywood."

Clarence Dillon's own departure from the film business—though not as dramatic or high-profile as Kennedy's—was equally well-timed. No one could accuse him of having "fleeced Hollywood." On the contrary. Dillon had played a significant role in underwriting the expansions of Universal Pictures, Educational Pictures, and Loew's, Inc. Dillon avoided high-risk loans and functioned as a principal banker for the profitable, conservatively run Loew's.

Joe Kennedy's reputation after leaving Hollywood—in no small part because Gloria Swanson publicly claimed that he'd "ruined" her career—was that of a cutthroat, callous, self-interested banker, a brilliantly astute financier with all the compassion of a great white shark. These personality traits did Kennedy no harm as he directed his bottomless ambition and fortune into the equally cutthroat realm of national politics.

Clarence Dillon, on the other hand, came out of his Hollywood sojourn with his reputation as an investor intact and, despite Upton Sinclair's unflattering portrayal of him in print, perhaps even somewhat enhanced. Not a whiff of Hollywood scandal followed Dillon back to Wall Street, and whatever liaisons he may have had with Ziegfeld chorus girls inside Otto Kahn's Ritz-Carlton suites were kept absolutely hush.

Stanton Griffis, Paramount Pictures chairman of the board from 1935 to 1942, described Dillon as having been gifted with "a psychic, Oriental mind," a mind uniquely "adapted to the business of buying and selling securities." It took a rare kind of brilliance to do what Dillon had done as Loew's investment banker, setting such a shrewd and cautious course that, alone among all the major studios, the company prospered during the darkest days of the Depression.

"Clarence Dillon," Griffis concluded, "was certainly the greatest financier of our times."

Chapter Eleven

STOCKS AND PYRAMIDS

LESS THAN A year after the spectacular Dodge Brothers purchase, Clarence Dillon was again making headlines. His latest coup involved something that today we all take for granted as part of everyday life—or at least did before the advent of credit card chips and contactless payments made with smartphones. The onomatopoeic exclamation *ka-ching!* entered the Oxford English Dictionary in 2005, the imitative sound of an old-fashioned cash register—meaning that someone is coming into a lot of money.

In 1871, James Ritty, a former Civil War cavalry officer, opened the Pony House saloon in Dayton, Ohio. The tavern thrived, but he faced a problem with employees pocketing cash during transactions. On a steamboat trip to Europe, Ritty observed a machine that was tracking propeller rotations and envisioned a similar device for counting cash transactions in his saloon. With his brother John, he designed "Ritty's Incorruptible Cashier," patented on November 4, 1879; it quickly became known as a "cash register." The Ritty brothers opened a small factory but sold their interests after a few years.

In 1884, John and Frank Patterson acquired the company and renamed it The National Cash Register Company (or "NCR"). Although initially costly with limited sales, the Pattersons believed millions of shopkeepers would see the value of a receipt-producing register to reduce employee theft. They established the "American Selling Force," using commissions and sales scripts from their NCR Primer manual—the first sales training guide—which led to NCR's rapid expansion by 1888 across America and into Great Britain and Germany. By 1905, NCR controlled 95% of the American market for cash registers.

By 1911 NCR had sold one million machines. By 1922 they'd sold two million.

NCR profits soared from $2.8 million in 1921 to $7.8 million in 1925.

Investment bankers had been urging the Pattersons to take NCR public, to allow investors to buy stock in this fast-growing business. John Patterson had been resistant to the idea of the stock market, but after his death, Frederick, John's son, finally agreed to go public in winter 1925 while aiming to retain control of their family-owned company—holding 51% stock alongside his sister.

Clarence Dillon gave the job of evaluating the NCR underwriting prospect to Karl Behr, who'd become a Dillon Read partner in 1925. Behr was one of Dean Mathey's new recruits. A fellow tennis star, he'd been on the US Davis Cup team in 1907, and ranked among the national top ten players for years; Behr and Mathey spent hours together on the courts and became lifelong friends. In a curious historical footnote, Behr had survived the *Titanic*'s 1912 sinking. He'd been on board pursuing a young woman whose parents tried to end their romance by taking her to Europe. Behr's resolve saw him rescued in the same lifeboat as her family. Within a year of the disaster they married.

Dillon sent the Columbia Law School graduate to Dayton

with a team of accountants. NCR had grown to twenty-three buildings over forty-four acres. Behr set up an office there to assess its standing in the business machine industry. He conducted two rounds of interviews with senior management and meticulously examined NCR's records to gauge managerial competence and operational efficiency. His analysis confirmed that their sales, warehousing, and distribution methods were robust, revealing NCR's strong financial health without any funded debt. Behr advised Dillon Read to proceed with a financing offer.

Clarence Dillon and his partners discussed the different goals of Frederick Patterson and the minority shareholders of the Patterson family. Dillon suggested restructuring NCR by issuing 1.1 million shares of Class A common stock and 400,000 shares of B stock to satisfy both parties. Dillon Read could buy all the Class A stock, selling it at $50 per share to the public and to Patterson's minority shareholders in exchange for their interests.

Patterson would keep the B stock, enabling him to control a majority of the board as long as he paid a $3 annual dividend on each A share. This plan would give good dividends to Patterson's minority shareholders while allowing Frederick Patterson to raise funds and keep control over NCR.

By early 1926, there was high demand from both within the US and internationally. On its debut at the New York Stock Exchange, NCR opened at $52⅞ instead of $50 per share. Dillon Read sold it for $54¼ per share, making a profit from this price increase along with its underwriting and sales commissions.

In January 1926, NCR went public with an issue of $55 million in stock, the largest initial public offering (IPO) at that time in United States history.

The mystique surrounding Clarence Dillon grew with another round of front-page publicity from the NCR deal.

GENIUS OF WALL STREET AT FORTY-THREE IS UNASSUMING

DILLON JOINS COMPANY OF ROCKEFELLERS AND MORGANS VIA GIGANTIC DEALS

Carefully cultivated reporters wrote about "the rise of a young man into a position never held before by any man this side of fifty." Dillon's youth and energy had him surpassing certain unnamed "slow-moving Wall Street dinosaurs" who were "highly indignant" at his success.

When his deals weren't being likened to those of great historical leaders—one writer trumpeted his "Napoleonic achievements"—Dillon was himself compared to celestial bodies: "Dillon New Meteor in Financial Skies," wrote *Forbes*.

Clarence Dillon projected an image of infallibility as a financial genius which bolstered the sales of any securities offered by Dillon Read. Rumors of any megadeal supposedly organized by Clarence Dillon could be readily believed—even if farfetched—due to Dillon's newfound reputation for doing the unthinkable. A secret of Dillon's success, according to the media, was his ability to ascertain "all the facts regarding a given project" then make "a lightning-quick, daring decision, which is nearly always right."

Reporters arriving for interviews at 28 Nassau Street found Dillon in his cozy library-like office, relaxing in a Queen Anne armchair, smoking an old black pipe "with a smile that suggests anything but cares," while modestly suggesting that "success came to him for no particular reason."

"The Wizard of Wall Street" became one of Dillon's favored appellations.

Even the physical descriptions smack of the kind of gushing prose normally reserved for film idols: a "suave, saturnine man with long, slender hands" and "poise in the fullest degree," who moved with deliberation and grace, peering at visitors from "under heavy-lidded eyes."

Financial writers who had access to Dillon in his private office were struck by its minimalism and simplicity: "just one or two sharp pencils and a paper pad on his smooth glass-topped desk."

As one columnist noted: "That's the way to be an efficient mysterious millionaire. Get rid of detail."

The reliable Dean Mathey, recognizing the long-term growth in the oil and gas industry, brought the firm what would be its most lucrative legacy account. In 1920 British industrialist Lord Cowdray—Weetman Dickinson Pearson, 1st Viscount Cowdray—had formed a new oil company called Amerada—combining "America" and "Canada"—for exploration and developing energy in North America. Advised to expand into Texas's mid-continental area due to its potentially huge oil reserves, Lord Cowdray found that US laws barred foreign-controlled companies from prospecting in Texas.

Leveraging Mathey's insights as an expert in oil and natural gas, Clarence Dillon negotiated Dillon Read's acquisition of 51% of Amerada on behalf of Lord Cowdray in early 1926. The deal granted Dillon "absolute control for ten years," including board majority rights—convincing his home state that Amerada was no longer foreign-owned. Mathey joined the board, and Dillon Read underwrote Amerada Corporation's initial public offering on February 2, 1926.

By the end of 1926, Amerada had a net income of $4.9 million. Dillon Read continued to transfer US oil properties from Europe to America, reselling Royal Dutch Petroleum's $30 million stake in Union Oil of California in 1924. Later, Dillon Read arranged the merger of Amerada Petroleum with Hess Oil to form Amerada Hess.

In 1927, representatives for the Louisiana Land and Exploration Company came to Dillon Read for funding; at that time, its revenue came from fur-trapping fees and selling shrimp. The company aimed to develop oil and gas reserves on its 1.8 million acres in southern Louisiana. Mathey consulted Everette DeGolyer, the Kansas-born world-renowned petroleum geologist and geophysicist who used reflection seismology to confirm a high potential for major oil finds on the land.

Dillon's strategy hinged on thorough research, which paid off handsomely. In late 1928, Louisiana Land partnered with Texaco for oil exploration on its land in exchange for a 25% royalty on production. Texaco discovered vast oil reserves—one of America's major finds. The royalties were extraordinary, sending Louisiana Land's securities soaring. Investors reaped huge profits and continued to do so for decades.

Louisiana Land and Exploration remained almost entirely a royalty-based company for the remainder of the twentieth century, its few employees mostly accountants in New Orleans.

"Investors have traditionally regarded Louisiana Land as a small money factory," *The New York Times* wrote in May 1974, "churning out ever-increasing and assured profits year after year."

In the mid-1920s, the oil business in Texas was booming as was the stock business in Lower Manhattan. By getting in at the right time, anyone could get rich. In the late 1920s, when Louisiana Land's shares were trading at 50 cents, one of the secretaries at Dillon, Read & Co. bought 3,000 shares. By the 1950s, the secretary's modest $1,500 investment had grown to over $6 million.

Ernest Tracy was the president of Dillon Read's investment trust, United States and Foreign Securities Corporation (or "US&FS")

when the trust purchased a significant amount of Louisiana Land and Exploration bonds and stock. The son of a stockbroker from St. Louis, Tracy had graduated from Yale in 1907 two years before Dillon Read's Robert Hayward, as well as Leonard Kennedy. Like Hayward and Kennedy, he was a member of Yale's secret society, Scroll and Key.

In October 1928, when Dillon Read launched another closed-end investment trust, United States and International Securities (or "US&IS"), Ernest Tracy also became its president.

This meant that Tracy was simultaneously serving as president of both of Dillon Read's closed-end trusts and of the Louisiana Land and Exploration Company. He took no salary from either of the trusts, instead receiving stock options at discounted prices.

Tracy was almost certainly using his position at LL&E to benefit US&FS—or the other way around. This would today be illegal, a clear conflict of interest. But it was not before the creation of the Securities and Exchange Commission in 1934.

After the Crash of 1929, financial author John T. Flynn—the same journalist who'd dissected Dillon's ethical conflicts in the Goodyear bankruptcy restructuring—began taking a closer look at these practices in his 1930 book, *Investment Trusts Gone Wrong!*

Clarence Dillon had marketed these two trusts—US&IS and US&FS—as a way for the public to access elite investment advice. Flynn describes how the trusts pooled large sums of money under the control of an "expert" manager, often investment bankers with securities to sell. This setup effectively created perpetual buyers for their products. Flynn argued that managing an investment trust was a form of trusteeship, since investors relied on managers to choose the best and safest stocks due to their own lack of expertise. He deemed it unethical for an investment banker focused on selling stocks to manage these huge funds. Instead, trust managers should objectively select promising stocks for investors.

However, Clarence Dillon's use of US&FS and US&IS as customers for Dillon Read securities that had become difficult to sell to the public was common practice. He didn't violate any laws, nor the accepted standards on Wall Street at the time. Clarence Dillon didn't treat the unsophisticated Main Street investor differently than any other leading financier.

John Kenneth Galbraith, in *The Great Crash 1929*, best summed up the spirit of the era.

"The sense of responsibility in the financial community for the community as a whole is not small. It is nearly nil."

Dillon also used these trusts as a form of pyramiding.

Dillon could draw on these closed trusts' assets for his firm's major financings, including the Dodge Brothers purchase. On May 1, 1925, Dillon, Read & Co. couldn't have written a check for $146 million—or even for $14 million. The firm didn't keep that kind of money liquid in a checking account.

John Flynn found Ernest Tracy's joint presidency of US&IS and LL&E to be particularly egregious, asking: "We shall have to judge here whether these trusts are acting as trustees of their investors or allies of the banking house of Dillon Read and Company?"

With each new success the adoration from the financial press grew to almost farcical heights. What distinguished Clarence Dillon from the typical investment banker? One writer posited: "His artistic approach."

Dillon was the sort of rare financier who preferred etching his own "landscapes for diversion." He set aside as much time for "leisure, travel, culture, and roaming in company with his schoolboy son in woods and hills and streams" as he did on "the hard facts and affairs of finance."

Nothing like this cultured sophistication had ever been seen in those grim gray canyons of Wall Street. "What other men make a labor, he makes an art."

A profile in the *Cincinnati Enquirer* in January 1926 described Dillon as almost Zen-like. He was, the paper wrote, "the apostle of relaxation."

This was, of course, a finely crafted facade. The partners who worked with Dillon saw behind the mask. If Dillon was an apostle of anything it surely wasn't the art of relaxation. As for his bringing a new sense of culture into the financial world? It all depends on whether one's definition of culture is flexible enough to include the dark arts of control and manipulation.

Dean Mathey's description of Dillon as "at times a hard taskmaster" seems generous; Dillon was dictatorial, Machiavellian, secretive, and cunning—hiding his plans even from his closest associates until he was ready to act.

He was the sort of man who appeared to have hundreds of trusted associates and confidants, but truthfully, had not a single real friend. Dillon was so coldly aloof that, as one senior associate recalled: "I don't think I had ten words with Clarence Dillon in the four years that I was with the firm in the 1920s."

At 28 Nassau Street, the door to Clarence Dillon's private office was always locked. Visitors had to make it past Dillon's personal secretary, Marjorie Wellbrock, a stern gatekeeper. Dillon had installed an ingenious secret electric system—today we might call it Bond-like. No one could enter his private sanctum unless Dillon pressed a hidden button on his desk to release the door lock.

A clash had been brewing for months between Clarence Dillon and perhaps his most gifted young partner. The two men were too much alike not to butt heads eventually. Just as Dillon had been styled "The Baron" at Harvard, Ferdinand Eberstadt was nicknamed "The King" at Princeton.

Dillon was inscrutable and autocratic, Eberstadt charming and thorny, once described as "a man whose manner is pleasantly abrasive, like a rough towel after a cold shower."

Both men were aggressive, impatient, convinced of their own brilliance. Ferdinand was deeply discontented with his position and remuneration at Dillon Read, especially given the immense legal and financial expertise he'd brought to bear while engineering the Dodge deal with Walter Chrysler in July 1928.

Dillon felt, of course, that he'd made Eberstadt's career by luring him away from his law firm partnership in January 1926 and making him a full partner in a thriving investment bank. Eberstadt, for his part, was aware of the profits he had accumulated for the firm and his own growing reputation on Wall Street.

The contest of wills between the two came to a head in December 1928.

Pressing his secret desktop button, Dillon buzzed the office door open; Eberstadt strode in and reviewed all of his recent contributions to Dillon, Read & Co. He needed no papers to cite precise statistics. He could quote chapter and verse about the numerous European financings while he was living in Weimar Berlin, where he used his fluency in German, his knowledge of German culture, as well as his legal and financial acumen to hugely benefit the firm. He calculated the exact amount that he'd earned for Dillon, Read & Co. during his years as a partner.

Eberstadt concluded by telling his boss his specific demand.

Eberstadt's current 3% partnership was wholly insufficient. He wanted 10%.

Dillon raised his eyes but not his voice. He stared back at Eberstadt.

"You're fired," he said.

Eberstadt's defiance was a rarity. The much younger man was like an exceptional rogue comet in Dillon's carefully controlled solar system. Why did all the other partners tolerate his overbearing and dictatorial ways? For no other reason than that Dillon was making them all wealthy. Extremely wealthy. In 1928, a partnership in Dillon Read was financially far more lucrative than a similar position at J.P. Morgan or Kuhn, Loeb. While their salaries were relatively modest, the partners became rich because of their shares in the firm's underwritings. Partners were able to get in on the ground floor of deals that were about to skyrocket.

The profits from Dillon Read deals enabled the partners to enjoy the most lavish lifestyles in New York. By the late 1920s, James Forrestal purchased a thirty-acre estate on the North Shore of Long Island—an area of such affluence and exclusivity that at the turn of the century it became known as the "Gold Coast." His manor house was staffed with a butler-valet, a lady's maid for Forrestal's wife, a nanny for the Forrestal children, a cook, and a gardener. Each day his uniformed chauffeur took Forrestal in a Rolls-Royce from his Old Westbury estate to his Wall Street office and back again. The Gold Coast of Long Island was dotted with magnificent homes surrounded by manicured rolling lawns, stables, tennis courts, and swimming pools.

Fitzgerald described the Jazz Age parties he'd attended in Great Neck and Port Washington—rendered fictionally as "West Egg" and "East Egg"—in his most famous novel:

"In his blue gardens men and girls came and went like moths among the whisperings and the champagne and the stars. . . .

On buffet tables, garnished with glistening hors d'oeuvres, spiced baked hams crowded against salads of harlequin designs and pastry pigs and turkeys bewitched to a dark gold. In the main hall a bar with a real brass rail was set up, and stocked with gins and liquors and with cordials so long forgotten that most of his female guests were too young to know one from another."

The novel vividly renders as "orgiastic" the Long Island revelry on Gatsby's expansive lawn, parties filled with Wall Street millionaires, flappers, and real-life bootleggers—like the Midwestern German American Max von Gerlach, said to be the inspiration for the titular character.

In Gatsby's garden-turned-nightclub, there were "old men pushing young girls backward in eternal graceless circles, superior couples holding each other tortuously, fashionably, and keeping in the corners—and a great number of single girls dancing individualistically . . . By midnight the hilarity had increased. . . . and all over the garden, while happy, vacuous bursts of laughter rose toward the summer sky."

It was, in fact, Ferdinand Eberstadt's desire to build a Gatsbyesque showplace to rival the elaborate estates of other Gold Coast multimillionaires that led him to confront Dillon about increasing his partnership interest from 3% to 10%.

Eberstadt had visited the glorious estate of his cousin, Otto Kahn, in Cold Spring Harbor, an eighty-room French chateau on seven hundred acres of beachfront land. Eberstadt sought to announce to the Wall Street establishment that he had arrived in his own right by developing an estate of similar grandeur. Eberstadt owned a sliver of land on the far side of Lloyd Neck for summertime use. In the fall of 1928, he purchased an eighty-acre tract called Target Rock Farm on the Gold Coast that extended to Long Island Sound. Over the next nine years, Eberstadt constructed a twenty-five-room mansion with two guest cottages, tennis courts, horse stables, and a series of magnificent gardens.

In 1931, Eberstadt established his own firm, F. Eberstadt & Co., Inc., located at 65 Broadway, just around the corner from 28 Nassau Street—and proved himself an enormously successful investment banker and mutual fund pioneer. In a matter of years, Eberstadt made a fortune almost equal to that of Dillon.

In 1967, he donated his eighty-acre estate to the federal government. Today, open to the public, it is known as the Target Rock National Wildlife Refuge and is operated by the United States Fish and Wildlife Service.

If there were a contest among Wall Street egos for the most magnificent home, Dillon could claim to have outdone everyone. No private estate was grander than his Dunwalke. By 1928, Dillon had built an elegant Georgian-style red brick mansion for himself and Anne on twelve hundred acres of bucolic foxhunting country in Bedminster Township, New Jersey. He created an aristocratic name for the estate by combining two familial lines from his wife's colonial American ancestry, the Duns and the Walkes.

Dunwalke is more than one mansion: it's a family compound that ultimately included separate homes for Clarence and Anne's children, Douglas and Dorothy, and their families. The estate included a caretaker's cottage and a sports complex with an indoor pool and tennis courts—a world unto itself. A world where Dillon could withdraw from public scrutiny.

Architecturally, Dunwalke is a masterpiece—massive but tasteful, quite the opposite of Charles Foster Kane's Xanadu, though the effect was much the same.

The entrance to the Dunwalke estate is a mile long, lined with more than a hundred elm trees. The three-story mansion, built of eighteenth-century red brick, overlooks lush countryside. Prize-winning Guernsey cattle roamed the lush grounds; well-bred horses grazed peacefully. The estate included a staff of liveried footmen and appeared to be the ancestral seat of an English aristocrat or a colonial Virginia planter—like some of Anne's ancestors.

To reach the estate, after passing through a constantly guarded gate, a visitor drove the elm-lined mile past Dillon's personal three-hole golf course, which was strictly for impressive display; Dillon had never touched a golf club in his life. Dillon's Rolls-Royce was customized for his six-foot height, with a raised roof so he wouldn't have to stoop when getting into his limousine before feeding the geese on Dunwalke, and then having his chauffeur drive him the forty-five minutes to Nassau Street in Lower Manhattan.

The excess of the ultrarich in the 1920s was but one side of the coin. The recklessness and overconfidence of the Jazz Age trickled down to the average American investor, too, leading to what we'd now call an "asset bubble."

The stock market had increased by nearly 20% each year from 1922 until 1929. At the same time, during the roaring twenties, there was a rapid growth in bank credit and easily acquired loans. Regular folks on Main Street, encouraged by the market's stability and seemingly endless growth, weren't afraid of going into debt. Why should they be? There seemed to be no downturn in sight.

The concept of "buying on margin" allowed ordinary people with little financial knowledge—let alone assets—to borrow money from their stockbroker with hardly any of their own money. In the 1920s, one could invest by borrowing 90% of one's investment. When times were good, it was hard to resist taking a seat at Wall Street's blackjack table or a spin at its roulette wheel. With only $1,000, for example, a small investor could borrow $9,000 and by buying on margin invest $10,000 in the market. If the stock prices doubled, his investment was worth $20,000.

The flawless image of his successes concealed the ways in which Dillon manipulated the game. While most Americans gambled with reckless abandon—like the dancers on Gatsby's lawn with their vacuous laughter floating into the summer sky—Dillon stood on the sidelines, aloof, like the bandleader waving his baton and watching with bemusement all the drunken rollicking to his "yellow cocktail music."

Dillon personally took almost no risks. He always hedged his bets.

Through inside information, as Charlie Schwartz had slipped him during the Dodge Brothers deal, or by using shell corporations fronted by loyal flunkies like Leonard Kennedy, as in his many dodgy high-yield international loans, Dillon was always gaming the system. He used advantages and methods that were unethical in spirit if not then illegal. Even the firm's hiring of Princeton professor Edwin Kemmerer to give academic buttressing (not to mention the US State Department's stamp of approval) for Dillon Read's flimsiest high-risk bond prospectuses in South America and Poland was not against any law at the time.

In fact, it's hard to pinpoint anything in Clarence Dillon's career that was, technically, illegal.

During the roaring twenties, Clarence Dillon was not *above* the law. He was ahead of it.

By the fall of 1929, Dillon knew that he had won more than enough—often at the expense of others—and it was time to cash out and leave the grand casino.

The end was near.

According to *The Day the Bubble Burst: A Social History of the Wall Street Crash of 1929*, a wire service reported that even the birds in Manhattan knew it:

"On Fifth Avenue, the police found a parrot screaming, 'More Margin, More Margin.'"

Chapter Twelve

BANKSTERS

IN EARLY SEPTEMBER 1929, twenty-two-year-old Paul Nitze was riding in the back seat of Clarence Dillon's chauffeur-driven Rolls-Royce in Somerset County, New Jersey. Nitze's economic report from his recent trip to Weimar Germany had impressed Dillon enough to earn the young man an invitation to spend the weekend at the Dunwalke manor in Far Hills. During their drive through the verdant countryside, the recent Harvard graduate made the most of his opportunity to probe one of the world's top financial minds.

The roaring twenties economic boom appeared to have no end in sight as millions of Americans speculated in the stock market, often with borrowed money. On March 25, there'd been a brief slump in reaction to the Federal Reserve's warning about excessive speculation. But the president of National City Bank, Charles Mitchell—known as "Sunshine Charley"—had blithely disregarded the Fed's advice and offered $20 million more to borrowers. This kept the stock market on an upward course for a while longer. On September 3, the market average reached its peak for the decade.

"Do you think America is heading for a recession?" Nitze asked.

Clarence Dillon's face was sober, and he reflected before answering Nitze's question.

"We won't have a recession," Dillon said at last. "No, we'll have a depression—one which will be far more serious than anyone now thinks possible."

Dillon had clearly been ruminating over this issue for some time.

"And it will be the end of an era," he said, reminding Nitze that empires and nations of the past had been dominated by royalty or clergymen, by military men or common-born politicians—and, occasionally, by wealthy financiers.

"History has shown us that periods dominated by men of finance have been of relatively short duration," Dillon said. "Just as in the city-states of Italy during the days of the Medici."

Since the US Civil War, Dillon noted, New York bankers had wielded more influence than Washington, DC, politicians. But now, he predicted, in a major economic depression, Wall Street would be reduced to a "secondary element" in the American power hierarchy.

Nitze listened, subdued, silent. Dillon's erudition and confidence were persuasive, but Nitze was still skeptical.

A depression? The *end* of an era?

Nitze was the last man hired by Clarence Dillon before the Crash of 1929. He began work at Dillon, Read & Co. on the first day of October. By October 21, there were signs of a stock market downturn. On October 22, Dillon opened the weekly partners' meeting with a reminder of his policy of "keeping the capital of the firm liquid and not using it for investment purposes except in rare instances."

The following day, Richard Whitney, acting president of the New York Stock Exchange and Dillon's neighbor in Far Hills, was absent from the trading floor. He was occupied presiding over the Essex Fox Hounds meet, an annual two-day horse racing event, concluding with a ball at the Somerset Hills Country Club, that attracted several thousand high-society members. An avid horseman, Clarence Dillon belonged to the Essex Fox Hounds and wouldn't miss the chance to enjoy that beautiful fall day among other well-dressed socialites. While the fashionable watched the thoroughbreds at the Schleys' Froh Heim estate in Far Hills, panic-driven trading in Manhattan resulted in the second-largest stock share volume in history.

Shortly after the opening bell on October 24, the market lost 11% of its prior value. At noon, an emergency meeting of bankers, including Thomas Lamont of J.P. Morgan, Albert Wiggin of Chase, and Charles Mitchell of National City Bank, came up with a hurried plan to stabilize the market. They picked Richard Whitney as their representative. When Whitney appeared on the Stock Exchange floor, he started placing orders to buy blue-chip stocks in huge quantities, "each at the price of the last previous sale," despite their plummeting value. Whitney's purchases had the desired effect, stopping the slide. The markets stabilized in time for the weekend.

But then came Black Tuesday. At 9:30 a.m. on October 29, terror-struck investors began a record sell-off of stocks. Now no efforts by the Rockefellers and other financial leaders to buy large amounts of stock could shore up confidence and avert the feared Crash.

Long before Black Tuesday, Clarence Dillon had prepared for a major correction of the overheated market. When the stock market crashed, Dillon Read had no loans. The firm had started to retreat from the markets long before other investment banks. In 1928, which had seen a brief collapse of Wall Street's bull market in June, Dillon Read had engaged in its lowest annual percentage of total American underwritings since the firm's activity in 1919. Dillon attributed the investment bank's late 1920s policy "in no small measure to [our] careful examination applied to prospective issues . . . and our rejection of many proposals of new financing presented to us."

In addition to his caution about new commitments, Dillon used his closed-end investment trusts, US&IS and US&FS, to buy unsold securities from his earlier underwritings. Dillon Read partner Henry Riter suggested on October 31 that "the retail sales department be authorized to make definitely reassuring statements" regarding US&IS and US&FS, when their share values declined during the market turmoil. Yet Dillon's investment trusts did better than most by surviving and outperforming the popular averages.

Dillon ordered Paul Nitze to sell all the Alcoa shares in the US&FS portfolio as fast as possible in the falling market. But, Nitze asked, wouldn't such sales drive the stock down further? Dillon waved aside Nitze's concern.

Dillon Read was never in serious trouble in late 1929, with $78.1 million in assets and $28.5 million in cash on its balance sheet. On its 1929 corporate income tax return, the firm reported a profit of $4.2 million, and a net loss of only $2,818.

By the early 1930s, as Dillon had forecast, the nation was in the depths of the Great Depression. Dillon Read held fewer meetings and pursued fewer proposed deals. Bonds performed better than stocks for about two years, until a major wave of defaults began. In 1931, twelve of Dillon Read's domestic issues and five of the firm's Bolivian and Brazilian issues were in default. By 1932, eleven of Dillon Read's domestic issues and six of its foreign issues followed suit.

Dillon's approach, including closing the Pittsburgh retail branch in November 1930 and cutting back on inessential staff, allowed the firm to survive. The firm's assets still dropped from $78.1 million three years earlier to $20.3 million in 1932.

Speaking at the American Club in Paris on May 13, 1932, Clarence Dillon sounded a note of optimism, emphasizing that economic declines are always cyclical.

"Today creditors everywhere want to be paid, and when paid that capital lies idle," he said. "But when confidence returns creditors will not want to be paid, paradoxical as that may sound, for they no longer want to hoard their capital but will want to reinvest it, and much of what today is frozen credit will again become gilt-edged."

In the wake of the Crash of 1929, most Americans blamed the Great Depression on Wall Street. Investors wanted answers from the New York banking titans who'd amassed riches. Dillon Read received its share of adverse publicity, singled out for its unethical methods in John T. Flynn's *Investment Trusts Gone Wrong!* (1930) and *Graft in Business* (1931). "The average politician," Flynn wrote, "is the merest amateur in the gentle art of graft compared with his brother in the field of business."

The large number of foreign defaults in 1931, including Bolivia, Peru, Chile, and Brazil, spurred the Senate Finance Committee to hold investigative hearings from December 1931 to February 1932, led by a California Progressive reformer, Senator Hiram Johnson.

Johnson, a prominent Republican who broke with President Hoover to support Franklin Roosevelt in the 1932 presidential election, believed that the big bankers on Wall Street had engaged in "massive fraud." Johnson claimed that New York bankers either "knew or should have known" that the foreign securities they'd been marketing to Main Street "were worthless and that they were bound to default."

The Wall Streeters who had to testify before the committee were of two distinct types, observed one financial reporter: "bankers of the old school, who spoke slowly, with a German accent," such as Otto Kahn, "or the crisp, younger, self-assured" and less tradition-bound men, such as Clarence Dillon.

The American public, more concerned with rampant unemployment and pocketbook issues, initially paid little attention to these hearings on the sales of foreign bonds—until one morning when Senator Johnson's committee dropped a bombshell big enough to make front-page headlines in *The New York Times.*

$415,000 TO A. LEGUIA AS AGENT FOR LOANS

J. & W. SELIGMAN & CO. PARTNERS
TELL SENATE INQUIRY ABOUT DEALINGS IN PERU

"The Senate Finance Committee was told today that $415,000 in commissions was paid to Juan Leguia, son of Augusto Leguia, former President of Peru for acting as agent in three loans to Peru totaling $100,000,000," the *Times* reported.

Frederick Strauss and Henry C. Breck, both partners at J.& W. Seligman, testified on Friday, January 8, 1932, about their now-defaulted bond issuing and their relationship with the now-deposed president of Peru.

Senator Johnson: Do you know how much the son of the president received?

Mr. Strauss: About $415,000.

Senator Johnson: What was the name, please, of the president of Peru and his son at that time?

Mr. Strauss: The president was Augusto Leguia.

Senator Johnson: And his son's name, if you recall?

Mr. Strauss: Juan Leguia.

Senator Johnson: Are you aware of the fact that the president of the Republic and his son are being prosecuted upon this very transaction?

Mr. Strauss: Yes, among others, I believe.

Senator Johnson: And are you aware of the fact that there has been any decision of the courts of Peru in respect to any of their activities in regard to these loans?

Mr. Strauss: A revolutionary tribunal has given judgment against the president and against his son.

Senator Johnson: Against the president *and* against his son?

Mr. Strauss: Yes. I am going to ask, if I may, to have my partner, who is more familiar with it, answer the question. I will adopt his answers.

Senator Johnson: I shall be very glad to have anybody answer concerning this transaction; and if you will do so, go ahead, sir.

Mr. Breck: The tribunal gave judgment against the president and his son for a great variety of acts of so-called "illegal enrichment" and found a very large—

Senator Johnson: You say "illegal enrichment." They called it bribery?

Mr. Breck: I do not know, sir.

Senator Johnson: "Illegal enrichment" will do.

Called to testify on January 6, 1932, Clarence Dillon read a carefully composed statement, in a calm and measured tone, expressing that the US had gone from a debtor to a creditor nation. Senator Johnson demanded to know why the firms' South American bonds were in default and whether Dillon, Read & Co. had ever bribed an official.

Senator Johnson: Do you recall, in conjunction with the Bolivian loan, that the minister of finance got into any difficulties?

Mr. Dillon: No, sir.

Senator Johnson: You do not know that he was accused of having accepted a bribe of $40,000 in respect to that governmental loan?

Mr. Dillon: No, sir.

Senator Johnson: You have no knowledge on that subject at all?

Mr. Dillon: No.

Senator Johnson: Do you recall making a loan to Milan, Italy?

Mr. Dillon: Yes. We did make a loan to Milan, Italy, in 1927.

Senator Johnson: What was the amount of that loan, please?

Mr. Dillon: $30,000,000. Our profit, as you call it, that is, our gross receipt, was $78,000.

Senator Johnson: Do you recall whether or not there were any court proceedings in Cremona with respect to that particular loan?

Mr. Dillon: My associate says there were.

Senator Johnson: Do you remember—if you do not recall it is not necessary for you to state—as to whether or not any particular official was charged in regard to that loan, with having received some portion of it, or having received some money in respect to it?

Mr. Dillon: I do not know.

Mr. Hayward: I am not sworn, Senator. Perhaps I had better not say anything.

Senator Johnson: You may state it, if you know.

Mr. Hayward: I understand he was so charged, and that he was exonerated. We made no payment, of course. We had nothing to do with it.

Exonerated after being charged? Hayward's testimony, if truthful, still smacked of legal parsing covering up something crooked.

Neither Senator Johnson, nor any other member of the committee, broached one issue while they had Clarence Dillon under oath. This was the still not publicly known story of how Princeton University's esteemed economics professor Edwin Kemmerer could simultaneously be paid by the US State Department, by various local and national governments in South America, *and* by Dillon, Read & Co. to act as the all-knowing "Money Doctor."

Perhaps that wasn't bribery—perhaps it wasn't even graft—but it certainly seemed to be a conflict of interest, didn't it?

Hadn't Professor Kemmerer's paid "expertise" helped Dillon, Read & Co. sell millions of these now-defaulted bonds to Main Street?

With so many similar questions still unasked, the Johnson hearings sparked public demands for a much broader investigation.

The Republican-controlled Senate had directed its Banking and Currency Committee to conduct a wide-ranging probe of Wall Street financial dealings in reaction to the nation's economic woes. But the proceedings got off to a rocky start in April 1932; Senate Democrats complained of a whitewash of Wall Street. Two chief counsels in succession were fired for ineffectiveness; a third resigned because he wasn't granted broader investigative authority by the committee.

Following Franklin Roosevelt's sweeping victory in the 1932 presidential elections, the committee's outgoing Republican chairman, Senator Norbeck, appointed a fifty-one-year-old New York City prosecutor named Ferdinand Pecora as chief counsel. Pecora had a reputation as being the most brilliant cross-examiner in New York.

Financial journalist John T. Flynn, who joined Pecora's investigative staff in August 1933, noted the irony that Wall Street millionaires, such as Richard Whitney, Jack Morgan, and Charles

Mitchell, had to justify their practices to an immigrant whose salary was less than $250 a month.

The son of a cobbler, Pecora was born in Sicily, and emigrated to the United States with his parents at the age of four. He'd been raised with six siblings in a cold-water flat in Chelsea. A dedicated student who had considered entering the Episcopalian ministry, Pecora had to drop out of college after his father suffered an industrial accident. The tenacious Pecora had clerked at a law firm across from the fabled J.P. Morgan & Co. bank on Wall Street. He had studied at night and graduated from New York Law School.

In the 1920s, Ferdinand Pecora had served as a New York assistant district attorney, establishing a reputation by prosecuting "bucket shops," shady brokerages often tied to organized crime figures like Arnold Rothstein.

Initially, Pecora had been an ardent Progressive Republican, supporting Theodore Roosevelt in the 1912 election. He later became a Wilsonian Democrat, sharing Supreme Court Justice Brandeis's view of the negative effects of concentrated economic power. In 1929, Pecora had failed to win the Democratic nomination for district attorney of New York. Pecora's desire for elective office was well-known and he hoped to use the hearings as a springboard for his political aspirations.

Street-tough, intellectually formidable, populist by nature, and as diligent as he was decorous, Ferdinand Pecora struck terror into the Wall Street tycoons when he appeared as the new chief counsel to the Senate Banking and Currency Committee in January 1933. It was as if Robespierre had been reincarnated in Washington, DC, with a team of lawyers.

Tall, with a thick head of wavy dark brown hair, the pinstripe-suited Pecora knew the value of publicity. He also had a prodigious memory, coupled with a remarkable ability to understand the most arcane aspects of financial transactions.

"I looked with astonishment at this man who, through the intricate mazes of banking, syndicates, market deals, chicanery of all sorts, and in a field new to him, never forgot a name, never made an error in a figure, and never lost his temper," John Flynn wrote.

Pecora collected massive amounts of detailed information prior to asking a question. Pecora also possessed a stage performer's sense of timing. He often brandished his cigar for dramatic effect during cross-examinations; he had a technique of asking seemingly mundane questions that drew his targets into his traps.

By the end of 1932, one-quarter of American workers were unemployed. Industrial production had dropped by half since the summer of 1929. Over 80% of the value of equity securities had been erased by the stock market crash. Banks were failing at a rapid rate.

When Franklin Roosevelt took office in March 1933, the administration conveyed to Pecora that if the public could be convinced that "the big violators" of banking laws were going "to be punished," it would be "helpful in restoring confidence."

Pecora set the goal of lifting "the veil on the clubby, secretive world of banking, a world to which he believed no one—government, investors, press—had adequate access."

The 1933 hearings, under the new Democratic chairman, Duncan Fletcher of Florida, began in a small room in the Senate with little fanfare. Once it became clear that Pecora was serious and that the investigation would be worthy of press attention, the hearings were moved to the Senate Caucus Room, which had rows of seats for the public and for the press, armed with cameras and flashbulbs. The show that followed would be theatrical, and it would play out for month after month with ever more national attention.

In June 1933, Pecora's team subpoenaed Dillon, Read & Co. for documents. Tens of thousands of papers belonging to Clarence Dillon's firm were photostatted by Pecora's assistants, indexed, and loaded into two large vans, each with a security guard, and driven back to Washington, DC.

The firm was cooperating with the prosecutors. The partners from Dillon Read were scheduled to appear before the committee in early October 1933 to be followed by Albert Wiggin of Chase National Bank, among other financial heavyweights, until the hearings ended in May 1934. By the summer of 1933, a number of abuses had been revealed through Pecora's skillful probing.

By June 1933, Ferdinand Pecora was on the cover of *Time* magazine, at a Senate table chomping on his cigar. Pecora seems to have personally introduced the term "banksters" to describe the financial "gangsters" who had jeopardized the country's economy. Although bankers and financiers argued that the Pecora Committee's dramatic approach would undermine trust in the US banking system, Senator Burton Wheeler of Montana said, "The best way to restore confidence in our banks is to take these crooked presidents out of the banks and treat them the same as we treated Al Capone."

Pecora had begun the hearings in February 1933 by questioning Samuel Insull, a utilities magnate, Charles E. Mitchell of National City Bank, and Richard Whitney of the New York Stock Exchange, followed by Wall Street leaders like J.P. Morgan & Co. in May and early June. He continued the hearings in late June with Kuhn, Loeb & Co.

Pecora's careful selection of early targets, such as the reckless "Sunshine Charley" Mitchell of National City Bank—later renamed Citibank—had brought national attention to the hearings. Senator Carter Glass, a former Secretary of the Treasury under President Woodrow Wilson, stated in November 1929 that "Mitchell more than any fifty men is responsible for this stock crash."

In critic Edmund Wilson's assessment, Mitchell had been "the banker of bankers, the salesman of salesmen, the genius of the New Economic Era . . ." Mitchell had sat "like an emperor . . . dynamic, optimistic and insolent, sending out salesmen in all directions as he preached to them, bullied them, bribed them."

The Amherst-educated son of a Massachusetts mayor, Mitchell had initiated an aggressive sales strategy at National City Company. A private investment affiliate of National City Bank, this company had been created to circumvent the prohibition on commercial banks selling securities. As president of both entities, Mitchell had dangerously intermingled the activities of National City Bank and National City Company. He had facilitated massive securities sales by providing bank loans to investors who counted on rising stock prices to cover their debts. Mitchell had trained his salesmen to hunt for neophytes—typical Americans with a bit of extra money but no experience as investors. He also had searched for new securities to sell, ignoring the risks inherent in shaky South American bonds.

Mitchell had rapidly expanded National City Bank and National City Company into the largest such American institutions, with branches in over twenty nations.

In the committee hearings, Pecora dramatically cornered the arrogant Mitchell who finally admitted that he had used National City Bank's securities affiliate to clear its books of over $100 million of questionable loans to Peru, Brazil, and Chile. Mitchell had dumped the bad investments on an unsuspecting public in the form of bond offerings. He had also "bulled" stock to manipulate the price of his company's large holdings of Anaconda Copper. Mitchell's real undoing was the shocking revelation during the hearings that he had generated a fictitious tax loss by secretly selling 18,300 shares of National City Bank stock to his wife, thus avoiding paying taxes in 1929.

Following these disclosures, Mitchell had to resign from all of his positions. Days later, the US Attorney for New York City launched an investigation into Mitchell's tax evasion. The banker had received bonuses of more than $1 million annually during the last three years of the stock market boom.

Mitchell appeared indomitable when he had first arrived in the Senate committee's hearing room "flanked by a retinue of senior associates." However, after his testimony, Mitchell became a shell of his former self. He was seen "walking to Union Station alone, carrying his own grip, a discomfited and beaten man."

In Pecora's own words, the fall of "Sunshine Charley" marked the moment when "a whole era of American financial life passed away."

Albert H. Wiggin of Chase was another kingpin to crumble under Pecora's penetrating gaze. According to the front page of *The New York Times* on October 31, 1933:

"Albert H. Wiggin admitted before the Senate Banking and Currency Committee today that he began to 'sell short' in stock of the Chase National Bank a month before the market crash of 1929."

Even as Wiggin ran one of the nation's largest banks, he served as a director or trustee of fifty-nine corporations, some of which he himself quietly came to control or were controlled by Chase or its supposedly independent investment arm, the Chase Securities Corporation.

"Many of these corporations from which Mr. Wiggin received . . . helpful additions to his regular earnings," Pecora recalled, "received large loans from the Chase National Bank."

The Wiggin operation "fell somewhere between back-scratching and extortion," according to journalist Alan Brinkley's in-depth *Vanity Fair* story about Ferdinand Pecora. "One such company, Metpotan, which Wiggin controlled, announced a total profit of a mere $159,000 in the years between 1928 and 1932; in the same period, Wiggin took out profits from Metpotan totaling more than $10.4 million. He was frequently offered stock from customers of the bank at a reduced price, in return for unspecified considerations."

One of the biggest scandals revealed during the Pecora hearings was that Wiggin, having retired from Chase, was receiving a salary of $100,000 *annually for life* from the bank—more than $2.5 million in today's currency.

After a great hue and cry, *The New York Times* reported:

"Albert H. Wiggin today asked the Chase National Bank to discontinue his salary of $100,000 a year for life, voted previous to his retirement last January as chairman of its board. The bank complied."

Pecora wrote about Wiggin: "In the entire investigation, it is doubtful if there was another instance of a corporate executive who so thoroughly and successfully used his official and fiduciary position for private profit."

Today, Albert Wiggin would go to jail. Instead, he retired wealthy.

While the ruin of "Sunshine Charley" Mitchell and the humiliating exposure of Albert Wiggin would prove to be the hearings' high point in terms of Pecora's clout, when it came to pure theater, nothing topped the testimony of John Pierpont Morgan Jr., universally known as Jack.

The House of Morgan had "a fetish for secrecy"—so having its leader subpoenaed to testify before an angry nation was deemed an intolerable imposition. Jack Morgan's father, the legendary founder of J.P. Morgan & Co., had died soon after enduring the humiliation of testifying before the Pujo Committee, which had been investigating Wall Street control of the nation's wealth in 1912.

Jack Morgan dreaded the prospect of testifying. He was livid about Pecora's demand for several years of his bank's balance sheets. Jack Morgan privately called Pecora "a dirty little wop" and a second-rate "criminal lawyer."

Morgan fought in vain to keep the powerful institution's doors at 23 Wall Street closed to Pecora's investigators. And the only concession given to the House of Morgan was that investigators would have to leave their offices by 6:00 p.m., while elsewhere, including at Dillon Read, "they combed through files as late as midnight."

The *Richmond Times-Dispatch* now summed up Morgan as "the twentieth-century embodiment of Croesus, Lorenzo the Magnificent, Rothschild; the lordly Mr. Morgan, financier and patron of the arts; the unreachable Mr. Morgan, with his impregnable castle at Broad and Wall Streets and his private army of armed guards; the austere Mr. Morgan, to whose presence only the mighty are admitted." The reporter noted gleefully that Morgan was now "in a committee room and upon his bare brow [rested] the gaze of the 'peepul.'"

"I state without hesitation," Morgan said at the conclusion of his well-crafted opening statement, "that I consider the private banker a national asset and not a national danger."

Pecora fired back a single question.

"What is your business or profession?"

"Private banker," Morgan said.

The audience burst into laughter.

Senator Carter Glass of Virginia, who would become the cosponsor of the Glass-Steagall Act, rolled his eyes at the crowded

Senate Caucus Room. He complained that the once dignified setting seemed like "a circus, and the only things lacking now are peanuts and colored lemonade."

The senator's words sounded great to a press agent at Ringling Brothers' Circus. On the second day of Morgan's testimony, while the senators were in an executive session, the Ringling Brothers agent took advantage of their absence to garner some publicity.

He marched into the Caucus Room with a twenty-one-inch-tall performer named Lya Graf.

"Gangway!" the agent shouted. "The smallest lady in the world wants to meet the richest man in the world!"

In moments, the tiny circus performer was sitting on the tall banker's lap—while the pressmen shouted questions and dozens of flashbulbs popped.

"Where do you live?" Morgan asked.

"In a tent, sir."

Morgan played along with the stunt, smiling down at her.

"Why, I've got a grandson bigger than you."

When the senators returned to the hearings, they were outraged by the scene and asked members of the press to show restraint by not publishing any pictures. Only *The New York Times* complied with their request. The photo, "Morgan and the midget," gained fame in newspapers across the country.

Pecora's investigation unraveled a complex, interlocking system that Morgan had built over the years. Morgan held 126 directorships in 89 industrial corporations with total assets of $20 billion. The House of Morgan directly or indirectly controlled an estimated *one-fourth* of all corporate wealth in the US, representing "incomparably the greatest reach of power in private hands in our entire history."

Pecora concluded, "The problem raised by such an institution goes far beyond banking regulation in any narrow sense. It might be a formidable rival to the government itself."

Nevertheless, Pecora could not point to any specific illegal activities by the House of Morgan.

Jack Morgan's reputation, however, was permanently damaged: Pecora revealed that none of the twenty Morgan partners, including the boss, had paid income taxes in the last two years.

A preferential client list also emerged, including former president Calvin Coolidge, adding to the public perception that access to Wall Street's riches was limited to a select few. Two days after the disclosure of Morgan stock share prices for "lucky friends," the Senate passed the Glass-Steagall banking bill without a single dissenting vote. The Glass-Steagall Act would separate commercial and investment banks for the next sixty years. After Pecora's grilling, Jack Morgan "seemed less the awesome figure" of Wall Street and "more like a Main Street banker with his eye on the main chance."

On October 3, after a three-month delay for Congress's summer "recess," Clarence Dillon and several of his senior staff, including James Forrestal, Robert Hayward, and Robert Christie, began what would become a grueling, sometimes tense, but for the most part cordial, ten days before the Senate committee.

Dillon, his partners, and his legal counsel had meticulously prepared for the hearings. They had pored over earlier witnesses' testimony for clues as to possible questions. Former partner Ferdinand Eberstadt asked an old Princeton friend, journalist David Lawrence, what topics might be covered. Lawrence, co-founder of the White House Correspondents' Association, advised Clarence Dillon to rehearse by going through several harsh cross-examinations regarding profits and influence from directorships, investment trusts, and foreign loans.

To prepare for the spotlight, Dillon hired public relations expert Ivy Lee who had burnished John D. Rockefeller Sr.'s public image by advising him to hand out dimes to children. The Dillon Read staff formulated responses to potential queries, working under Lee and Robert Christie, who assumed that because of the Johnson hearings, Pecora would concentrate on the firm's foreign underwritings.

Members of the press anticipated a dramatic spectacle like previous showdowns. The *New York World Telegram* described Clarence Dillon as a "shrewd, brilliant man about whom legends have grown," and assumed that it would be painful for Dillon "to project his tall, lean figure and quizzical face under the spotlight of a Senate investigation."

The *New York Daily News* described "Manhattan's lean, black-eyed, soft-spoken Clarence Dillon, skilled juggler of millions in the Wall Street whoopee days before the crash," noting that "the tanned and healthy-looking Dillon" had handled "more money in the dizzy decade than did the late J. Pierpont Morgan at any similar time in his career."

In contrast to Jack Morgan's attempt to bar any investigation of private banks, Dillon's strategy was quite the opposite. Pecora opened the hearing by thanking Dillon personally and his firm generally, acknowledging that from the very outset Dillon Read had offered Pecora's staff "the fullest possible measure of cooperation, aid, and assistance that we have asked for in our investigation of various matters connected with their business. At no time has there been the slightest hindrance or obstacle placed in our path by their office; but on the contrary they have extended every courtesy and accommodation." Pecora said he was "very happy" to make this statement.

The Senate committee eventually focused on the Dillon Read investment trusts, US&FS and US&IS, for which Clarence Dillon had a prepared statement. Emphasizing the motive of benefiting the small investor in his formation of the trusts, he testified: "The thing that moved us most . . . was the fact that the small investor cannot get diversification." Dillon spoke agreeably about the importance of giving "more information to the investing public."

In response, Senator James Couzens, a Michigan Republican who'd accumulated $30 million from his investment in Ford Motor Company, homed in on the fact that Dillon Read had formed US&IS with the funds of US&FS to further augment their firm's profits, rather than those of the small investors. Couzens characterized their scheme as "reprehensible" and an example of "rotten ethics."

The public had contributed five times as much to US&FS as Dillon Read but had received only one-third of its common stock.

Clarence Dillon knew that he'd violated no existing laws; he was unfazed.

"We could have taken one hundred percent," he replied. "We could have taken *all* that profit. We could have bought all the common stock for $5,000,000."

Senator Alva Adams—making a sardonic reference to Lord Clive, who'd conquered much of eighteenth-century India—stared at Dillon.

"Do you remember what Lord Clive said? 'When I consider my opportunities, I marvel at my moderation.'"

Robert Christie was interrogated by Pecora the next day, and Pecora tried unsuccessfully to get him to characterize the investment trust as a "pool." Pecora clearly sensed that pursuing the US&FS deal could elicit newspaper publicity. He succeeded in achieving coverage when Christie admitted that Dillon Read partners had been able to purchase US&FS securities at 20 cents per share in 1924, with some selling their holdings at an average price of $56 per share in 1928–1929.

The Christian Science Monitor ran a scathingly critical editorial:

"The examination by a Senate Committee of Dillon Read,

the third private bank to disclose its operations to public gaze, yields an unpleasant story about the investment trusts, those mushroom growths of the boom period."

In those "years when the sky was the limit," the editorial concluded, "the financial columns teemed with feature stories on how John Doe of Squeedunk had multiplied several hundred times an original outlay of $100 in an investment trust. Unfortunately for John Doe, the profit was all on paper. In the tale that unfolded to the senatorial committee, most of the members of the firm cashed in on their winnings. They not only got rich, but they got out."

By October 6, other compelling stories had eclipsed the Dillon Read testimony. Pecora had been trying for weeks to subpoena Howard Hopson of Associated Gas and Electric, America's largest utilities holding company. Hopson had finally agreed to testify. Pecora also boldly announced to the press that he would run for the office of New York district attorney in the 1933 election. With Pecora's attention apparently focused on other matters, he failed to probe as deeply as he might have done when Ernest Tracy, the president of both US&FS and US&IS, admitted to creating a loss to offset profits or disingenuously answered a question about whether the trusts had been used as "a dumping ground" for unsold securities. Tracy simply replied that when US&FS's board decided to buy certain securities, Dillon Read had offered them.

Robert Hayward was evasive under oath as he testified about Dillon Read's lucrative Brazilian and Bolivian bond deals, initially denying that he knew Clarence Dillon had a financial interest in Leonard Kennedy & Co.

Pecora again did not delve into these matters as thoroughly as he had done in other cases. Dillon Read had been fortunate in their late scheduling on the committee's calendar. For the public, the novelty of the hearings had worn off; interest in the daily press reports was waning and the number of spectators was dwindling. Many felt that what had emerged was only "a mass of dreary details" in comparison with the "fireworks and histrionics" that had marked the "Sunshine Charley" Mitchell and Jack Morgan testimonies.

On October 13, the firm's final day in the Senate Caucus Room, James Forrestal was unlucky to be the only Dillon Read partner singled out for Pecora's relentless investigation of personal, rather than business, finances.

Forrestal was forced to admit that he had avoided $95,000 in US income taxes by transferring securities to a Canadian holding company that he owned. Such transactions were legal and not uncommon for Wall Street, but the disclosure of economic deviousness during the climate of the Great Depression was embarrassing for Forrestal. Douglas Dillon noted that although Forrestal "seemed very strong . . . whenever he was criticized publicly, not privately, he sort of fell apart."

Following Pecora's grilling, Forrestal "thought what he had done was godawful, which it certainly wasn't," but "it upset him terribly, and he just sort of vanished from the scene for several days." No one could find him. Forrestal's friend, Eliot Janeway, felt he had experienced "a sort of temporary breakdown."

Despite the revelation of Dillon Read's incredible profits and Forrestal's humiliation, no investment banker would come out of the hearings as unscathed as Clarence Dillon.

Dillon had seemed unperturbed by the questions and benignly fed Pecora much of what he wanted to hear from a financier who offered a historical perspective.

While other issues dominated the media, newspaper coverage of Dillon Read's testimony on South American underwritings—such as the October 13, 1933, *New York Times* article, "Dillon

Group Made 6 Million on Loans; Brazilian and Bolivian Bonds Now in Default"—helped to solidify the perception that the firm had been exploitative in South America. This coverage later stimulated some antisemitic responses, such as the book *Brazil: Colony of Bankers* (1936), by South American fascist writer Gustavo Barroso.

"Sunshine Charley" Mitchell was the only witness in the Pecora investigation found guilty of violations of the law.

In an ironic twist, Richard Whitney, the patrician president of the New York Stock Exchange who led the public fight against Congress's efforts at regulation throughout the period leading up to the passage of the Securities Exchange Act, would be convicted of embezzlement in 1938 by New York District Attorney Thomas E. Dewey.

According to *The Nation* magazine: "Wall Street could not have been more embarrassed if J.P. Morgan had been caught helping himself from the collection plate at the Cathedral of St. John the Divine." Whitney, seeking clemency, admitted to embezzling funds from the Exchange, from his firm, from the New York Yacht Club, and even from his father-in-law. Six thousand people turned out to watch the handcuffed Whitney begin his journey at Grand Central Station, as he was transported upstate to Sing Sing prison.

Clarence Dillon gave Whitney's wife and children the use of one of the smaller houses at his Dunwalke estate. When Richard Whitney was released from prison several years later, he joined his family there. Paul Nitze believed that Dillon's action was primarily motivated by his social ambition in Far Hills rather than by friendship with the now-disgraced Whitney. Also, Anne Dillon was a close friend of Richard's wife, Gertrude.

The vicissitudes of the Great Depression and the new atmosphere of governmental regulatory reform on Wall Street led to the end of an era for Dillon Read. By 1930, longtime partner

William Read Jr. withdrew from the firm. On January 1, 1931, his brother Duncan, the last representative of the Read family, retired. In November 1933, partner Henry Riter departed to form Riter & Co., taking over Dillon Read's retail offices across the country. Clarence Dillon loaned $100,000 to Riter to assist with the organization of his new company, as he was no longer interested in having Dillon Read function as a distributor of securities.

In quick succession other key members of Dillon Read retired: Edward J. Bermingham in 1933, William Charnley in 1934, and Bill Phillips in 1935. Robert Christie, who helped with the formulation of the code of fair competition for investment bankers required by the National Recovery Administration in 1934, suffered a heart attack and died at the age of forty. President Franklin Roosevelt and other Washington, DC, officials sent condolences to Christie's widow. Robert Hayward died within two months of Christie in 1934. Leonard Kennedy died from lobar pneumonia at age fifty in 1936.

With the sense that Wall Street's days of independence were over, Clarence Dillon avoided anything that might invite even the remotest chance of renewed government investigation. Always meticulous in his preparations, he became even more focused on following regulations to the letter.

After the Crash, Dillon Read diminished its public profile, stopping all advertisements except for the announcements listing them as underwriters of new securities issues.

Only fifty-two years old in 1934, Dillon was losing much of his taste for public day-to-day management of the firm. Yet he could not loosen his controlling grip; he maintained an unyielding authority over its operations. In the mid-1930s, Clarence

Dillon ran US&FS from a suite at 40 Wall Street, across the street from the Dillon Read offices.

James Forrestal nominally took over Dillon Read's management, but he sent a memo to Dillon summarizing each day's activities and talked with him regularly by telephone. Dillon Read underwritings finally began to increase in 1935, but the firm was more conservative and reluctant to be associated with any bank that was not highly respected.

When Dillon named Forrestal as the president of Dillon Read in 1938, the firm's outward image had changed from "something of a pirate ship roaming the market for booty" at the start of the roaring twenties to the quintessential "establishment investment bank" by the late 1930s.

Both Dillon and Forrestal recognized that restoring public confidence was necessary for Wall Street to survive. They supported the establishment of the Securities and Exchange Commission if it could achieve that goal. A Democrat, Forrestal sympathized with the Roosevelt administration's reform efforts, but he only wanted to operate behind the scenes, covertly raising money to help with the passage of the 1935 Public Utility Holding Company Act. The act entailed the breakup of the utilities empires, but it also meant more refinancing business for investment banks.

The most lasting consequences of the Pecora hearings were the new regulatory laws and their enforcement bodies. Congress passed the Securities Act of 1933, the Glass-Steagall Banking Act of 1933, and the Securities Exchange Act of 1934.

In 1939, Pecora wrote: "Forgotten, perhaps, by some are the shattering revelations of the Senate Committee's investigation; forgotten the practices and ethics that the Street followed and defended when its own sway was undisputed in those good old days. After five short years, we may now need to be reminded what

Wall Street was like before Uncle Sam stationed a policeman at its corner, lest, in time to come, some attempt is made to abolish that post."

Much as the roaring twenties marked the birth of modern Wall Street, the Pecora hearings marked the beginning of government regulation of financial practices. What had been unethical but legal now became illegal.

After the creation of the SEC, on June 30, 1934, President Roosevelt appointed its first chairman: Joseph P. Kennedy.

Kennedy's personality—forceful, confident, but always with an easy smile—served him well in the position. Journalists took to the optimistic SEC chairman, and favorable coverage helped spread the message that market regulation was a good thing for the country.

In a July 1934 profile, *The New York Times* headline gushed: "Kennedy Started As Candy Vendor: Worked Way Through Harvard and Graduated into State Banking Post," stressing the self-made Boston millionaire's charm, good looks and affability:

"Joseph P. Kennedy, 45, sandy-haired, freckled, usually smiling New York financier, who has just been named chairman of the Federal Commission for Regulating of Stock Exchanges, first entered the business world in Boston [as] a candy vendor on an excursion boat."

Absent from any news story about Joseph Kennedy was a deep analysis of his role as an investment banker at Hayden, Stone & Co. His expertise in the unregulated market of the roaring twenties had been insider trading and stock price manipulation. Kennedy's personal specialty was to buy a stock at ever increasing prices to drive up the trading price; he'd then dump the shares on the unsuspecting public.

When Kennedy engaged in such stock manipulation, it wasn't

illegal. Now it's the crime of Federal Securities Fraud under 18 U.S.C. § 1348. Known as a "pump and dump" scheme, widely exposed in the 1990s as many "boiler room" operations—often fronts for Mafia figures—sprang up in New York with rooms full of young broker-fraudsters duping average investors with aggressive cold calls.

The choice of Joe Kennedy to head the SEC was, to say the least, controversial. Ferdinand Pecora, for one, had expected to get the appointment, while many assumed that legal expert James M. Landis, who'd clerked under Supreme Court Justice Louis Brandeis, was the best-suited man. Those who remembered Joe Kennedy's days at Hayden, Stone & Co. saw the appointment as almost ludicrous.

Jerome Frank, the pioneering legal philosopher, said that the appointment of Kennedy to run the SEC was like "setting a wolf to guard a flock of sheep."

Franklin Roosevelt, of course, was nobody's fool. He appointed Joe Kennedy to be the first director of the SEC for good reason.

Kennedy was a man who knew all Wall Street's tricks.

The pinnacle of Clarence Dillon's social success in the United States was his son's ascension into Washington's highest echelons of power. Clarence himself had, of course, briefly served in the capital under Bernard Baruch during the First World War but had come to despise Washington bureaucracy.

To his great disappointment Clarence realized that his son Douglas wasn't suited for investment banking—despite his repeated efforts to push him into the firm. However, the younger Dillon did excel in politics, diplomacy, and especially foreign and fiscal policy.

After writing foreign policy speeches and being active on Republican county and state committees, President Eisenhower appointed Douglas Dillon ambassador to France on February 27, 1953.

Fluent in the language and familiar with French culture, he performed his duties with aplomb. When Douglas completed his diplomatic post in 1957, his domineering father still opposed his decision to continue his career in government—he'd been appointed by Eisenhower to be Under Secretary of State for Economic Affairs.

Clarence viewed such public work as less important than the private sector's "real work," and was still hoping his son would take the helm at Dillon, Read & Co.

When John F. Kennedy won the 1960 presidential election with a razor-thin victory over Richard Nixon, JFK was under pressure to show moderation and balance by his cabinet selections and alleviate conservatives' fears of a perhaps too-far left-wing inclination.

What better way to do so than for the first Democrat elected to the presidency since Harry Truman to choose a well-known Republican for one of the most powerful cabinet positions?

The appointment of the soft-spoken fifty-one-year-old made headlines on the front page of *The New York Times* on December 17, 1960:

> DILLON APPOINTED SECRETARY OF THE TREASURY
>
> WASHINGTON, Dec. 16—President-elect John F. Kennedy designated a Republican, Douglas Dillon, as his Secretary of the Treasury today and named his brother, Robert F. Kennedy, as Attorney General.
>
> . . . While the new Treasury Secretary was a heavy contributor to the Nixon campaign this year, Senator Kennedy said he had sought in the three top Cabinet positions—State, Defense and Treasury—"The best people available in the United States regardless of their party."

The circle was now complete. Two outsiders, sons of immigrants from Irish Catholic and Polish-Jewish ancestry, had cemented their places in the American aristocracy—albeit through their sons.

Two men of questionable ethics and morality who knew each other well in the frenzy of roaring twenties Wall Street and had both prospered as investors in the nascent era of Hollywood, had watched as their sons brought "luster" to their families' names.

Joseph Kennedy's son, Jack, worked closely with Clarence Dillon's son, Douglas, to deftly steer the economy; after JFK's assassination in 1963, Dillon continued to lead the country's fiscal policy under President Johnson.

By many assessments Douglas Dillon was one of the finest secretaries of the treasury to ever serve this nation.

Epilogue

FRANKLIN ROOSEVELT AND Clarence Dillon graduated from Harvard within two years of each other. Both belonged to the Institute of 1770 after not being able to join the prestigious Porcellian Club. There's no record of them having been friends in Cambridge, though they surely were acquainted.

A dyed-in-the-wool Republican, Dillon voted for Calvin Coolidge in 1924 and Herbert Hoover in 1928 and in 1932. But in 1936, Dillon crossed party lines to support Franklin Roosevelt, contributing to his reelection campaign. Dillon was drawn to Roosevelt's foreign success just as he would later support Eisenhower and then Kennedy.

Free from the stress of the Pecora Hearings, by the mid-1930s, Dillon began visiting frequently with Roosevelt. By 1936 they'd formed a strong relationship. Leading up to the war, they exchanged letters, met at official and unofficial White House meetings, and lunched at Hyde Park. Dillon served as an unofficial economic advisor on European and Japanese matters. Both shared internationalist views, a love for European culture, an appreciation for the finer things, and pragmatic negotiation skills.

After one visit to the White House, Dillon cagily told the press it was just "a meeting between two old friends."

On September 30, 1936, in a letter labeled CONFIDENTIAL, Roosevelt wrote: "Dear Clarence—I wonder if you would be willing to write out for me, during the next month, your ideas or suggestions for changes in the tax laws." Roosevelt knew that a Wall Street wizard like Dillon would understand all the loopholes and borderline legal tax tricks. He assured Dillon: "I would not, of course, use your name in any way but I should like to have some of your ideas for my personal assistance."

"Dear Franklin," Dillon wrote back, "I shall be delighted to undertake the work you have suggested and sincerely hope that my thoughts on the subject may be of service to you."

Dillon's expertise contributed to the Revenue Act of 1937, which revised tax laws and reduced tax evasion. Roosevelt knew how to return favors. Clarence and Anne received an invitation to a gala luncheon for Roosevelt's second inaugural.

The two men shared a deep appreciation for the fine arts. Roosevelt asked if he could use a famous painting in Dillon's art collection—*Washington as a Statesman* by Junius Brutus Stearns—in the design of the red-violet 3-cent stamp, issued on September 17, 1937, which marked the 150th anniversary of the signing of the Constitution.

After Neville Chamberlain's Munich Agreement with Hitler in 1938, Roosevelt leaned even more heavily on his friendship with Dillon. The banker, well-connected through his business and social ties in Europe, was one of the best-informed Americans on European affairs. He and Roosevelt realized that strengthening Britain and France was key to US defense if another world war erupted. In 1939, their collaboration increased to support these allies through discreet measures, including five official White House meetings.

Dillon recognized that isolationist sentiment limited US aid to France and Great Britain. His value to Roosevelt was as a behind-the-scenes confidant and intermediary. Joseph P. Kennedy, now the outspoken ambassador to Great Britain, was becoming a persistent headache for the president. Kennedy publicly stated that Britain had no chance of winning a war against Nazi Germany. He didn't hide his admiration for Hitler's totalitarian regime and shared the Führer's belief in a sinister worldwide Jewish cabal. Following Germany's invasion of Poland and Britain's declaration of war in September 1939, Kennedy remained defeatist, telling journalists that Britain was "finished as a world power" and that a German invasion of the UK was inevitable. In Washington, Roosevelt was enraged; he couldn't risk having his rogue ambassador in London mislead the British government.

The president cleverly circumvented Kennedy by asking Dillon to convey a private message to Britain's new prime minister, Winston Churchill, via the banker's friend, Lord Lothian, who was serving as the British ambassador in Washington.

Roosevelt had yet to get to know Churchill well; Dillon already did. Before meeting with Lord Lothian, Dillon arranged for the president to be ready to take a call from him. Dillon told Lord Lothian he believed Roosevelt was "fully committed to all-out help for the Allies." The British ambassador replied that he would like "to reassure London on that," but wondered if this was only Dillon's opinion.

Dillon then asked to make a phone call privately to the White House, knowing the British Embassy would tap his conversation with Roosevelt after Lord Lothian left the room. Although Dillon only told the president he wouldn't see him until the following week, the British understood clearly that the Wall Street financier enjoyed Roosevelt's confidence. The message indicating Churchill had Roosevelt's strong support was sent to London within an hour.

Dillon had been influential with Japanese industrialists since the 1920s. Yoshisuke Aikawa, founder of Nissan, saw him as a key American financier with ties to Roosevelt and hoped he could facilitate communication between Japan and the White House. Dillon Read was seen as more sympathetic to Japan than the House of Morgan. Dillon informed President Roosevelt about developments in Japan before Pearl Harbor.

In his business life Clarence Dillon was many things, but he was also undeniably a patriot. So were the men he hired and mentored in his firm. Dillon Read partners and associates contributed immensely to the war against the Axis powers. The most prominent was airman Billy Fiske. Son of partner William Fiske, at age sixteen Billy had been the youngest gold medalist at the 1928 Winter Olympics and won a second bobsledding gold in 1932 before attending Cambridge University. In September 1939 he was a young banker at Dillon Read's New York office. He wanted to immediately see combat and, since the United States was neutral, Fiske pretended to be Canadian when he volunteered for the RAF.

On July 12, 1940, Fiske became a member of No. 601 Squadron RAF, famously dubbed the "Millionaires' Squadron." On August 16, 1940, during the Battle of Britain, Fiske piloted a Hawker Hurricane and his squadron downed eight Stuka dive-bombers. But after only minutes in the air, a German gunner managed to hit Fiske's fuel tank. Fiske landed his badly damaged Hurricane and was fatally injured from burns—becoming the first American serviceman to die in WWII. Fiske earned high praise as "the best pilot I've ever known," memorialized by Churchill at St. Paul's Cathedral on America's Independence Day. A plaque was unveiled in the crypt of St. Paul's Cathedral, London. The inscription reads: "An American citizen who died that England might live."

Clarence Dillon later directed E.I. Treasure to close Dillon Read's London office and Seymour Weller to leave Paris; however, Weller stayed and joined the Resistance after marrying a French woman and becoming a citizen. He protected Château Haut-Brion from the Nazis by concealing its antiques and wine cellar after France's collapse.

In 1940, Clarence Dillon's thirty-one-year-old son briefly joined Forrestal in Washington to prepare a report on Navy Department procurements. In July 1941, President Roosevelt suggested in a memo to his aide that Douglas Dillon could assist Colonel William J. Donovan, who was creating the Office of Strategic Services (OSS), the precursor to the CIA. Unsatisfied with his OSS desk job, Douglas requested a release for navy active duty. He graduated first in his naval aviation training class and served as an assistant operations officer for the Seventh Fleet in the Pacific. Douglas rose to lieutenant commander, earning the Legion of Merit with Combat Device and the Air Medal before returning to Wall Street in 1946.

Another Dillon Read partner, William Draper, went on active duty in June 1940 after years in the Army Reserve following his distinguished World War I service. Draper was first assigned to the Army General Staff in Washington, working with Dillon Read associate Paul Nitze on creating the Selective Service Act. Nitze later earned the Legion of Merit as vice chairman of the Strategic Bombing Survey during the war. In 1945, Colonel Draper became a brigadier general, taking key roles in postwar Germany and Japan. Paul Nitze held influential government positions for decades, including the secretary of the navy and Deputy Secretary of Defense under President Johnson.

Clarence Dillon served his country as a civilian in Washington, DC, during the Second World War, much as he had in the First. He left his close friend, Charles McCain, as the "caretaker" of Dillon Read for the interim. Soon after Pearl Harbor, the fifty-nine-year-old Dillon was asked by Vice Admiral Andrews to be chairman of the National Committee of the Navy Relief Society. Dillon raised money for families of naval officers killed or seriously disabled in the war. He worked with Stanton Griffis, head of Paramount Pictures, who arranged a special train that transported popular movie stars across the country for fundraisers.

In 1941, he undertook the national chairmanship of a drive that raised more than $10 million (over $150 million in today's dollars) for the Navy Relief Society, for which he received a Presidential Certificate of Merit and a citation from the navy.

James Forrestal, meanwhile, had long been feeling stifled as Clarence Dillon's successor. Despite being the firm's titular president, he had little real power—from his home in Dunwalke, Dillon made all the important decisions. By 1940, now a multimillionaire, Forrestal could see a more promising future for himself in Washington. President Roosevelt was recruiting astute businessmen for war preparedness and economic mobilization. Hearing of Forrestal's organizational skills, he called Dillon in June 1940 to request Forrestal's service as an administrative assistant at the White House.

Forrestal brought Paul Nitze as his aide while keeping him on the Dillon Read payroll. By August 1940, Roosevelt appointed Forrestal under secretary of the navy. Forrestal discovered that his investment banking skills of analysis, problem-solving, and adaptation were especially effective in breaking up war production bottlenecks. He reached out to his former Dillon Read partner, Ferdinand Eberstadt. Eberstadt became vice chairman of the War Production Board.

By now—decades after the fiery end to their business relationship—Clarence Dillon and Eberstadt were cordial. Eberstadt wrote to Dillon in September 1942: "You did not overestimate the degree of non-organization—not disorganization—and confusion" in the government bureaucracy. Dillon responded,

"I want you to know how deeply grateful we all are for the job you are doing."

Forrestal, compulsively overworking himself, rarely accepted Dillon's frequent invitations to dinners or to his Maine summer retreat. He occasionally reached out to his former boss, such as in a December 1945 letter where Forrestal mentioned discussing with Vice President Henry Wallace how to revive business and trade.

In August 1947, Forrestal requested names from Dillon for potential candidates to fill key positions under the new bill unifying the armed services. Forrestal had asked Eberstadt to conduct a detailed study of the nation's postwar security needs, which became the basis for the National Security Act of 1947. Although a Democrat, Forrestal also met privately with Republican candidate Thomas E. Dewey, who was expected to win the 1948 presidential election, and agreed to continue as secretary of defense in his administration.

Weeks before the election, an exposé revealed Forrestal's meetings with Dewey. After Truman unexpectedly won the election, already troubled by rumors of Forrestal's fragile mental health, the president asked for his resignation on March 31, 1949. Forrestal was distraught, believing he had failed in his duty to the nation. Always prone to depression, he entered inpatient psychiatric treatment. He underwent extensive pharmacological and psychotherapeutic treatment for weeks and seemed to be on the road to recovery. But in the early hours of May 22, Forrestal's body, clad only in his pajama pants, was discovered on a third-floor roof. The jump from his window on the sixteenth floor had killed him.

Clarence Dillon's grandson, Philip Allen, once said that the famous banker had two primary goals in life: amassing wealth and gaining social acceptance. Dillon had devoted the 1920s to the former, and for the rest of his life he devoted all his energy to the latter. Dillon realized that the surest path to social acceptance lay in his development of luxurious homes in select enclaves, his cultivation of friendships with members of old-moneyed families, the education of his children at exclusive institutions, and his philanthropic endeavors.

Through his marriage to Anne, Clarence Dillon had already gained a listing in the Social Register. However, his lineage disqualified him from joining certain private social clubs, like the Knickerbocker Club of New York, where Wall Street financiers Richard Whitney and Winthrop Aldrich were members. Despite this, Dillon could socialize with the Winthrops, Aldriches, and Whitneys by building homes in Far Hills, New Jersey, and Dark Harbor, Maine—areas favored by the ruling class of the wealthy descendants of early English colonists in America.

When he built his estate in Far Hills in the late 1920s, Dillon paid attention to every construction detail. To connect further with the Anglo-American establishment, he used brick walls from an eighteenth-century Virginia home built by George Washington's cousin; these bricks had arrived in Colonial Virginia as ship ballast. Clarence and Anne collected early American and eighteenth-century British silver, furniture, and portraits for decoration. Dunwalke soon became filled with museum-quality paintings and antiques.

The Dunwalke mansion had seven master bedrooms with private bathrooms on the second floor and its grand staircase seemed to float in midair. Thirteen staff members worked in the main house: a butler, two footmen, a cook, two kitchen helpers, two chambermaids, a parlor maid, a laundress, Dillon's valet, his wife's maid, and a houseman. The footmen wore green-and-gold waistcoats under green tailcoats with buttons engraved with the initials C & A.

During meals, one footman stood attentively behind Clarence's chair and the second behind Anne's. The outside staff included chauffeurs, stable boys, gardeners, a kennel man, and a tennis professional who dutifully instructed Douglas and Dorothy.

Far Hills is unlike any other residential community in the United States. This exclusive enclave of mostly Republican Episcopalian multimillionaires first developed in the nineteenth century. A few wealthy families from New York City had bought large tracts of land for weekend country estates. In an area reminiscent of the English countryside, these New Jersey gentlemen farmers had then engaged in the aristocratic sport of foxhunting. They were not landed gentry with centuries of farming history. Many were first-generation creators of wealth through industrial ventures and financial institutions. Other families of long-established social prominence, such as the Whitneys, soon joined them. The Essex Fox Hounds Club remains as a core community institution.

As an Essex Fox Hounds member, Dillon later hosted hunt breakfasts at Dunwalke. In 1923, he invested in several thoroughbred steeplechasers with Bayard Tuckerman Jr., a Harvard-educated horse racing promoter, and Marshall Field III, heir to the Marshall Field department store fortune. A private road provided access to the local train station, where residents would travel in an exclusive parlor car to Manhattan. There Dillon resided at his fully staffed townhouse mansion.

Clarence Dillon first attended the Metropolitan Opera with his employer, William A. Read. At that time, Jews were not eligible to own opera boxes at the Met, although they could later lease them. Owning a box was the pinnacle of social success. Even younger members of established box-holding families had to wait years for a place in the Diamond Horseshoe, the first circle of boxes for wealthy patrons like the Astors and Vanderbilts. During the 1920s, Dillon rented a box for several opera seasons. When in New York, Anne attended the opera every Monday evening. Dillon was elected to the Metropolitan Opera board of directors in 1931 and helped with the company's financial turnaround. His sixteen years of service on the board further cemented his status in New York. By 1950, Mr. and Mrs. Clarence Dillon were on an "Elite 400" list compiled by Igor Cassini who wrote the famed *Cholly Knickerbocker* society gossip column for the Hearst newspaper chain.

Dillon had achieved his goals in the United States, but he wanted the respect and admiration of Europe's nobility and old money. The purchase and careful restoration of the historic Château Haut-Brion and its vineyards in 1935 was part of his entry into privileged society. When Dillon bought the famous twenty-acre property near Bordeaux for $160,000, it was in disarray and unprofitable. The estate was centuries old; Thomas Jefferson had visited in 1787 and shipped cases of wine home to Monticello. Dillon took pleasure in renovating the château and vineyards.

In 1938, Dillon was designated a commander of the Legion of Honor as a foreigner who'd served France with distinction in the wine trade. During World War II, Clarence Dillon offered Château Haut-Brion to the French government for use as a hospital. When the Nazis occupied France, the Luftwaffe used it as a rest home for pilots. Many German officers shared Dillon's taste for the wines. The finest vintages, however, were hidden behind rubbish. A bold French woman on staff complained about the pilots taking fruit, resulting in German guards being posted with bayonets to defend the trees.

In 1957, Clarence Dillon was listed as one of the fifty wealthiest Americans by *Forbes* with assets estimated at between $150 million to $200 million (between $1.71 billion and $2.2 billion today). The previous year, he'd built another spectacular vacation retreat, High Rock, on the north coast of Jamaica. The airy villa sat at the summit of Round Hill, a peninsula thirty minutes from Montego Bay. Anne's health began to decline in the 1950s and Dillon built High Rock so that she wouldn't have to travel to Europe for their seasonal vacations.

At High Rock, the Dillons took pleasure in hosting many prominent guests; Secretary of State John Foster Dulles arrived on one of President Eisenhower's Lockheed Constellation planes for a much-needed rest.*

After Anne suffered a heart attack in 1957, Dillon hired nurses to care for her around the clock and kept a doctor on call. When Anne died in 1961, Dillon created a memorial for her at Dark Harbor, placing a granite stone with an epigraph from John Hall Wheelock's poem in their private garden:

On the shores of Gilkey's harbor
In her garden by the sea
There amidst the flowers she loves
She comes again to me

The second stanza ends with the poignant lines:

And lays her precious hand in mine
There ever to abide.

In Anne's honor, Dillon funded the Patriot Memorial Chapel at the Washington Cathedral, and the Conference Hall and Tapestry for the Assembly Hall of the World Council of Churches

---

* Decades after Dillon's death, High Rock was bought by designer Ralph Lauren, renovated, restored, and featured in *Architectural Digest* as one of the "ultraglamorous" vacation homes in the world.

in Geneva, Switzerland. After Anne's death, Dillon saw himself more than ever as the patriarch of a future dynasty. To make that happen, he had needed his children to join the ranks of America's highest social strata, to become true "Episcocrats." So, he had enrolled both in private Episcopalian schools where they socialized with Biddles, Auchinclosses, Vanderbilts, Mellons, and other scions of powerful families. Dorothy followed the path of an upper-class young woman from Far Hills after attending the exclusive Miss Chapin's School for Girls in Manhattan, followed by the Foxcroft School in Virginia's horse country, before debuting at a glittering dance hosted by the Dillons at The Ritz-Carlton ballroom in New York City.

Clarence initially sent Douglas to a small New Jersey school that William A. Read's sons had attended. Douglas befriended two fellow students, John D. Rockefeller's grandsons, Laurance and John III. Later, Douglas graduated second in his class at Groton, a bastion of privilege whose alumni traditionally achieved top positions in government and finance. At Harvard, Douglas easily surpassed his father academically, graduating magna cum laude and joining one of the prestigious final clubs, the Spee. Douglas Dillon married a Boston debutante, a descendant of Oliver Ellsworth, a 1787 Constitutional Convention delegate and the third chief justice of the US Supreme Court. The society wedding was attended by Boston Brahmin families such as the Saltonstalls and the Welds.

And yet Dillon was only partly successful. Despite Douglas's impeccable establishment credentials, he nevertheless had great difficulty when he applied for membership in the exclusive Chevy Chase Club near Washington. The club had previously turned down Senator Barry Goldwater, based on his being half

Jewish. Goldwater quipped: "What if I agree to play only nine holes?" Even as the Secretary of the Treasury, Douglas was admitted only after he assured the club authorities that he was no more than 25% Jewish—and even then, it took years for the membership committee to agree with that exception to club policy. (It was a small fib: just like Goldwater, Douglas Dillon was in fact half Jewish.)

Clarence Dillon wanted his son to succeed him as head of Dillon Read. Douglas was far more diplomatic than his father, and much kinder to his associates. He shared, however, his father's disciplined nature. After Douglas's graduation from Harvard in 1931, Clarence Dillon purchased a seat on the New York Stock Exchange for him. At first, Douglas had mainly functioned as a liaison between his father working at the US&FS offices and Forrestal at the Dillon Read offices. But Douglas had chafed under his father's stern hand while working at Dillon Read in the 1930s. Eventually, Douglas played more important roles as a US&FS director and as a Dillon Read partner in the American Viscose deal in the spring of 1941.

Dillon was delighted when Douglas was appointed US Ambassador to France by President Eisenhower in 1953, but he didn't openly express his admiration to his son. Only after Douglas had served in the Democratic Kennedy and Johnson administrations as Secretary of the Treasury did Dillon revel in his son's accomplishments. In his draft autobiography Clarence copied out verbatim President Lyndon Johnson's 1965 letter of praise written to Douglas upon his resignation as Secretary of the Treasury. Then he copied out his own 1965 letter to his son, referring to Douglas's "magnificent career."

"You have added lustre [sic] to the family. It will someday be yours to carry on and see to it that the family shall endure; that your grandchildren and your grand-nephews and niece are brought up and trained so that in their turn they may add to the prestige and dignity of the family."

Even within his own firm, Clarence Dillon had been one of the most solitary men on Wall Street. He demonstrated his social skills through his brilliant ability to attract and mentor talent. He was charming and voluble, but few could say they truly *knew* him. Ever the poker player, he was never a man to let down his guard.

To keep his growing family nearby, Dillon built a Mott Schmidt–designed brick American Colonial home, known as Dunwalke East, for Douglas in 1936, and in the late 1950s, Dorothy and his granddaughter, Phyllis, added their homes in French Country style and American Colonial, respectively, to the acreage.

By the late 1950s, Clarence would see his two children in their nearby houses, his large staff, and his even larger flock of geese. It was too late in life to form close friendships.

When there were occasional visitors, Dillon's granddaughter, Phyllis, recalled, he enjoyed "making fools of them quietly just for his own amusement." During one luncheon at Dunwalke, "there was a fellow whom he encouraged to go on about photography without disclosing that he knew a lot himself." When another guest claimed to be expert at brandy, Dillon "brought out three bottles and three small glasses and had the fellow comment on the relative merits of each. The guests didn't know that my grandfather was pouring from only one bottle for all three glasses."

Dillon maintained a vigorously active lifestyle well into his late '80s and early '90s. He exercised with the same discipline he once applied to pursuing deals. He walked miles daily and lifted medicine balls to maintain his strength. Besides using the indoor pool at his Far Hills estate, Dillon also had a pool built at his

Dark Harbor retreat; he swam laps at both residences, moving a stone from one end of the pool to the other after each lap. He had regular medical examinations and kept his personal doctor on call for house visits.

Dillon was unique among his peers with this dedication to wellness. Few Wall Street moguls of his era looked after their physical condition. Few lived as long as Dillon.

On April 14, 1979, Clarence Dillon died peacefully at age ninety-six of natural causes in his Dunwalke home. He was laid to rest after a service at St. Luke's Episcopal Church in the local town, the chapel he'd built in honor of Anne. Family filled the first three pews.

Wall Street figures and neighbors from nearby estates were amongst the three hundred attending the service in the small stone church.

At the time of his death, Dillon's fortune was one of the largest in the United States. His assets increased to over $1.5 billion in value by 1979. He'd given much of his wealth away during his lifetime. Charitable by nature and no doubt having observed the reverence with which Jacob Schiff had been treated by New York's high society, Dillon became a devoted and well-known philanthropist. In 1930, when Douglas was a junior at Harvard, he informed his father that the fieldhouse had burned in a fire. Dillon pledged $500,000 to build the majestic neo-Georgian replacement designed by noted Boston architectural firm Coolidge, Shepley, Bulfinch & Abbott. To this day, Dillon Fieldhouse is the hub of Harvard athletics programs.

For decades Anne and Clarence Dillon contributed generously to the Metropolitan Museum of Art, the United Hospital Fund of New York, the New York Zoological Society, the Somerset Hills Visiting Nurse Association, the Italy America Society, and the State Charities Aid Association. Dillon's philanthropic donations also included a Princeton University library to house the diplomatic papers of John Foster Dulles and the Clarence Dillon Public Library in Bedminster, New Jersey. Princeton also has a square near Mathey College and the Forrestal Campus named in his honor. As the Dillon Fieldhouse at Harvard and numerous gifts to private schools attest, the word "anonymous" was not part of Dillon's philanthropic lexicon.

In his will, Dillon bequeathed 118 acres of his Far Hills estate and its main Georgian house to Princeton University, with the condition that Dunwalke be used as an academic center for twenty-five years. In 2001, Princeton University sold Dunwalke to John L. Thornton, former copresident of the Goldman Sachs Group, for $18 million. Dunwalke Preserve, 85 acres owned by Dillon's great-grandson, Andrew Allen, is now one of the nation's premier destinations for deer hunting and pheasant shooting.

Today, the name Clarence Dillon resounds most prominently not on Wall Street or Ivy League campuses but in the vineyards of France. Dillon, Read & Co. no longer exists as a bank, but the French company Clarence Dillon bought in 1935 to manage his beloved Haut-Brion wine estate is still thriving. Headquartered in the 8th arrondissement of Paris, Domaine Clarence Dillon produces vintages of the prestigious Bordeaux wine. Domaine Clarence Dillon is presided over by Dillon's great-grandson, Prince Robert de Luxembourg. The French company's board of directors includes several of Clarence Dillon's descendants. The family still treats the winery of Haut-Brion as a trust, albeit a profitable one, with its shop in Paris, La Cave du Château, offering bottles of its best Bordeaux vintages at thousand-Euro prices.

There is a darker side to Clarence Dillon's legacy. The prominent obituary which ran in *The New York Times* on April 15,

1979, lacks any mention of Dillon's well-publicized legal troubles or his congressional testimony about profiting handsomely by selling scandalously high-risk bonds to the American public. Yet, the repercussions of the darker side of Dillon's innovative mind reverberated in the financial world—even after his death.

As the *Times* obituary glowingly noted, "in the 1920s, Dillon, Read underwrote billions in securities, including the financing for a number of European and South American countries. For these services, Mr. Dillon was decorated by the French, Italian, Belgian and Polish Governments." Curiously absent is any mention that the bonds issued in South America were irresponsibly risky and defaulted with disastrous consequences both to the entire South American economy and for the consumers in the United States he'd duped.

History doesn't repeat itself, as Mark Twain once said, but it often rhymes. In 1970—with the amoral financial practices of Clarence Dillon and Professor Edwin Kemmerer seemingly forgotten—a new generation of bankers was laying the foundations in Latin America for the greatest economic crisis since the Depression. The loan spigots were opened for funding development projects and social programs throughout the region.

External debts by Latin American borrowers increased at an annual growth rate of about 20% for a decade. Brazil, the region's economic colossus, was once again in first place—increasing its foreign debt by twelve times to about $71 billion by 1980 and exceeded $100 billion within the next three years. The debt burden, rising interest rates, and the crash in oil prices soon led to widespread defaults by the South American nations with economic consequences globally.

Clarence Dillon achieved an American dream. He'd made a meteoric rise to fortune on Wall Street in the roaring twenties and fully assimilated—a Polish-Jewish immigrant's son—into the dominant Episcopalian establishment of the United States.

Clarence Dillon may have been a flawed man in some ways, but he was also an innovator who did much to create our modern financial world. Despite the autocratic way he ran his firm, Dillon had a keen eye for talent. He recruited, motivated, and trained a group of remarkable young men who made major impacts both in the financial sphere and in government service. Many of these men helped lay the foundations for postwar American security. That, indeed, may be Clarence Dillon's most enduring legacy.

Bibliography

Note:

Clarence Dillon was a very private and guarded man. He gave only a handful of interviews to the press in his life, primarily in the mid-1920s. When quoting from his recollections, primarily about his family life, my source was the unpublished draft autobiography written by Dillon. Although titled *The Story of Anne Douglass Dillon*, most of it revolved around Clarence. Throughout the early chapters, I have quoted and paraphrased many of Dillon's recollections of his early years in Milwaukee from this manuscript; I am grateful to the Dillon family for giving me access to this document. Some of the information from his later years came from former business associates and family members who did not wish to be acknowledged.

—William Loomis

Albion, Robert Greenhalgh, and Robert Howe Connery. *Forrestal and the Navy*. New York: Columbia University Press, 1962.

Allen, Hugh. *The House of Goodyear: A Story of Rubber and of Modern Business*. Cleveland: Corday & Gross, 1943.

Auletta, Ken. *Greed and Glory on Wall Street: The Fall of the House of Lehman*. New York: Random House, 1986.

Barroso, Gustavo. *Brasil: Colonia de Banqueiros; História dos Emprestimos de 1824 a 1934* [*Brazil: Colony of Bankers; History of the Loans from 1824 to 1934*]. 5th ed. Rio de Janeiro: Civilização Brasileira, 1936.

Baruch, Bernard M. *American Industry in the War: A Report of the War Industries Board (March 1921)*. New York: Prentice-Hall, 1941.

———. *Baruch: The Public Years*. New York: Holt, Rinehart & Winston, 1960.

Beauchamp, Cari. *Joseph P. Kennedy Presents: His Hollywood Years*. New York: Vintage Books, 2009.

Benson, Michael, and Craig Singer. *Moguls: The Lives and Times of Hollywood Film Pioneers Nicholas and Joseph Schenck*. New York: Kensington, 2024.

Berg, A. Scott. *Goldwyn: A Biography*. New York: Knopf, 1989.

Birmingham, Stephen. *Our Crowd: The Great Jewish Families of New York*. New York: Harper & Row, 1967.

Bispo, Antônio, Arthur Peluso, Barbara Gigante, Flávio Moraes, Mayara Tosta, and Wladimir Valladares. "From Icon to Dust: 100 Years Since the Destruction of Downtown Rio de Janeiro's Morro Do Castelo." *RioOnWatch*, February 12, 2023. https://rioonwatch.org/?p=73465.

Brady, Nicholas F. *A Way of Going*. Privately printed, 2008.

Bulmer-Thomas, Victor. *The Economic History of Latin America since Independence*. Cambridge Latin American Studies. Cambridge: Cambridge University Press, 1995.

Castles.nl. "Castellammare Castle." Castles.nl. Accessed April 9, 2025. https://www.castles.nl/castellammare-castle.

Chaplin, Charlie. *My Autobiography*. London: The Bodley Head, 1964.

Chernow, Ron. *The House of Morgan: An American Banking Dynasty and the Rise of Modern Finance*. New York: Atlantic Monthly Press, 1990.

Chisholm, Anne, and Michael Davie. *Lord Beaverbrook: A Life*. New York: Knopf, 1993.

Chrysler, Walter Percy, and Boyden Sparkes. *Life of an American Workman*. New York: Dodd, Mead & Company, 1937.

cityseeker.com. "Castello a Mare Archaeological Park, Palermo." cityseeker. Accessed April 9, 2025. https://cityseeker.com/palermo/652989-castello-a-mare-archaeological-park.

Cohen, Naomi Wiener. *Jacob H. Schiff: A Study in American Jewish Leadership*. Hanover, NH: Brandeis University Press, 1999.

Cuff, Robert D. *The War Industries Board: Business-Government Relations During World War I.* Baltimore: Johns Hopkins University Press, 1973.

Dawes, Charles Gates. *A Journal of Reparations.* London: Macmillan, 1939.

Dorwart, Jeffery M. *Eberstadt and Forrestal: A National Security Partnership, 1909–1949.* College Station, TX: Texas A&M University Press, 1991.

Douglas, Ann. *Terrible Honesty: Mongrel Manhattan* in the 1920s. New York: Farrar, Straus and Giroux, 1995.

Ferguson, Niall. *The House of Rothschild: The World's Banker: 1849–1999.* New York: Penguin Books, 2000.

Fitzgerald, F. Scott. *The Great Gatsby.* New York: Charles Scribner's Sons, 1925.

———. *This Side of Paradise.* New York: Charles Scribner's Sons, 1920.

Flynn, John T. *Graft in Business.* New York: Vanguard Press, 1931.

———. *Investment Trusts Gone Wrong!* New York: New Republic, 1930.

Forrestal, James. *The Forrestal Diaries.* Edited by Walter Millis and E. S. Duffield. New York: Viking Press, 1951.

Gabler, Neal. *An Empire of Their Own: How the Jews Invented Hollywood.* New York: Crown, 1988.

Galbraith, John Kenneth. *The Great Crash, 1929.* Boston: Houghton Mifflin, 1955.

Geisst, Charles R. *Wall Street: A History.* Oxford: Oxford University Press, 1997.

Goldman, Herbert G. *Fanny Brice: The Original Funny Girl.* New York: Oxford University Press, 1992.

Goodwin, Doris Kearns. *The Fitzgeralds and the Kennedys.* New York: Simon & Schuster, 1987.

Grant, James. *Bernard Baruch: The Adventures of a Wall Street Legend.* New York: Simon & Schuster, 1983.

Grayson, Theodore Julius. *Investment Trusts: Their Origin, Development, and Operation.* New York: J. Wiley & Sons, 1928.

Gurda, John. *The Making of Milwaukee.* Milwaukee: Milwaukee County Historical Society, 1999.

Hall, Robert C. *Dean Mathey: Essence of the Man.* Privately printed, 2010.

Heller, Deane Fons, and David Heller. *The Kennedy Cabinet: America's Men of Destiny.* Derby, CT: Monarch Books, 1961.

Hemingway, Ernest. *The Sun Also Rises*. New York: Charles Scribner's Sons, 1926.

Higham, Charles. *Trading with the Enemy: An Exposé of the Nazi-American Money Plot, 1933–1949*. New York: Delacorte Press, 1983.

Jeffreys, Diarmuid. *Aspirin: The Remarkable Story of a Wonder Drug*. New York: Bloomsbury USA, 2004.

Kemmerer, Donald L. *The Life and Times of Professor Edwin Walter Kemmerer, 1875–1945, and How He Became an International "Money Doctor."* Champaign, IL: Privately printed, 1993.

Kennedy, Joseph Patrick. *I'm for Roosevelt*. New York: Reynal & Hitchcock, 1936.

Konolige, Kit, and Frederica Konolige. *The Power of Their Glory: America's Ruling Class, the Episcopalians*. New York: Wyden Books, 1978.

Latham, Caroline, and David Agresta. *Dodge Dynasty: The Car and the Family That Rocked Detroit*. San Diego: Harcourt Brace Jovanovich, 1989.

MacKay, Malcolm. *Impeccable Connections: The Rise and Fall of Richard Whitney*. New York: Brick Tower Press, 2011.

Mathey, Dean. *Fifty Years of Wall Street with Anecdotiana*. Princeton: Privately printed, 1966.

Meyer, Richard H. *Bankers' Diplomacy: Monetary Stabilization in the Twenties*. New York: Columbia University Press, 1970.

Morris, Edmund. *Edison*. New York: Random House, 2019.

Mussolini, Benito. *My Autobiography [Ghostwritten by Richard Washburn Child]*. New York: Charles Scribner's Sons, 1928.

Oppenheimer, Jerry. *The Other Mrs. Kennedy: Ethel Skakel Kennedy: An American Drama of Power, Privilege, and Politics*. New York: St. Martin's Press, 1994.

O'Reilly, Maurice. *The Goodyear Story*. Edited by James T. Keating. Elmsford, NY: Benjamin Company, 1983.

Pak, Susie J. *Gentlemen Bankers: The World of J. P. Morgan*. Cambridge, MA: Harvard University Press, 2013.

Paris, Barry. *Louise Brooks*. New York: Knopf, 1989.

Parrini, Carl P. *Heir to Empire: United States Economic Diplomacy, 1916–1923*. Pittsburgh: University of Pittsburgh Press, 1969.

Pease, Neal. *Poland, the United States, and the Stabilization of Europe, 1919–1933*. Oxford: Oxford University Press, 1986.

Pecora, Ferdinand. *Wall Street Under Oath: The Story of Our Modern Money Changers*. New York: Simon & Schuster, 1939.

Perez, Robert C., and Edward F. Willett. *Clarence Dillon: A Wall Street Enigma*. Lanham, MD: Madison Books, 1995.

———. *The Will to Win: A Biography of Ferdinand Eberstadt*. New York: Greenwood Press, 1989.

Perino, Michael. *The Hellhound of Wall Street: How Ferdinand Pecora's Investigation of the Great Crash Forever Changed American Finance*. New York: Penguin Publishing Group, 2010.

Rogow, Arnold A. *James Forrestal, a Study of Personality, Politics, and Policy*. New York: Macmillan, 1963.

———. *Victim of Duty: A Study of James Forrestal*. London: Hart-Davis, 1966.

Ronald, Susan. *Hitler's Aristocrats: The Secret Power Players in Britain and America Who Supported the Nazis, 1923–1941*. New York: St. Martin's Press, 2023.

Schlesinger Jr., Arthur M. *The Crisis of the Old Order: 1919–1933 (The Age of Roosevelt, Vol. I)*. Boston: Houghton Mifflin, 1957.

Schulman, Daniel. *The Money Kings: The Epic Story of the Jewish Immigrants Who Transformed Wall Street and Shaped Modern America*. New York: Knopf, 2023.

Seligman, Jocl. *The Transformation of Wall Street: A History of the Securities and Exchange Commission and Modern Corporate Finance*. Boston: Houghton Mifflin, 1982.

Sinclair, Upton. *The Moneychangers*. New York: B. W. Dodge, 1908.

———. *Upton Sinclair Presents William Fox*. Los Angeles: Privately printed, 1933.

Smith, Adam. *An Inquiry Into the Nature and Causes of the Wealth of Nations*. London: W. Strahan and T. Cadell, 1776.

Sobel, Robert. *The Age of Giant Corporations: A Microeconomic History of American Business, 1914–1992*. Westport, CT: Greenwood Press, 1972.

———. *The Great Bull Market: Wall Street in the 1920s*. New York: Norton, 1968.

———. *The Life and Times of Dillon Read*. New York: Truman Talley Books/Dutton, 1991.

———. *N.Y.S.E.: A History of the New York Stock Exchange, 1935–1975*. New York: Weybright & Talley, 1975.

Sutton, Antony C. *Wall Street and the Rise of Hitler.* Seal Beach, CA: '76 Press, 1976.

Thomas, Dana L. *The Plungers and the Peacocks: An Update of the Classic History of the Stock Market.* New York: G. P. Putnam's Sons, 1989.

Thomas, Gordon, and Max Morgan Witts. *The Day the Bubble Burst: A Social History of the Wall Street Crash of 1929.* 1st ed. Garden City, New York: Doubleday, 1979.

United States, 72nd Congress, 1st Session. *Sale of Foreign Bonds or Securities in the United States: Hearings Before the Committee on Finance, United States Senate.* Washington, DC: US Government Printing Office, 1931.

United States, 73rd Congress, 1st Session. Senate Committee on Finance. *Stock Exchange Practices. Part 4, Dillon, Read & Co. October 3–13, 1933.* Washington, DC: US Government Printing Office, 1934.

United States, 73rd Congress, 2nd Session. Senate Committee on Banking and Currency. *Stock Exchange Practices Report.* Washington, DC: US Government Printing Office, 1934.

———. *The Pecora Commission's Final Report.* Washington, DC: US Government Printing Office, 1934.

United States, 76th Congress, 3rd Session. Temporary National Economic Committee. *Investigation of Concentration of Economic Power.* Washington, DC: US. Government Printing Office, 1940.

United States, Department of Commerce. Bureau of Foreign and Domestic Commerce. *American Direct Investments in Foreign Countries.* Washington, DC: US Government Printing Office, 1930.

Wasko, Janet. *Movies and Money: Financing the American Film Industry.* Norwood, NJ: Ablex, 1982.

Wechsberg, Joseph. *The Merchant Bankers.* Boston: Little, Brown & Co., 1966.

Index

E

K

Y

Z